MW00897973

Best wishes
to Fred Ernst
from Helmut Zittier,
a Survivor of III/Z.G.
Vancouver, B.C.
September 2, 001

WE WENT WHERE THEY SENT US

AND DID AS WE WERE TOLD

(MOST OF THE TIME)

SEE PAGE 73

We went where they sent us
... and did as we were told
(most of the time)

Edited by Gordon Bell

OOLICHAN BOOKS
LANTZVILLE, BRITISH COLUMBIA, CANADA
2000

Canadian Cataloguing in Publication Data

Main entry under title:

We went where they sent us and did as we were told (most of the time)

ISBN 0-88982-194-1

1. World War, 1939-1945—Personal narratives, Canadian. I. Bell, Gordon, 1923-
D811.A2W42 2000   940.53'71   C00-911173-5

We gratefully acknowledge the support of the Canada Council for the Arts for our publishing program.

THE CANADA COUNCIL | LE CONSEIL DES ARTS
FOR THE ARTS | DU CANADA

Grateful acknowledgement is also made to the BC Ministry of Tourism, Small Business and Culture for their financial support.

BRITISH
COLUMBIA
ARTS COUNCIL

We acknowledge the financial support of the Government of Canada through the Book Publishing Industry Development Program for our publishing activities.

Canada

Published by
Oolichan Books
P.O. Box 10, Lantzville
British Columbia, Canada
V0R 2H0

Printed in Canada

Contents

Introduction / 13

Beginning

Miracles / 17
Tony Hennig

My Life During World War Two / 20
Aniela Plonka

Light Duty / 25
Archie Byatt

The Fairmile / 27
Norm Rosewall

Right Turn Murphy / 29
Frank Murphy

Atlantic

Not A Brilliant Move / 33
Alex Burton

HMCS Iroquois / 36
Ray Kynock

Murphy s Law / 36
Hugh Robinson

Torpedoes Ahead! / 39
George Milford

Life In The Merchant Marines / 40
Bill McFadden

Ding Dong Bell / 40
Ronald W. Bell

Of Such Stuff Are Heroes Made / 42
Frank Horner

The Grand Old Lady Of The RCN / 42
Gordon R. Calam

The Ship That Voted Itself Out Of The
War / 44
Ross Carnduff

Friday the Thirteenth / 46
Arnold Bernard Klayh

Disobedience Rewarded / 47
Lloyd Smither

Mediterranean

Peace In Our Time / 51
Thomas Gates / 51

Landing Ship Tank / 52
Derek Harvey-Smith

Torpedoed / 53
George A. Horne, R.C.A.S.C.

A Trip Down Memory Lane / 54
Warren Shaddock

Professional Coward / 55
Tet Walston

They Were Just Kids / 55
Guy Trenholm

Yak, Anyone? / 56
Phillip Redman

Africa

Life In The Royal Air Force / 63
Edward E.C. Beaven

Shoe-Shine Scabbards And Exploding
Biffies / 68
Ron Buxton

Bombs And Beer / 70
James (Stocky) Edwards

An Egyptian Cadet's War / 71
Mohammed Sidky

Eggs Stronger Than Buildings / 72
Helen Sidky

The Other Side Of The War / 72
Helmut Zittier

Italy

Bare-Assed In The Dugout / 77
Gordon Bannerman

from *Mines And Bridges* / 78
Bob Cameron

Italian Interludes / 79
Sam Deane

Remembering Pozzallo / 82
Harry Greenhough

Recollections Of Ortona / 83
K J. Gourlay

The Ten O'Clock News / 86
Jim Hurford

Raw Chicken / 87
Lemie Lacouvee

Eating Peacocks / 88
Joe Morton

A Long Walk / 88
Clarence Murphy

An Incident in the Bari Opera House / 90
Stan Scislowski

Saved By The Cross / 93
Otto Wuerch

Brown Boots And Scottish Accents / 93
Hector Young

The Edge Of No-Man's Land—The FOP / 94
Roy McKinley

Canada

Confined To Barracks / 99
Gelda Bell (Ingalls)

Marching Band / 99
Gord Bell

Roughing It / 100
Donna Chapman

Dangerous Drill / 100
Helen Henning

The War Years In Nanaimo / 101
June Jackson

How Ruthie Won The War / 102
Ruth Masters

Paper Balloons / 107
Kay McCaskill

It Came Home Alone / 108
Peter Dawson

A Time To Question / 109
Ross C. Morton

My First Flight / 110
Everett E. Sponaugle

Shades of War / 112
A.C. (Fred) Rogers

Too Young To Join / 114
Bud Stevens

A Taste of EATS—Empire Air Training Scheme / 115
H. L. Symon

A Friend For Life / 117
Shirley Williamson

Winnie's Cigars / 118
Lorraine (Wilkinson) Bonar

Battle of Britain

Everything That Goes Up Must Come Down / 123
Peter Cornfoot

Fire Watch / 123
Marjorie Miller

Bomb Raid / 124
Gary Noland

National Fire Service in Hull, UK / 124
Irene Duff

Hurricanes in the Defense of London / 126
Doug Haynes

Our Avenue: 1939 to 1946 / 126
Iris Heywood

The Plymouth Blitz / 129
Bob Williams

England

Boffins And Doodle-Bugs / 133
Maria Bowering

Military Police / 134
Henry J. Gagne

You're Not In Canada Now / 137
Dick Jackson

Love In The Water Tank / 137
E. Ted Leeson

American Hospitality / 138
Sid Philp

A Knockout, An Unhappy CO, And A Toe
/ 138
Bill Pineo

A Day To Remember / 139
Gordon Quinn

Target Practice / 140
Georgina Rosewall

London Adventures / 141
Margaret Ruston

Santa Wore Blue / 143
Ken Stofer, RAF

Memories / 145
Iris Francis Nichol

VE Day in Milford Haven, Wales / 145
Roy Hinder

Eleven Plus One / 146
Hilda (Ingalls) Whitehead

Lucky Escape / 150
Stan Walpole

My Story / 150
Harold A. Tomlinson

VE Day in Trafalgar Square / 154
Hugh Noakes

My Life as an Army Nurse / 157
Terry Gallacher

War Bride / 158
Pat Dunlop

.A Sweet Memory / 160
Edith Measure

Flying Fortresses / 161
Vic Childs

An Aged Kid / 161
Vic Childs

Dieppe

A Survivor of S.S. Lancastria / 165
J. F. (Joe) Sweeney

The Warren Twins: Gemini Flight / 173
Doug "Duke" Warren

Operation Jubilee (Dieppe Raid) & the
Essex Scottish / 175
Roy A. Jardine

Meeting Queen Elizabeth, now the
Queen Mother / 177
Roy A. Jardine

Sniper / 178
Bill "Boots" Bettridge

Remembrance of Dieppe / 185
Del McFadden

I Remember the Joys of a Missed Youth /
189
Ronald K. Haunts

Enemy Counter Attack? / 190
Frank Sellers

Liberation of Europe

Carpiquet / 193
James Woodrow Blakely

Our Last Days / 195
Howard Benn

Ada / 197
Clifford Bolton

Fear In France / 200
A. E. Brock

219 Days in the Hands of the Germans /
201
Translated by Jacques Aubin

219 Jours Aux Mains des Allemands /
203
Hervé Courture

Letter, Written to a Daughter, to Educate
   School Children / 205
   Allison Chute

Children in Harm's Way / 207
   Art Enger

Memories of D Day / 208
   Edwin Woollard

Billie Goat Goes to War / 210
   John Grainger

1st Canadian Parachute Brigade / 211
   Jim Kingsley

A Slit Trench Too Far / 211
   G.N. (Bud) Schaupmeyer

Wartime Photographers / 213
   Lloyd H. Thompson

Letter from the War to My Brother. / 215
   Raymond "Tony" Wallace

War Starts and Ends a Friendship / 218
   Truman Wilcox

Attack on the Normandy Dry Dock, St.
   Nazaire, Mar. 1942 / 220
   David Lloyd Davies

Fogbound / 225
   Ted Hutton

We Done Good / 227
   Charles Clark

Dutch Resistance Fighters / 229
   Karel Berkman

Special Operations Executive Len
   Mulholland / 230
   Gordon Bell

My Time in Europe During the War Years
   / 232
   D.F. (Doug) Beasley

The Sound of Bagpipes in Holland / 233
   Sietske Van Houten

My Momentary Claim to Fame / 233
   Bernard Quigley

Reflections / 235
   Ernie Ratelle

VE Day / 235
   John A. Spence

Denmark Occupation / 236
   Ely Bull

My Brother's Last Letter Home / 236
   Jon Robert McQuay

Germany

Life in Nazi Germany / 241
   Peter Buttuls

Navigating Wellington Bombers / 241
   Howard Dale

Riddled Bomber / 242
   James A. Duff

Joining the Luftwaffe / 242
   Walter Gulick

Life as a Tail Gunner / 244
   Gordon Hunt

A Canadian Family Trapped in Germany
   / 245
   Rosaline Mandalik

A Soldier's Diary: Brief Notes to Give my
   Mom / 246
   Tom Mansfield

My Father's War / 249
   Goody Niosi

Behind Enemy Lines / 250
   Goody Niosi

Moment of Compassion / 251
   Franz Stigler

Lucky Wrong Turn / 252
   Tom Crawshaw

A German Perspective / 252
   Alex Maldacker

Life in the R.A.F. / 257
   Ron Bull

Prisoners of War

Organ Music / 261
   Lorne Shetler

The Escape Committee / 263
   Max Sikal

Shot Down over Russia / 263
   Tony Ruppert

Wartime Wings / 265
   Ted Barsby

Pacific

High Jinks in Northern India / 269
  Maurice Lonsdale

The Forgotten War / 270
  George Maycock

Life in the Forgotten Air Force in South
  East Asia / 271
  Gil Green

Commonwealth Air Training Plan / 273
  John Mills

VE Day and Other Reminiscences / 274
  W. E. (Bill) Howell

A Funny Experience / 275
  Peter J. Eastick

The 'Forgotten' War / 276
  Peter J. Eastick

HMCS UGANDA / 277
  Fred H. Broadbent

Nagasaki / 278
  Koos Van Houten

After

Just A Penny Note / 281
  H.J. 'Pat' Barron

Military Units Mentioned / 284

Military Terms & Abreviations / 286

Acknowledgements / 289

Image courtesy of Vancouver Island Military Museum & Ron Buxton

Introduction
Gordon Bell

Tony Hennig of Ladysmith B.C. was in action on the first day of World War II. Therefore, it seems the logical way to start this account of the experiences of Canadians who served during those perilous times, and who have chosen to share their memories so that future generations may have a means of knowing what it was like for the ordinary people who donned their uniforms, served in their nation's armed forces, and came back to Canada to grow old.

Seventeen years old when Poland began to mobilize for the expected Nazi invasion, and too young for the draft, Tony Hennig volunteered and was assigned to duty as a dispatch rider. One week later, on the first day of World War Two, when the road came under attack by a STUKA dive bomber, he was blown off his bicycle and landed, unconscious, in the ditch. When he came to, he saw, all around him, the mangled remains of women and children, along with the bodies of a few men too old to fight. They had been trying to flee from the front. These were the first victims of Hitler's Blitzkrieg. Tony says, "This was the first time in my life that I really prayed and sincerely meant it. From that ditch, as mother had taught me, I knelt down and offered my thanks to Holy Mary, Queen of Poland. I sure believed, and still do, that she was with me from that time on."

Twenty-one days after experiencing his first miracle, with his regiment decimated and the Nazi victory nearly complete, Tony's commander told him to try to get to the Polish embassy in Budapest, where he would be given a train ticket to Paris, to join the free Polish army being formed in France.

❧

Dedicated to our our fallen comrades.
We will remember them.

Beginning

Miracles

Tony Hennig

I was in a summer uniform. Walking across the Carpathian mountains in September is not a warm-weather journey. But I kept on going, and was one tired, cold, and hungry teen-ager. When I finally reached Budapest I faced another problem – no one understood me when I asked for directions.

That night, I was standing at a corner trying to figure out where I was and how to find the embassy. A pretty lady overheard me asking passers-by, stepped out of the shadows, and enquired in Polish, "Little boy, would you like something to eat?" I was led to a house occupied by several more ladies, given a big meal and a warm bed. There, beside the first real bed I had seen in weeks, I knelt again to thank Holy Mary. The following morning my worn and dirty uniform was gone; the girls had bought me a new suit. I didn't know till later what kind of a house I was in—my mother had never told me about those places. I was cared for almost as though I were a little brother, until the embassy arranged transportation to Belgrade. There is still a soft spot in my heart for the ladies who choose that life and I always include them in my prayers.

In Yugoslavia I met up with more volunteers and new orders. Marshall Petain had surrendered; France was now under Hitler's control and our new destination was Damascus, where the French Foreign Legion was recruiting and preparing to fight. The train ride through Greece, Turkey, then on into Syria was uneventful, and being with other Polish volunteers was comforting, but I had never been away from home before and I was homesick and worried about my family. We were in Damascus just

Tony Hennig with fellow Polish veteran Bogden Sawel

long enough to get our Legion uniforms. Because Rommel's Afrika Korps was battering the demoralized British Army, and we Polish volunteers wanted to fight as a unit, we were hastily formed into the Carpathian Brigade, transferred to British command at Alexandria, Egypt, and sent into battle. I lost many friends, but came through without a scratch.

I was still fighting the Afrika Korps as a foot soldier when the RAF signalled all units that they were looking for volunteers, to train as pilots. Figuring I had done enough walking for one war, I applied immediately, and a few months later was en route to flying school in Britain.

On the night of March 13, 1943, just south of the equator, we were torpedoed by the Italian submarine *Leonardo Da Vinci*. I was one of the lucky ones who got off before she went under. As the sun rose, we could see swimmers being devoured by sharks. A state of panic existed aboard the raft. I just prayed, grateful to be afloat in a calm sea and sure that this was just another miracle. Thus when the Navy rescued us fifty-four hours later, I was not surprised; I knew they would come. However, after being picked up, while all the others were in sick bay being treated as survivors, I was in such great shape that I was put to work. I completed the trip as a deck hand on the British (Flower class) destroyer HMS *Primrose*.

I met Canadians for the first time when I arrived in Cheshire and was billetted in a barracks full of them. My new friends helped me decide that after the war was over, Canada would be almost as nice a place to live as Poland; but in the meantime there was elementary training on Tiger Moths, Miles Magisteres, and Harvards, then posting to # 318 Polish fighter squadron of the RAF as a Spitfire pilot.

Polish pilots had earned an awesome reputation for aggressiveness and courage during the Battle of Britain. Those early pilots had fought the Luftwaffe over Poland, had flown to France, and fought there till the French gave up, then had taken off for England to join the RAF. They had seen their country destroyed, and their families brutalized and murdered by the Nazis. For many of these airmen there was nothing more to lose, and revenge was a powerful motivator. In the Battle of Britain alone, between August 8, and October 1, 1941, twenty-one of the eighty-six Polish pilots who joined in the defence of London were lost. Together, they were responsible for 12 percent of the 2600 losses the Luftwaffe suffered in the Battle of Britain. However, by the time I was trained and joined the squadron, Bomber Command was carrying the war to Europe, and German fighters were kept busy over their own country.

While Allied fighter squadrons escorting bombing operations over the continent were in action nearly every time up, # 318 was given the task of escorting for a VIP transport squadron. We never knew who we were protecting, but we sometimes had as many as six escorts on a mission, and when a half dozen Spitfires surrounded a DC3 in flight, it must have been somebody awfully important. In addition to the protection we provided, we were routed to avoid dangerous airspace on all of our trips, so I never felt that I was in much danger while flying escort. But then another busy time came along for Mother Mary.

I was sent to Number Sixty-One Operational Training Unit on Hornington RAF Station, at Bury St. Edwards, to train new pilots on Spitfires and Hurricanes. This was possibly the most dangerous part of the war for me. I was promoted to Assistant

Adjutant at Hornington, and was still there when the war ended. Shortly after the war I learned from my younger brother, who had just escaped to Britain, that Father had been killed. Together, we arranged to bring Mother to live with us. This was no easy task, as the Russians had taken over Poland, but we finally convinced the communists that an old widow would only be a burden.

Some months later, when we had her settled in, I still hadn't found suitable employment, so I decided to try my luck in Canada. I started out as a door-to-door salesman in Alberta, selling pots and pans. People had lots of money and not much to spend it on. Factories were slowly switching over from war production and I lucked in, earning a fair living and improving my language skills. One evening, near Lethbridge, I was stopped by a policeman because I had no tail-lights. I not only got off with a warning, but was taken home for dinner, and sold a set of cookware to the cop and his wife.

Canada has been good to me. I have been allowed to prosper here, and I love my country. Furthermore my miracles have never ceased - in fact the biggest miracle of my life happened in 1991.

It started when I attended an estate sale on Reid Island (one of the smaller gulf islands in Georgia Strait.) I bought a tractor to use around my place, and was persuaded by a friend to take the old bell too, because nobody else wanted it, it was going cheap, and I had lots of room. The bell, which may have been from a buoy, or a shipwreck, sat in my front yard as an interesting ornament, and no one was able to explain its origins—nor was I able to explain why I kept it. The only reason seemed to be that it was too heavy to move.

That bell sat in my yard for three years, till one day I went to a reception for a priest from Poland, and he told me about the new church he was building. When I asked him where, he said, "You wouldn't know the place, it is so small."

Then I asked, "Do you have a bell?"

"Oh no! We are a small poor parish; it would take a miracle for us to be able to afford a bell."

"Father," I said, "you have your miracle."

With the help of friends in the shipping industry, and of a Polish sea captain, the bell now calls the people to worship in Holy Mary, Queen of Poland church, in the town of Nasuto. I was there for the dedication in 1993. After the service, I walked five miles over the same path my mother had walked, and visited her birthplace.

It was a very satisfying homecoming for a happy pilgrim who still believes in miracles.

I offered my thanks to Holy Mary Queen of Poland. I believed then, and still do, that she was with me.

My Life During World War Two

Aniela Plonka

On the last day of August, 1939, I said goodbye to my mother. She had tears in her eyes, and asked when she would see me again. I said, "Mom, I am going to Przemysl, only a few kilometres from home." I was going there to stay with my auntie, who was expecting twins, and whose husband was away in the army. She lived close to my high school, and my living with her made it more convenient for me to travel to school.

Thirty-two years passed before I saw my mother again.

On August 28, 1939, the ten-year Treaty on Non-Aggression was signed in Moscow by Germany's Joachim von Ribbentrop and Russia's Vyacheslav Molotov. On September 1, 1939, the German army attacked Poland, bombarding cities, towns and villages. Not only did they attack the Polish army, but they shot civilians who ran in panic. Injured and dead people were scattered everywhere. It was a horrible thing to see and live through.

On September 17, 1939, the Russian Army invaded eastern Poland, and the Germans and Russians divided Poland in half. The river San, which flows through the middle of Przemysl, was made the German-Russian border. My mother's house was on the Russian side. I worried about my mother and my family. I had not heard from them since I had left to go to school. I tried to get home, but the Russians didn't let people go through their border. They dynamited the bridge, so I decided to wait until the river froze.

On the morning of January 19, 1940, I crossed the frozen river, but two Russian soldiers grabbed me. They took me to their headquarters for questioning, and kept me there all day. Although I pleaded with them to release me and let me go home to my mother, when night came, they took me to prison.

The prison cell was full of people: older ladies, school kids and children. There was no room to sit down. At night we had to take turns to lie down on the floor. Once a day they gave us some soup. We were starved, longing for a piece of bread. There was no place to wash either.

After two weeks, they loaded us in the canvas-covered trucks and took us to the rail station. I wanted to let my mother know what had happened to me, so I wrote a note, then tore a strip from my dress and tied it around the note. While the truck was moving, I cut a hole in the canvas with a razor and threw my note out. Then I looked through the hole and saw somebody pick it up and run away. Whoever it was let my mother know what had happened to me.

At the rail station, they loaded us into freight wagons. The wagons had some straw on the floor and a can standing in the corner. We travelled like that for two days and nights. We stopped at the town of Nikolayev, in Russia, and were brought to the prison door, where they gave us some water. I drank three quarts of water at once.

At Nikolayev prison, many times, and always after midnight, they called me for questioning.

After six months, they put us in covered trucks, in separate partitions, and drove us far away to some other prison. At that prison they let us out of the truck one at a time, then put each of us in an upright position in a separate cupboard-like box in the wall. In front of me was a door, with a few holes for air to come in. If ever I fainted, I couldn't fall because there was no room to fall. The Russians were very advanced in their cruelty. Sometimes they kept me standing there for three to four hours before they called me for questioning. By then I would be totally exhausted, and I just didn't care any more. The Russian Commander would insist that I admit I was an enemy of Soviet Russia. He would yell at me to scare me. "Why don't you cry? For Pilsudski you would cry, but you will not cry for me!"

Aniela Plonka, age 22.

I answered, "Yes, for Pilsudski I would cry, but I will not cry to please you." [Joseph Pilsudski was a Polish patriot and leader during World War One. Also, he was Poland's first Head of State.]

The next prison they sent me to was in Kharkov. I will never forget the Kharkov prison. They put me in a large cell with Russian women who were hardened criminals. They were in prison for murder, assault, theft and many other crimes. They swore and fought between themselves. I was so scared, I thought I had died and was in Hell. Every night, two Russian guards came to the cell to count us. I kept asking them, "Please put me with Polish women."

They asked, "Why?"

"Because," I replied, "I can't speak Russian."

"You have to learn," they answered. "Learn from these women."

Every night, the guards asked us what we had done before we came to prison. The Russian women answered that they had been thieves, or pick-pockets. One night, when they asked me again, I said I was a pick-pocket. The guards looked surprised and smiled. Next day they put me in a cell with Polish women.

I remained in Kharkov prison for another six months. Then one day they called me to the Commander's office and read me their sentence. As an enemy of Soviet Russia, I was sentenced to five years of hard labour in a women's camp called Akmolinsk. It was the winter of 1941.

We came to Akmolinsk on a prison train with bars on the windows and armed guards. They gave us salty fish to eat, but there was no water to drink. As far as we could see, there was nothing but snow. Finally, they brought some snow for us to eat. We travelled like that for a week.

The camp was north of Akmolinsk, Siberia. There were no railroads, so we had to walk through the deep snow for ten hours to get to the camp. Some people were so tired that they fell in the snow. The soldiers swore, and pushed the prisoners with their rifle butts. Over three hundred Polish women were transported this way.

The camp was full of Russian prisoners, mainly wives and daughters of Tsarist officers who had been shot when the communists took over. These prisoners were there for life. I was put to work digging frozen ground, because they planned to build a railroad. The work was hard, and the hours were long—fourteen to sixteen hours every day in temperatures of forty-five degrees below zero. To keep warm we had to work fast, for when you stood up to rest for half a minute, your sweat would freeze on your back. My feet were frozen so terribly that for many years it was difficult for me to find shoes which wouldn't hurt.

Every prisoner had to dig a "norm"—so many meters long, and so many wide. If somebody managed to dig the "norm," he or she received more bread the next day. I could never make the "norm." I was too weak, so I received only small portions of bread. Also, we got a bowl of soup once a day, made of grain and fish heads.

For one and a half years I worked in that camp, doing hard work outside, building railroads and digging canals. Many of my friends didn't make it. They died of starvation and diseases. My brother also died somewhere in Siberia.

I lost all hope of survival. But then, in June, 1941, the German army attacked Russia and the two "partners in crime" were now at war. Polish General Wladyslaw Sikorski tried to save the Polish people from Russian prisons. The terms of agreement were signed in London, England, on July 30, 1941.

On December 4, 1941, The Declaration of Mutual Assistance and Collaboration was signed in Moscow by Polish General Sikorski, and Joseph Stalin. Stalin agreed to release Polish prisoners. There were over a million Polish prisoners of war, and many thousands of civilian families had been deported from Poland to Russia.

In May, 1942, I was released from the Russian prison. Two Polish ladies and I decided to go to southern Russia by train. Some Russian prisoners asked us to convey messages to their families, to say that they were alive. When we reached their families, they were so afraid that they said, "No we don't know anybody who is in prison."

It was very difficult to get a seat on a train. The trains were full of Russian army personnel, and the railway stations were full of Russian refugees from the front, whose homes had been destroyed by bombs.

After a long wait at the Akmolinsk rail station, my two friends and I managed to get on the train. We didn't have money to buy tickets, so the conductor threw us out. We clung to the rails of the steps, while the train was running. On the next rail car steps, some Russian men were also hanging on. I had a little bag on a string, which the man from the next car tried to steal. He pulled and jerked at the bag, but the string wouldn't break. I couldn't release my grip to let the bag go, because the train was going very fast and I would have been killed if I had fallen. The string of the bag cut my arm, and for many years I had a big scar from that cut. When the train stopped, we walked to a village in Kazakhstan, (a country occupied by Russia,) and asked for jobs because we were very hungry. The Kazakh people let us work on their farms and paid us with flour and potatoes.

After a few weeks, we tried to get to Alma-Ata. Some Russian men from the village were going to Alma-Ata. They said they could take one of us, if we paid them. We had fifty roubles between us, so my friends decided I would take our belongings and ride with the Russians, while my friends would walk.

On the way to Alma-Ata, the Russian men stopped by a bar for drinks, while I waited on the wagon. When they came back they yelled at me to give them more money, but I didn't have any, so they started hitting me and tearing off my clothes. I was very scared and I didn't know what to do. There was a little Kazakh man with the Russians. He asked them to leave me alone, but they were drunk and wouldn't stop. When the wagon continued down the hill, the Kazakh man pushed me off the wagon. I rolled down the hill. Then he threw my bags down. He saved my life.

I didn't know where I was, or what to do. I sat on my bags and cried, and prayed. After a long time, somebody came by and asked if he could help. He was a Kazakh man riding on a donkey, and he spoke only Kazakh. But somehow, we understood each other. He let me borrow his donkey. I put my bags on the back of the donkey, and started off. The donkey was going steadily, until we came to a creek. The donkey sat down right in the middle of the creek, and my bags of flour got wet. I jumped off and started pulling the rope, but the donkey refused to move. I was so upset, I ran behind the donkey and grabbed her tail and pulled it very hard. She jumped, and started running.

Finally, I got to the place where I was supposed to meet my friends. They said, "We walked, and we have been waiting here for you for a long time. You had a ride, and you are so late."

In Alma-Ata, we worked on the cotton fields. We lived in a small cottage built from clay and straw. When we laid down at night, we could see the stars shining through the holes in the roof. There, I got sick with a severe case of dysentery. I thought I wouldn't survive. One morning, a Russian soldier came to our door and said that he was collecting all the Polish people he could find, to get them to one place for transporting. The place was near Tashkent. He was sorry to see me so sick, and he put us on a wagon and gave us some bread and boiled water to drink. Gradually I got better. We called that soldier an angel of mercy, sent by God to help us. He was the first Russian I met who acted like a human being.

From Alma-Ata, we travelled to Tashkent, a town in Uzbekistan. The Polish army was forming near Tashkent, in a town called Jangi-Jul. There, in August, 1942, I enlisted in General Wladyslaw Anders' army. The army camp was full of Polish men and women just released from Russian prisons, who had joined the Polish army.

There were also some Polish Catholic priests. The following Sunday, we gathered in an open field to hear the Holy Mass, for the first time in three years. There were thousands of people, men and women, young and old. It was very emotional; our tears flowed, as we prayed and sang, *"Boze Cos Polske"* (God save our Poland).

In October, 1942, I was transported with the Polish army to the Middle East. We travelled from Port Krasnovock through the Caspian Sea and arrived in Port Pahlevi, in Iran.

For eight months, I worked in a Teheran hospital as a volunteer. I worked night shifts. I started two hours early, because I took classes in nursing. It was a crash course, but it helped my work in the hospital. The hospital was a new building, not yet finished. There was no electricity, no telephones. We had to use lanterns. There was a shortage of doctors and nurses. Transports of Polish civilians were coming from Russia. People had diseases like typhoid fever and tuberculosis. Most of those people died in that hospital.

I was transferred to Iraq, Seventh Division, Polish army, where I worked in the YMCA canteen. We were in a place called Quizi-Ribat, near Baghdad. Iraq is very hot—no rain or clouds, only sun, sand and palm trees. When the wind blows, the sand hangs in the air. We lived in big tents with nets tied around our beds to protect us from scorpions, tarantulas, and other poisonous creatures. Many Polish people got sick with malaria from mosquito bites.

The Polish army in Iraq didn't have any entertainment, so another soldier and I were asked to sing. We were sent to many camps and divisions, where we sang solos and duets. If we put on a play, I took part in it.

In Iraq, I met my husband, who was a Polish army officer. He too had been a prisoner of war in Russia. He left for England, to join the RAF, a few days after we met. I didn't see him for a year, but we kept in touch by writing letters. From England, the RAF sent him to Canada for nine months of navigation schooling. When he returned to England, he was stationed at Newcastle–on-Tyne, and flew a two-person plane called a Mosquito. They were also called Night Fighters. His duty was to spot the German bombers flying towards England, and shoot them down.

In July, 1943, I was transferred to Palestine (Israel). Travelling to Palestine, we saw a mirage. It looked as if there was a big city, and a body of water lying ahead, but when we got to that location, there was nothing. Yet the mirage remained in the distance.

In Palestine, I continued working in the YMCA canteen. Our camp was located on the Mediterranean, at a place called Haifa. It was hot there, so we swam in the sea. Also, we took bus tours to Jerusalem and Tel-Aviv. I went to Jerusalem four times, visited the Holy Land and the churches, and went to Bethlehem and Nazareth. There was also a tour to the Dead Sea. I enjoyed every minute of it.

In December, 1943, I was accepted into the air force. Our transport left for England around Christmastime. We travelled by train to Alexandria, and took a big ship across the Mediterranean Sea. The ship had to move slowly and carefully, be-

24

cause there were mines in the water. We had to stop for a week at Gibraltar, and wait until the Navy fished out all the mines.

The first week in January, 1944, we arrived in Glasgow, Scotland. In February, I enlisted with the WAAF. They sent me to the Halton station, near London, for a mechanics course. In eight months, I finished the course and began working as a Flight Mechanic E, working on engines in Lancaster bombers. I was stationed at Silloth, located between England and Scotland.

Living in England for four years, I visited many cities and made a lot of friends. I was also married in England, and my son, George, was born in Edinburgh, Scotland.

Since August, 1939, when I had last seen my mother, I had no knowledge of what had happened to my family. It was useless to write a letter, because the Russians and Germans were fighting on Polish territory. When the war was over, we got a letter from my husband's mother, who warned, "Stay where you are. If you come back, you will be sent to Siberia."

She told us that my mother was alive, and had been ordered, by the Russians, to leave her house and go to the Polish side of the border, because her house was in the newly acquired Russian territory. She also said that my brother had been captured by the Russians, beaten, and taken to prison somewhere in Siberia. My two younger sisters had been taken to Germany for hard labour.

When I heard the news, I cried so much, I thought my heart would break. Because my husband and I knew how dangerous it was to return to Poland, we decided to come to live in Canada.

Light Duty
Archie Byatt

I joined the Royal Canadian Navy on April 4, 1938, as a boy seaman, and after initial training was sent to HMCS *St. Laurent*. We went on an exercise in the South Pacific. A short time after returning to Canada in late August, we were instructed to leave for Halifax. As we passed under the Lions Gate Bridge, the captain cleared lower decks and, with all hands assembled about him, announced in terse tones, "Men, we are at war."

It was only after we had cleared the Panama Canal that Canada declared war on Germany. Our government had held back, fearing that, as we would be belligerents, the neutral USA might close the canal on us before we had made our way through. We traveled seven thousand miles in fourteen days to reach Halifax, and were immediately put to work on convoy duty. Conditions were horrific, as we were still in tropical gear and had not received warm clothing before heading out on the North Atlantic.

During the spring of 1940, sixteen of us volunteered to go to gunnery school and become anti-aircraft gunners for the RCN. It was pandemonium when we arrived at Victory Barracks, Portsmouth, just as the battered and bloody survivors were returning from the ill-fated *Narvik* expedition in Norway. In the faces of those poor men, we saw what war was really all about.

The conditions endured on the North Atlantic contributed to a lot of illness amongst us sailors. One morning I awoke in my hammock to find that my left leg was stiff, and I could not move. I was taken to sick bay, where the doctor informed me, "You have rheumatic fever."

Shortly after I was admitted to hospital, the Luftwaffe began bombing west coast ports and patients were moved to Idsworth House, Portsdown Hills. There were seventeen of us with the same disease, when a man from the Air Ministry came and asked for volunteers to be tail gunners in RAF bombers. We were all terminally ill, and they figured we could still be useful. One man did volunteer. I don't know what happened to him, but all the others died. The doctor couldn't understand how I survived.

Our hospital overlooked Portsmouth and we were able to watch the Luftwaffe in action. They would send Stukas in to shoot down barrage balloons; then the bigger bombers would come to work over the harbour.

Eventually the doctor said I was to go on light duty.

"Where?" I asked.

"Down in Portsmouth," he replied.

I thought, some light duty, where the Germans were bombing around the clock!

I worked in the barracks by day, and stayed with my relatives at night. Our Anderson shelter saved our lives many times, as we were bombed night after night and, at the beginning, during the day. The Luftwaffe blitzed Portsmouth one night, while I was on another AAA course at Eastney. The whole city was in flames. We were called upon to put out fires, and to try to comfort elderly victims. It was three days before I was able to get off duty and search for my relations. Thank goodness, they were not injured. (In a later raid a time- bomb landed in their yard and the house was destroyed.)

From my own neighbourhood, out of ten volunteers only two of us came home. My friend George Corbett had been in pilot training in England, as a reservist. He was home when war was declared and returned to the RAF as soon as the war started.

I was convoying from Liverpool to Iceland at the time of his death. I share with you the last letter received from George. It is one of my most memorable treasures.

Officers Mess
RAF Station
Coltishaw, Norfolk
Aug.12/40

Greetings Arch;

And salutations! Boyoboy, was I glad to get your letter today & pretty surprised as well. Well sport, before I go any further, can you get up to London sometime next week? I'm due for 4 days leave but don't know just when - I'll let you know as soon as possible & we should be able to have some fun if you could come up for a few hours.

That London address is my Aunt's - all my Canadian mail comes through her because my addresses are so uncertain.

I'm here with a Spitfire Squadron having a helluva time. The Jerries are not bothering us very much at the moment but we've got plenty to do & do a lot of flying. You'll hear all about what goes on if we can get together in London. We're on the East Coast here & our job is to prevent any Jerries from crossing over. Also we escort a lot of convoys out in the North Sea. These Spitfires are wonderful planes & the Jerries know it & keep pretty clear, unless they're in numbers giving them odds of over 10 to 1. I've only been with this squadron for about 3 weeks & things have been very quiet up to now.

Well, Arch, I haven't time for any more now. Drop me a line soon, letting me know if you can get to town, & I'll by then be able to tell you when I'll be in London.

Are you on the St.Laurent? If so, where's Freddie Gorwall?
S'long Pal,- hope to see you soon

George Corbett
P/O R.A.F.

The Fairmile

Norm Rosewall, Nanaimo, Asdic Operator on Fairmile ML Q080

Eighty of the Fairmile ML Q080 boats were built in Canada—fifty-nine in the Great Lakes shipyards, fourteen on the West coast, and seven in Weymouth, USA. The Fairmiles played a vital role as escorts in the St. Lawrence River and the Gulf of St. Lawrence, and as convoy escorts between Newfoundland and the mainland.

Transferred from Naden to Halifax, I reported to the Reg Office and was promptly shipped out on a train journey to no-one knew where. The train was so slow that you could have walked alongside. We were dropped off in the dead of night at a train station, where we waited until daylight for the train to take us to our new base in Gaspe.

Our Flotilla consisted of the Seventy-second, Seventy-fourth, Seventy-ninth, Eightieth, Eighty-second and Eighty-third. Shore crews were not amused when they had to refuel us, as we had Sterling engines that used high-octane airplane fuel. The Eighty-second was very badly damaged and two of her crew died as a result of an explosion during refuelling.

Norm Rosewall circa *1943*

A pleasant diversion for the flotilla was being sent down the east coast of the USA, with stops at Boston, New York, Norfolk, (where they changed our camouflage to American colours,) Savannah, and Miami. We were based at the Miami Yacht Club. Three of the flotilla were sent to the Bahamas, and three of us went on to Cuba. Tying up in Havana harbour, we had a chance to go ashore and look around, and we saw a whole different way of life. On a second trip, we went around Cuba and had to anchor off the Isle of Pines, a prison island. The water was so shallow we could not go on shore; the boat would go in but there was not enough depth for the Asdic dome on the bottom.

One of my hairiest experiences took place when we were following another Fairmile, on our way from Gaspe to Halifax, through the Northumberland Strait. We were caught in one of the fiercest storms I ever encountered; the waves were so high that we lost sight of the mast tops of the lead ship. We were the only two in the Strait at the time, and in the middle of the night the lead ship signaled that they had ended up on the rocks off Prince Edward Island. When I got off watch it was so rough I could not even sling my hammock, and ended up sleeping in the Asdic well. After eighteen hours of battling the storm we found shelter in Pictou, Nova Scotia and tied up alongside an old World War One four stack destroyer, on lend-lease from the American navy.

The skipper of that ship was a compassionate man, and sent over hot rum, enough for doubles. After that, we went downtown to a restaurant and got something to eat. The storm had been so bad that the galley had been impossible to work in, and we had not eaten for a day and a half. As we trooped into the restaurant everyone thought we were survivors; we must have looked a scurvy, bedraggled lot.

28

Right Turn Murphy

Frank Murphy

I went to work for the RCAF in 1941, as a courier at Number One Equipment Depot in Toronto. In 1943, I joined the RCAF as an air crew trainee and was posted to the Manning Pool, in Brandon, Manitoba. We certainly traveled first class—each airman had a private compartment.

After one month at Manning Pool, I was posted to a pre-Air Crew Educational Detachment in Vancouver where I was billeted in a private home; I paid four dollars per week for bed and breakfast, which consisted of bacon, sausage, eggs, toast, cereal and pancakes. We were paid $1.25 per day living-out allowance, so we were well compensated.

The next stop was back to Toronto, and Little Norway Camp of the Norwegian Air Force. This was our Initial Training School, where air crew selection was made. I didn't make pilot, mostly because,e when the Link Trainer said, "Turn left," I turned right, and knocked the instructor on his ass by hitting him in a vital spot with a wing tip.

So off I went to Number Four Wireless School, in Guelph. Six months later, I went to Number One Bombing and Gunnery School where, in August, l944, I graduated as a Pilot Officer Wireless Air Gunner. After a short leave, I headed for Number Thirty TU at Patricia Bay, BC, for flying boat training.

Flying boat training was handled by the Royal Air Force, so many of the officers didn't think much of the "colonials." I got into trouble when I was caught teaching poker to a group of sergeants—and playing with real money. Five of us admitted to gambling, and court-martial procedures were started. On December 6, 1944, a Canso, with the other four miscreants in the crew, crashed. All on board perished. As I was the only one left, the charge of gambling with enlisted personnel was dropped.

January, 1945 saw me at Sydney, Nova Scotia flying with 116 Squadron in the Battle of the Atlantic. We did convoy escort, Leigh Light Patrols, Search and Rescue, general patrols and, for a time, flew with the International Ice Patrol. Pictures that stay in my mind are the sight of a hospital ship with lights ablaze, alone in the middle of black sea and black sky, and the sight of a convoy, with ships as far as the eye could see. When winter came, pack-ice filled the sea from horizon to horizon.

I left Cape Breton Island on June 9, 1945, with ice still in the harbour at Glace Bay.

Frank Murphy

Atlantic

Not A Brilliant Move

Alex Burton

We are now the faceless, problematic, older population. But it was not always so. There was a time when Hitler's mighty forces challenged us, and we cried, "Me too!" By the millions we rushed to pick up the gauntlet and accept the fight, many to the death. We all went marching off to war, and while some did so in lock step, to the sound of bands, the waving of flags and the smiles of pretty girls, my entry into the fray was different.

I joined a cable ship, and went into the U-Boat infested Atlantic to steal enemy under-sea cable. It was not a brilliant move.

Why steal cable?

By the end of 1941, the last of the Allied cable reserves had been used to maintain a vast worldwide cable network. Replacement supplies from Germany, Italy and France were no longer available. The English factory had been destroyed by enemy bombing, and the United States did not have a cable industry. Repairs to existing lines were required constantly, but a cable ship without cable was useless. So it became necessary to steal the 450 miles required, even at the risk of losing the ship and its crew.

I was on the Newfoundland ferry, *Caribou*, which had docked in North Sydney. We were herded into a make-shift immigration office in an old, windowless warehouse. It smelled of salt fish, hemp rope, spilled molasses and a thousand other Maritime odors.

I was the last to be interviewed. When I appeared at the rough wooden counter, cap in hand, it was to face an immigration officer who wanted to get back into his office, where the electrical heaters were. Here I was, a sixteen year old from the fishing village of Harbour Buffett, apprehensive, and low on cash. The booming voice saying, "Papers!" sounded unnaturally loud, in the hollowness of the empty warehouse.

The officer must have expected more documents; when I handed him my baptism certificate, he screamed, "Oh, no! Please. No. Is this some kind of a joke? And what's this? A church certificate of some kind? Stay there."

As he turned to walk away, he muttered aloud, "When will these people understand we don't just let anyone into Canada? When will they realize that we are very, very careful about who we let in?"

By then he was next to another officer, this one with gold stripes up to his elbow. I remember thinking, "Boy, that one must have been born into the office."

My officer said to him, "Mr. Jones, sir, I have another that, perhaps, should be sent back."

"No, Kelly," was the immediate reply. " We have no budget. Give him a ninety-day visitor's permit. Let him go on to Halifax, and if they want to send him back, let them pay for it."

As Kelly turned to leave, Mr. Jones barked, "And Kelly, make sure your records read that this is an ordinary, normal entry."

For a moment I wondered if Canada was being invaded by Newfoundlanders.

I joined the cable ship, *John W. MacKay,* in Halifax on March 9th, about twelve days after the ninety-day permit ran out. I began to think that, as an illegal immigrant, every RCMP officer and Military Police patrol in Canada was looking for me.

The *John W. MacKay* was not only a ship, but also a floating factory. This combination required a special navigational crew, a ship's crew, and a complete factory staff—a total of ninety-two personnel, all crammed together on a 2000 ton ship for long periods at sea.

It took a number of months to acquire ninety-two volunteers, willing to sail out of Halifax at the height of the Battle of the Atlantic, to find and steal 450 miles of enemy cable. Finally, in a typical east coast fog, we slipped out of Halifax on May 22, 1942.

We learned, after the war, that the Merchant Navy lost 898 British, Allied and neutral ships through enemy action, during the first six months of that year. This loss represented over four million gross tons of ships and their cargo.

Let me recount just three such incidents, where an enemy submarine was within hours of the *MacKay.*

On June 6th, the ship arrived at the location of the cable line, which was on the ocean floor. The crew then commenced trolling , finding, lifting, and manipulating the cable over the rollers at the bow, along the deck, on to the lifting machinery, and into a tank, ready for coiling. This process took two days.

While this activity was going on, there was a lot of unavoidable noise: powerful main engines, pumps, running water and electrical generators, as well as the noise created by ninety-two crew members. Added to that was all the cable-factory noise, such as steam generators, and lifting machinery, which was outside on the deck.

I can still see the gloom of the hooded lights over the outside work stations, and hear the running feet and urgent orders, when an accident took place. I can feel the pain and helplessness. We had nowhere to hide.

On that date, our location was approximately five hundred miles south of St. Vincent, Cape Verde Islands. The *MacKay* was either stopped, or moving at less than one knot an hour. The submarines, on the other hand, could attain speeds of up to twenty knots per hour, depending on the type.

JUNE 6/7	006' 53' N 028' 13' W CIS	*John W MacKay*	Stopped
JUNE 7	004' 17' N 013' 48' W MN	*Chile*	Torpedoed
JUNE 10	000' 08' N 018' 52' W S/S	*Alioth Netherlands*	Torpedoed
JUNE 13	005' 30'W 023' 30' W SIS	*Clan MacQurrie*	Torpedoed

Because of all the noise and light, if a submarine were to surface near us to investigate, I would not expect its commander to be very understanding when he found us stealing fifty million dollars worth of irreplaceable property.

We were scared. We began sleeping on deck, and secretly storing extra food and water in our lifeboats. As the days went by, the captain would, without notice, call for boat drills, night and day. It seemed important to him that every member of the crew become efficient in getting the boats away. We wondered if he believed that we were running out of luck.

At our speed, we could lower the boats all the way down the side, to touch the water. It reassured us to know that when and if the hit came, the boats could be in the water in minutes. The rafts were left uncovered, and set to drop at a single pull on a lever.

I was seventeen years old, so I tried out all the prayers I could think of. I even remembered my dad's advice on my leaving home. "Son," he said, "when you are alone and afraid, don't be shy to say to Him, 'Lord please stand watch with me, because the night is dark and I am far from home.'"

Don't knock it. I'm still here!

The theft of cable went on until June 30, when all 450 miles of enemy cable were coiled in the tanks. The *MacKay*, heavily loaded, sailed to Freetown, Sierra Leone, at a mad 12.3 knots an hour. After moving at one mile an hour for so long, we felt as though we are flying.

As we arrived off Freetown on July 3, we were buzzed by two American Hurricane airplanes demanding our recognition signal, which we could not find. We began to think we would be sunk by friendly fire. In desperation, we fired our distress flares, which must have confused the pilots no end; but it worked, and we were free to enter harbour.

On July 9, we received congratulations from the Lords of the Admiralty. But there was no shore leave. We were only there for provisions and fresh water, then out we went again to repair desperately needed Allied cables.

The *John W MacKay* did cable laying and repair work in the Persian Gulf for improved Eighth Army communications, and as an aid to American war supplies bound for Russia, using that route. The ship also worked at the Allies' secret Port T, in the Addu Atoll, (Maldive Islands) Ceylon, (Sri Lanka) the Indian Ocean, and in the Mediterranean Sea.

The ship departed Halifax NS on May 22, 1942, and returned May 5, 1944. My signing on a cable ship to steal enemy cable in the Atlantic, was not a brilliant move. But in our youth we do many things that, in old age, we realize were foolhardy. However, these actions do create our dreams, and we were rewarded by congratulations from the Lords of The Admiralty, a body that does not historically honor Merchant Navy personnel.

It seemed, somehow, worth it. After all, I'll never be seventeen again.

HMCS *Iroquois*

Ray Kynock, Nanaimo, RCN

I served aboard HMCS *Iroquois*, a proud ship, with a great crew. Her keel was laid in September, 1940. It took another year to complete, and another two years before she entered active service. On November 30, 1942, *Iroquois* was commissioned into the Royal Canadian Navy.

Although completely manned by Canadians, our first tour of duty was with the RN's Home Fleet, on escort duty on the treacherous Murmansk convoy run. During our first operational mission, the troopship SS *Duchess of York* was sunk by German bombers. Our ship's company rescued more than six hundred survivors from the frigid Arctic waters, establishing a reputation synonymous with our name.

During numerous offensive sweeps of the English Channel and the French coast in preparation for the D-Day invasion, Canadian ships earned a reputation for excellence and fearlessness in battle, and became known as the Deadly Destroyers. While being refitted in Halifax, *Iroquois* missed most of the early action. It was to be a fortuitous pause, for, during this period, she was fitted with the latest radar and Action Information centre—the precursor of the modern Operations Room.

This new equipment was put to good use in the Battle of the Bay of Biscay, during the summer of 1944. On two occasions, *Iroquois*, along with another destroyer and a cruiser, destroyed two German convoys. These successes were largely due to the foresight and tactical innovation of our second captain, Commander J.C. (Jimmy) Hibbard. In a break from tradition, he moved from the bridge, and drove his force from the newly fitted AIC, using radar. These were some of the earliest examples of radar coordinated attacks, which would soon become standard in the post-war era.

We spent the winter of 1944/45 escorting troopships in and out of Plymouth. Returning to the Home Fleet in March, we participated in anti-shipping operations off the Norwegian coast. Ironically, *Iroquois'* closest brush with death occurred during our last mission of the war, when we were reassigned to the Murmansk run. Outbound from the Kola Peninsula, a U-boat fired an acoustic torpedo at us. It was heard by the stokers in the Engine room. Had it not been for a last minute, full speed astern, emergency engine movement, the torpedo would have surely found its target.

Murphy's Law

Hugh Robinson

Even war has its lighter side. My most humorous experiences occurred during basic training with the Royal Canadian Navy, (RCNVR) during World War Two. We were a pretty awkward bunch, very green, and vulnerable. We were taking our training in a shore establishment, and we stood Duty Watch every third night, mine being the Red Watch. We slept in hammocks on the top floor, in a room down a long hall from the Officers' wardroom.

We had fire drills periodically, and were told it was the equivalent of Action Stations at sea. When the bell went, we were to report to our assigned stations on the double. This situation gave the officers an opportunity for fun, at our expense. They had a party in the wardroom every Friday night. After the booze was really flowing, they would ring the fire bell, gather at the wardroom door with their girl friends and watch, with big grins on their faces, as we poor slobs raced down the hallway in our night attire. Great fun for them, and humiliation for us. We dreaded Friday nights!

Things were about to change, however, and the man who brought it about was a young, ordinary seaman by the name of Murphy. It was Friday, when Murphy announced that this was the last time the officers would be playing their little game.

You should know something about Murphy. Nature had been extremely kind to him—he must have been the most generously endowed man in the Canadian Navy.

We awaited the miracle. Sure enough, about midnight, that cursed fire bell went. Out of our hammocks we jumped, some in pajamas, some in shorts— except for Murphy, who was about to become the original streaker. The officers had said that fire drill was the equivalent to Action Stations, and a casual glance showed that Murphy was ready for action. Away we went, out of the door, with Murphy in the lead, and the rest of us streaming out behind him like a pack of blood-hounds.

Down the hall, gathered outside the wardroom doors, were the grinning officers with their giggling girl friends. They didn't grin for long. It was worth a week's pay to see their faces. The girls started to shriek, and made half-hearted attempts to cover their eyes, but the look on the officers' faces was something to behold. Shock, amazement and astonishment, accompanied, I'm sure, by the awful awareness of their own shortcomings. They pushed their girl friends back through the door, and closed it as we galloped past.

Murphy was as good as his word. We never had another fire drill on a Friday night.

I don't remember being frightened during the fourteen months that we were on H.M.S. *Puncher*. U-boats were our main threat, and, while we encountered them often, we couldn't see, hear or feel them. We weren't attacked by them, and none of the ships in our convoy were sunk. When we encountered real danger, I wasn't aware of it until long afterwards.

It happened in the Arctic Ocean or the North Sea. I had just come on watch at midnight, and had gone to the carrier's flight deck to check that the aerial depth charges were secure in their racks. It was blowing a gale, and bitterly cold. I checked the charges, first on the starboard side, and then on the port rack. They were secure.

I turned around, and all hell broke loose. The five-inch gun below me was the first to open up, and I was hit by a muzzle blast that almost knocked me down. I was furious at the gunners. I thought we'd been hit by a U-Boat, but while U-Boat captains were known for their courage, they wouldn't be crazy enough to surface amid this flotilla. I went on cursing what I thought were trigger-happy gunners, as I made my way below deck. I was in a towering rage, half deaf, (it turned out I had a broken ear drum,) and still fuming about the gun crews, when I got to the torpedo room. There, a seaman told me that enemy aircraft had attacked us, but had been driven off. I thought he meant that fighters from our other carrier had driven them off, but it didn't make sense to me, so I put it all down to just another crazy rumour.

Forty years later, I was in Ottawa, attending a Naval Reunion. A former shipmate gave me an old copy of the *Crow's Nest,* a navy paper, in which our former Captain—by then Admiral—Bidwell had an account of his command of the *Puncher*. He said, "The *Puncher* . . . was attacked several times, but she held to her luck. On one occasion, a determined night attack was made by aircraft flying low, to avoid radar. However, this particular attack was repulsed by our five-inch battery, which were not A/A guns at all, but could put up large splashes, which proved highly inconvenient to the low fliers, and discouraged their approach when still out of torpedo range."

When I got home from the reunion I phoned John Hunter, a former ERA on *Puncher,* and asked him about it. He said, "Sure, didn't you know? They piped it over the PA system that we were under attack by seventeen enemy aircraft."

Well, I finally got it. Because of the howling wind, and being at the far end of the flight deck, I just hadn't heard the pipe. If you think I had been mad at the gunners forty years previously, it was nothing compared to how mad I was at myself then. Think of it—forty years of lost opportunity to brag in Legion lounges about my brush with certain death. The original seventeen aircraft would have ballooned into one hundred and seventy, with a couple of pocket battleships thrown in for good measure. Think of all the free drinks that would have generated; and now I can't drink!

If any of you old gunners read this, thanks for saving my ungrateful neck.

We crossed the Arctic Circle on April 7th, 1945, on our way to conduct raids on the U boat pens in Narvik. It was from these pens that the subs attacked the Allied convoys going to northern Russia. These are among the most desolate seas on earth, and in wartime, some of the most perilous - the northern reaches of the Murmansk run. The storms were the worst I had seen, towering waves pushed on by the incessant gales blowing down from the Pole. Anyone who has ever been in the Arctic Ocean in those conditions knows what the term "high seas" means. Outside of the Drake Passage in the Southern hemisphere, they have to be among the worst on the globe.

We sailed north as far as the Greenland Sea, and returned before dawn each day to Norwegian waters in order to get our strike-off. We did this repeatedly without success due to the terrible weather. There were U boats around at all times, but we kept a close watch and the destroyers patrolled constantly. I thank God for those magnificent ships. War can have its rare moments of stark beauty. Anyone who has ever seen a veteran wartime destroyer slicing through a raging northern sea while going flat out with her tattered old battle flag flying, will know what I mean.

After about a week, we finally had to abandon the strike. The hard-working destroyers kept running low on fuel, and it became increasingly difficult to supply them from the carriers. We headed for our base at Scapa Flow, one thousand two hundred miles to the south, through the most heavily sub-infested waters in the history of U boat warfare. Germany had recalled almost all of her submarines to this area, but we made it through without incident, due in large part to our destroyer screen.

That was our last trip out of Scapa. Altogether we lost ten flyers to enemy action. We then went south to Glasgow, where we entered the huge KG5 dock for repairs. I got a week of leave and was in Scotland on V.E. Day, May 8th, 1945.

It was an unforgettable time. Nearly six years of war, with its terror and privation, had finally come to an end for the inhabitants of this stubborn little island. We celebrated with these wonderful people: street dances, bonfires, milling crowds, all to the accompaniment of church bells.

We remained in the U.K. for a month or so, then left for home. We arrived in Halifax on July 1, my twenty-first birthday.

Torpedoes Ahead!

George Milford

My longest trip was thirty-four days, on the NewfieJohn to Derry run, in the Frigate HMCS *Montreal*. It was in the middle of winter, and so rough, that half the time the deck would be underwater. Like all convoys, we could only travel as fast as the slowest ship. There were lots of subs around, so we had to go north to Greenland, then past Iceland.

One foggy day in February, 1944, while I was on watch, I caught a glimpse of a raft in the water, and informed the skipper. We ended up rescuing a Swordfish crew. The Swordfish was a biplane torpedo bomber, which, though obsolete, served throughout the war. Affectionately called the "string bag," they could fly low and slow, so, in spite of their vulnerability, they served well. It was a Swordfish that crippled the German battleship *Bismarck*, and had it going round in circles because its steering gear was seized up.

We got one U-Boat off Land's End, on that trip.

One of my scariest trips was near the Azores. I saw something speeding toward us and screamed, "Torpedo!" I felt stupid when it turned out to be a dolphin; they like

George Milford

to play and the darn thing bumped its nose against the ship. I took a lot of razzing on that one.

I was on the *Assinaboine*, (we called it Old Bones) based in Jamaica, to escort ships from the Panama Canal to New York. I bought over-proof rum at seventy-five cents a gallon, cut it half-and-half with water, and sold it in New York in twenty-six ounce bottles for $7.50. Unfortunately, the NYPD didn't like me cutting into the Mafia's bootlegging business, but they let the Navy handle it. So, when we got to Halifax, everybody else got twenty-eight days' leave, and I spent twenty-eight days in the Brig.

One of our traditions was that, on Christmas Day, the Captain brought a tot of wardroom rum for each of us sailors. If we could drink it down and then say thank you sir, we got another shot. Not too many of us got two shots of rum for Christmas.

Life In The Merchant Marines

Bill McFadden, Merchant Navy

I steered the merchant navy ships hauling supplies across the North Atlantic. We were the prime targets of the German U-Boats trying to stop the flow of war materiel and food to Britain, and their attacks were so effective that one in ten merchant marines died at sea—a higher ratio than any other branch of the service.

We were sitting ducks, once, when a German plane tried to bomb us in mid-ocean. The captain was yelling, "Hard right, then hard left," but I was as hard over as I could get. We escaped that attack, but saw a nearby ship go down. That was a scary time.

Merchant Marines were all volunteers. We served on 180 ships. More than seventy of our ships were sunk by enemy action, but we still didn't qualify for any of the benefits received by people who served in the other branches of the service.

Ding Dong Bell

Ronald W. Bell

I joined the Royal Canadian Navy (RCNVR) in 1943, at HMCS *Nonesuch*, and was trained as a stoker. At the same time, my brother joined as an Ordinary Seaman and became an ASDIC operator. Since our surname was Bell, and we were in the same group, we got the nicknames Ding and Dong. I was Ding, and the name stuck with me through my time in the service.

In September, I was sent to HMCS *Cornwallis*, Nova Scotia, for my stoker course, and then was transferred to Halifax in November, and put in a boiler party. I classify this as being my worst month in the Navy. The ships came in for servicing, and they couldn't wait long enough for the boilers to cool down before we had to open them up, and clean the tubes and tanks. A real dirty, hot job.

Just before Christmas, we went to Boston to commission a destroyer escort, to take her to Scotland and turn her over to the Royal Navy. While in Boston I got to meet my aunt, whom I had never seen before. She introduced me to her friends as her nephew from the far northwest, just as if I had come down there by dog-team.

We did sea trials out of Charleston's Navy Yard, Boston, then sailed for Scotland with other warships and a fleet of merchant ships. We arrived at Greenock, on the Clyde River, where we turned the ship over to the RN. I was able to get a week's leave to visit my Dad, who was a sergeant in the Royal Canadian Engineers, stationed in Southern England. He had spent time in England in World War One, and knew London pretty well. One night, he suggested that we trade uniforms. He said he had always wanted to wear bell-bottoms, and I was proud to go out pub-crawling, at age eighteen, wearing a sergeant's uniform.

I spent about eighteen months on the Castle class corvette, *Coppercliffe,* doing escort work between St. John's and Londonderry, North Ireland. I will never forget the wonderful voices of the young Irish boys, who would come into the pubs and sing.

One September evening in 1944, we were at action stations in the mid-Atlantic. Stoker Petty Officer Al Brokman and I were on duty in Number One boiler room. The orders from the bridge were quite erratic: "Full speed ahead! Stop. Half-reverse!"

Our orders were to fire those boilers without making smoke, in order not to give away our location. Orders came down from the bridge through the voice pipe: "Stop making smoke!"

After the third time this happened, Al Brokman got aggravated and hollered, "You are God damn lucky to get any."

We were in the middle of the ocean on VE Day, so we dead-headed it into

Derry, fuelled up, then dead-headed back to St. John's, where I volunteered for the Pacific and got fifty-eight days' leave.

While I was home, Japan surrendered, but I had to go back to Halifax and work on a sea-going tug boat, towing ships from different locations to Sydney, Nova Scotia, for decommissioning.

By volunteering for the Pacific, I missed out on the trip of a lifetime. My old ship, *Coppercliffe*, went from St. John's, through the Panama Canal and up to Vancouver. My mate, Jack Craig, didn't volunteer; he stayed with the ship and made the trip, stopping and going ashore at many places.

Of Such Stuff Are Heroes Made

Frank Horner

Picture a bunch of seventeen and eighteen-year old, middle-class British boys, fresh from school, still somewhat self-conscious in their RAF blue uniforms, visions of flying Spitfires uppermost in their imaginations. Not really interested in girls, and easily embarrassed by "naughty" words and deeds in mixed company.

Place these innocent youths on the RMS *Andes,* bound for Canada and the USA, and the prospect of days of doing what AC Plonks do best – nothing!

Suddenly: "Action Stations! Passengers to boat drill, army crew members to their guns!"

Balloons are released from the forward upper deck on which the gunners practice training with their weapons. Some of the balloons fail to float, and fall to the decks. Shrieks of laughter from a group of WRNS, (upstairs in segregated quarters) as a balloon descends on them.

Oh, horrors! Red faces, averted eyes; such embarrassment on the lower decks, down among the 'erks, as they discover the balloons are inflated condoms.

Of such stuff are heroes made.

The Grand Old Lady Of The RCN

Gordon R. Calam

HMCS *Skeena* was built in 1931, in Southampton, England. Miss Mildred Bennett, sister of the then Prime Minister of Canada, was accorded the honour of releasing the bottle of Empire wine, and declared, "I name you *Skeena,* and wish you, and all who sail in her, the best of luck."

She was a River Class destroyer and was probably named after the Skeena River. Her displacement was 1320 tons. She was 322 feet long, with a beam of 32 feet. Her armament was: four 4.7 inch guns, two two-pounder pom-poms, five machine guns, and eight torpedo tubes. A complement of 138 men was increased to over two hundred during the war, being jammed in like sardines! We slept in hammocks which were head-to-toe, and directly above the eating table. I remember a sailor who stepped out of his hammock and his foot landed in a plate of dehydrated scrambled egg.

Skeena arrived on the west coast in August of 1931, and in 1937, the two warships, HMCS *Skeena* and HMCS *Fraser,* visited my hometown of New Westminster. After visiting the ships, I knew I wanted to join the Navy. In 1940, I joined the RCNVR in HMCS *Discovery*, in Vancouver. The following year, I joined the permanent RCN, in Esquimalt.

I was a torpedo man, and spent some very cold, wet watches whilst on convoy duty between Newfoundland and Londonderry, Ireland. Mountainous seas, between ten and thirty feet, were the norm. I regularly had six meals a day—three down, and three up. Our navy clothing wasn't fit for the tropics, let alone the North Atlantic. After spending four hours on and four hours off duty, you would inevitably hear: "Action stations!" when it was your time off and you were trying to catch up on sleep.

HMCS *Skeena* was brought to the English Channel for D-Day, to sweep the Channel for submarines. On June 7, 8 and 9, there were eight torpedoes fired at *Skeena*. I saw one acoustic torpedo skim alongside us about twenty feet away; it blew up our cat gear. (Cat gear consisted of two bars of steel, towed about one hundred yards astern, which caused a high frequency sound—higher than our propellers—so the torpedos would head for them and blow up.)

On 6 July, HMCS *Skeena*, *QuAppelle*, *Restigouche*, and *Saskatchewan* sailed to within two miles of Brest harbour, France, and sank four German flak ships. *Skeena* had three seriously, and eleven slightly, wounded. There were four dead in the other destroyers.

On 24 July, we were attacked by four Junker 88's. One bomb came so close to our ship, that the explosion in the water heeled the ship over ten degrees.

On 12 August, just south of Brest, in Audierne Bay, we encountered three armed trawlers and two larger ships. Only one large ship got away; the rest were sunk. The *Skeena* rammed *Qu'Appelle* during manoeuvres, on a pitch-black night, cutting seventeen feet off our bow. We both managed to get back to Plymouth without any degausing gear, and for the next month or so we were in dry-dock, getting a new bow.

October 24 saw us outside of Iceland, where we encountered a fierce storm. The senior officers decided that the four destroyers would come into Reykjavik harbour to anchor. Shortly after midnight, our anchors slipped, and we were on Videy Reef. Half an hour later, the order was given to abandon ship. The ship tossed around in the storm, rolling back and forth, and it was difficult to hang on to the guard rails at our life raft stations. The decks were awash with waves and oil. When he saw that it was hopeless, the captain stopped the abandon ship procedure. We lost fifteen men that night; they are buried in Fossvogur Cemetery in Reykjavik, except for one who was never found. The hulk was sold to three Icelanders for $6,000. They towed it to Reykjavik for dismantling. Parts of *Skeena* were loaded on a Dutch vessel, the *Liberty*, and towed to the United Kingdom. The towline broke and both vessels sank. HMCS *Skeena*, the Grand Old Lady of the RCN, now lies permanently on the bottom of the North Atlantic.

May she rest in peace forever.

The Ship That Voted Itself Out Of The War

Ross Carnduff

Our father had served in the Navy in the First World War, so my brother Russell and I went Navy too. I was seventeen when I reported to HMCS *Naden*, in December 1940. It was the lure of adventure, and scary at times, but I still have it in my blood.

In June, 1941, I was in a draft of 150 sailors to Halifax. I boarded the destroyer HMCS *St. Croix*—a four-stack World War One destroyer acquired from the USA on a lend-lease arrangement with Britain, whereby the USA got bases on a ninety-nine year lease, in exchange for fifty of these ships, and Canada got seven of them.

I got my sea-legs from making a raft and sailing it on a slough on my grandfathers farm; but nothing, not even the training, prepares a prairie boy for North Atlantic storms. The first time I went to sea, we were standing at attention out on the quarter-deck, and many of us were having a hard time standing upright.

I was on convoy duty till June, 1943. I can't remember how many trips I made in three years, on the run from St. John's, Newfoundland, to Londonderry, Ireland, (we called it the NewfieJohn to Derry) escorting merchant ships and tankers. An average trip would be about fourteen days across, three days to re-fuel and re-ammunition, and then return, picking up a convoy off the Irish coast.

Although we were not involved, we were on duty in the area where the *Bismarck* sank HMS *Hood*; but the bigger danger was from submarines. We were attacked by U-Boats nearly every trip, and lost many tankers—they seemed to be the target of choice, followed by the merchantmen. At the time, the U-Boats were mostly interested in sinking war supplies. Merchant seamen were the true heroes of the war, and it is incredible how they always signed on for the next trip, knowing that their casualty rate was the highest of any of the services, and that they stood little chance of survival if a U-Boat skipper got their ship in his sights.

Paddy Price (l) & Ross Carnduff pictured with the HMCS Uganda, Jan 1945

My most frightening experience was on a convoy back to Canada, in 1942. We were in what we called the "Black Hole," an area in mid-Atlantic where the aircraft of that time didn't have enough range to give us cover. U-Boats gathered there, and we were attacked by about a dozen of them. HMCS *Ottawa* took a torpedo in the magazine, and she went down in two minutes. The sub that got her was only 1200 yards in front of *St. Croix,* and we were ordered to stand by to ram. They crash-dived, and we could see them closing the hatch as we took our first run with depth charges; our second run blew her up.

In that same action we, and the corvette *Shediac,* sank U87. We then tried picking up survivors, but, with so many subs in the area, we couldn't stay long enough to get all of them out of the water; a stopped ship was too easy a target. It was terrible to have to sail away, and I wasn't the only one with tears in my eyes.

In June, 1943, fate played a big part in my life when I was drafted off *St. Croix* to take a torpedo course, and on September 20th, south of Iceland, she was torpedoed. Only five officers and seventy-six men, from a crew of 140, were rescued by HMS *Etchen.* Two days later, *Etchen* was torpedoed, and all but one survivor from *St. Croix* perished, along with *Etchen's* crew. I knew every member of *St. Croix's* crew, except the two that were drafted to replace me and one of the stokers, and I cherish the full list I have of their names. It is still painful to talk about losing so many friends all at once.

After my course, I was drafted to HMS *Glasgow*. We took part in Overlord, the D-Day invasion of France, supporting the American landings at Omaha and Utah beaches, where we exchanged fire with German guns at Cherbourg. One shell hit our afterdeck, destroying the aft gun turrets, and we were sent back to Newcastle-on-Tine for a refit, then I was drafted aboard HMS *Belfast,* along with several other Canadians. We sailed to Boston, then to Halifax and a fourteen-day leave, after which I was sent to Charleston, South Carolina, to join HMS *Uganda,* with a completely Canadian crew for the first time since leaving *St. Croix*.

We went back to Halifax, then Newcastle-on-Tine and tied up beside the *Glasgow,* still undergoing refit from the D Day shelling.

We sailed to Gibraltar, Malta, Egypt, and through the Suez Canal to the South Pacific. After re-supplying in Sydney, Australia, we became the only Canadian warship to fight against the Japanese when we joined the US First, and British Third Fleets in bombarding Truk Island, the Admiralty Islands and Sakishima, en route to Japan.

From the time we left Sydney, we were on board *Uganda* for eight months without going ashore. Then a circular came through saying the eight hundred member crew hadn't volunteered for the Pacific, and the Canadian Government had passed legislation that only volunteers would go to the Far East. So we all got to vote on whether we should stay in the Pacific, or go home.

We were probably the only ship that ever voted itself out of a war.

Friday the Thirteenth

Arnold Bernard Klayh

I applied to join RCNVR shortly after Pearl Harbor. Although the quota was filled, I was accepted for a special new branch, having earned a diploma and gained experience in radio training.

In March, 1942, I was sent to Ottawa. I was attached to the National Research Council, to train in HDF operations and to monitor transmissions of U-Boats in the Atlantic. Later, I was sent to Lambeth, Ontario to work on high frequency operations with Foreign Intelligence Services. A new branch was formed for radio specialists, and I was enrolled in school at Hyacinth, Quebec, where I attained top marks. Given a choice of posting, either on Vancouver Island or a sea draft, I chose the sea draft and was posted on a new frigate, HMCS *Magog,* as an artificer. The *Magog* was dispatched to Bermuda for workups, to familiarize crew with wartime functions. Upon completion, I was assigned to an escort group, patrolling the North Atlantic and approaches in the Gulf of St. Laurence and Newfoundland.

On Friday, October 13, 1942, the *Magog* set sail from Gaspe to pick up a convoy, and was torpedoed on Saturday, October 14, at ten twenty-seven a.m. (See footnotes **) Casualties were light, because earlier, there had been a donnybrook in Gaspe with crew from a naval escort, and many of the sailors were up on charge and weighed off, causing them to not be on the afterdeck where the torpedo struck. The HMCS *Shawnigan* was called upon to tow the *Magog* to a protected bay, with two RCAF patrol boats shielding her from further attacks. Subsequently, a sea-going tugboat from Levis, Quebec was dispatched to tow her into salvage at Lauzon shipyards, where it was learned she was not repairable, and the crew was sent to Stadcona, Halifax, and given survivors' leave.

While home on survivors' leave, we learned that the *Shawnigan* was torpedoed off Iceland, and there were no survivors. After our leave, the majority of the crew was assigned to HMCS *Waskesiu,* which was dispatched to the Azores to intercept a convoy from the Mediterranean, for protection across the Bay of Biscay. After the convoy was safely deposited to Cardiff, Wales, the *Waskesiu* was ordered to Greenwich to escort and provide safe cover to another British sub, to an Atlantic destination.

Our ship was then dispatched to Londonderry, Ireland, for repairs and refueling. While we were there, Germany surrendered, and orders were to return to Canada for further assignments.

When we arrived in Halifax, we were not allowed leave, because there were riots going on. After completing our refueling and getting new supplies, we were ordered to Vancouver for a Pacific refit. Danger occurred on the way to Panama, when a violent hurricane nearly capsized the *Waskesiu*. Once in Panama and through Lake Gatun, we were towed by donkey engine through the canal. The ship suffered minor damage when a cable snapped, and she was put in dry dock in San Diego for repairs. After repairs, the ship was sent to Burrard shipyards, where home leave was granted to the ninety per cent of the crew that had volunteered for Pacific duty.

While I was on leave, the Americans dropped the A-Bomb, resulting in the surrender of the Japanese.

A.B. Kenneth Kelly had a premonition of his death. He had read a passage in the Bible that claimed Magog and people of Magog were doomed. That, coupled with the sailing on Friday the thirteenth, he felt, was a definite omen. Unfortunately, he was killed during the torpedo attack. I was very lucky. I had been discussing post-war plans with a shipmate, Thomas Davis, when I was called to the radar cabin to correct a problem. I was there when the torpedo struck.

Disobedience Rewarded
by Lloyd Smither, 129 Hurricane Squadron

I was practicing camera shooting in the Harvard we used for gunnery training, when we crashed in a swamp. My pilot and I got out and away as fast as we could hobble. After several minutes, when it became apparent that there was no danger of explosion, I went back to turn off the ignition. It was raining lightly, so I pulled the rubber dinghy out of stowage, dragged it over to the harder ground, and we got under it to wait for rescue.

They started searching for us that evening, and before dark we were spotted by Cap. Leonard. They dropped a doctor and nurse in to patch us up, but, as daylight was almost gone, there was no attempt to bring us out. Next morning, they had the Norseman and an SAR crew ready to go when control tower decided it was too foggy, and refused permission to take off.

Jim Westwood took off anyway. There was bright sunshine where we were, and they landed in a nearby pond. The rescue crew trekked in with their gear, and the stretcher bearers carried us out to the float plane.

I was in hospital for two weeks after we got back to base. Jimmy was put on charge for disobeying orders, but several weeks later he was awarded the Air Force Cross.

Mediterranean

Peace In Our Time

Thomas Gates

My war started in 1938, when Prime Minister Chamberlain returned from Munich declaring, "peace in our time." I was serving on aircraft carrier HMS *Hermes,* in the China Fleet. After Pearl Harbour, we placed lookouts at Kranji radio station, Paula Brani and Blaka Mali. Each lookout was equipped with silhouette pictures of Japanese warships, while at the same time we were being told, "We're not expecting the Japanese to attack British Outposts."

In January, we left Singapore on HMS *Terror* and arrived at our new base, in Bombay. The German pocket battleship, *Von Scheer,* was roaming around the Indian Ocean, sinking unarmed ships, mostly oil tankers. So we**,** with only two fifteen-inch guns and eight 4.7 dual-purpose guns, were expected to take her on. Fortunately, we never found her.

We were ordered to the Mediterranean, first to Alexandria then to Malta—convoys came and went without any serious trouble. We found ourselves secured in Lazaretto Creek until 10 June, when Italy declared war. One hour later, they raided Malta, breaking the Sunday service.

Our total defense were the Maltese AA gunners, HMS *Terror* and three Gloster Gladiators, (old 1920s bi-planes, with great maneuverability) named Faith, Hope, and Charity. Once the raids started, they never stopped; in fact, the official log showed us having been subjected to over five hundred raids, up to the time we left to go to the defense of Crete, eight months later. Again, we were the only ship to defend Suda Bay, and to assist the retreating Greek Army. Then we had to face a different enemy, the Stuka dive-bombers. We had to re-ammunition at night. On one occasion we had an oil tanker on one side, and an ammunition lighter on the other; that was one of the most frightening experiences of my life. Our luck ran out on 23 February, during an attack by German and Italian aircraft. The bomb that got us, missed—but went under, and exploded upwards.

When the order to abandon ship was given, a sailor locked the canteen door. The candy and cigarettes were going to the bottom of the sea, and he locks the door!

I was rescued after spending four hours in a lifeboat. Then, I was sent to Port Tewfik, Egypt. We heard what was happening back home, and wondered if we would have a country to go home to. Only essential shipping was allowed in the Suez canal, so I was sent on an ocean liner bound for South Africa. At Capetown, I joined the battleship HMS *Nelson*, enroute to England, and got involved in the hunt for the German battleship, *Bismarck*. We ended up sinking four of *Bismarck's* supply ships, but never engaged her. We were devastated when we heard that she had sunk HMS *Hood,* with only three survivors.

After that, I was on convoy duty in the North Atlantic, aboard HMS *Maplin*. One night, we lost sixteen ships to U-Boats in the middle of the ocean (called the Black Hole, before long-range aircraft took away the worst of the submarine menace). After half a year on that job, I joined the Royal Marine commandos and trained in Scotland, where I spent some time with the Americans. They were generous, and supplied us with everything that was otherwise impossible to get. We had visits from General Patton—I didn't like him, I think his rank went to his head—and General Bradley, who was a real gentleman and who talked with us for quite a while.

Then I was assigned to the First Canadian Division, in the invasion of Sicily, where, after a few days in foxholes, we were billeted in a castle that had been Mussolini's summer home. I ended up with malaria, and was shipped to a French hospital in Algiers. When I was able to travel, I became a soldier without a unit, and had to work my way along the coast hitching rides on anything going west. I finally joined a convoy in Phillipeville. That wasn't the end of my problem.

When we got back to Britain, the captain of the ship I was on reported one refugee, and I was sent to London for investigation and interrogation, until they finally identified me. I was then sent to Scotland, where I was an instructor on landing craft and steel pontoons, designed for landing tanks on the beaches of Normandy on D-Day. I spent the rest of the war as a commando instructor.

We were ordered back to Alexandria. Same old harbour, filled with the same ships, swinging around the buoys. The flagship, *Queen Elizabeth*, and her escorts, the battleship HMS *Warspite*, the *Terror*, and two tough little Yangtze gun-boats, were classified as a Bombardment Squadron. It seems funny now, but if it weren't for the fact that attacking the port of Bardia had taken the pressure off the Hungarian troops and the Seventh Indian Division, (really great soldiers!) the day bombardments, night bombardments, and seemingly never-ending task of fighting attacking planes would have worn us down.

Landing Ship Tank
Derek Harvey-Smith, Royal Navy, HM LST 1021

I served on her from 1944 to 1946, operational in the Mediterranean and Far East theatres. I was in the Indian Ocean, sailing east, on VE Day, and sailing west, on VJ Day.

Among my most memorable experiences: both my school and my church were bombed and burnt out; rescuing my aunt, age eighty, who was pinned to her bed when the ceiling plaster came down, due to a bomb that landed at the bottom of her garden. I never knew she could swear like a sailor.

I arrived in Canada in 1949 and served in the Royal Canadian Navy and in the RCN Reserve from 1949 to 1977.

Torpedoed

George A. Horne, R.C.A.S.C.

We embarked on the SS *Santa Elena*, a ship of about eight thousand tons, at Liverpool. We had only been at sea a few days, when Lord Haw Haw (a German propaganda broadcaster) announced that there was a large convoy bound for Naples, Italy. We joined the rest of the convoy, not far from the Irish Sea. There were approximately twenty-six ships in the convoy which included the Fifth Canadian Division and the First Canadian Corps, along with ancillary troops, and a complete Canadian Hospital Unit on our ship.

We were proceeding off the coast of Algiers. One evening, about dusk, the alarm sounded and it was announced that German aircraft were approaching. A few minutes later, the anti-aircraft guns began blasting. When the pom-pom guns opened up, we knew that the plane was after us, as these guns are used for short range. There was a terrific noise as the plane passed over us. Then the aerial torpedo hit, and our ship listed badly to the port side. The lights went out and the air was filled with dust and smoke from the explosion. We were knocked to the floor.

The Captain immediately gave the abandon ship signal. We did not stop to pick up any of our belongings, but made for the deck. There was no panic. We found only two decks above the water. The plane that attacked us was brought down, but there were still others about, so we had to lie down on the deck, on account of the flak.

After the lifeboats had been lowered from the deck above us, we went down the ladder into the sea. We were fully clothed, and had our life jackets on. I saw a raft about a hundred yards from the ship,

Sgt. George A. Horne with boat, made by German POWs, found in escape tunnel.

and decided to swim for it. The heavy swell kept carrying me back, but I finally made it to the raft. This raft had no paddles—apparently, they had fallen off when the raft was thrown into the sea—so we had to use our hands. Looking at the ship behind us, and knowing the terrific suction caused when a ship goes down, we paddled as fast as we could.

A short time after, we saw something looming; it was hard to figure out what it could be. Then we realized it was a big ship, coming through the smoke- screen. It was dark, and we were sure that the ship would not be able to see us in the water. However it finally stopped—and were we thankful!

After we had been in the water for two hours, a Royal Navy lifeboat picked us up; but we might as well have stayed on the raft, as the boat was half full of water. The name of the ship was the SS *Monterey,* built in 1939, and about 23,000 tons. It was sixty feet up the side of the ship, so we had a problem getting on board, when we got alongside. You had to grab the scramble net whilst the lifeboat was on the top of the swell, and then hang on when the lifeboat dropped away from you.

Once we made it on board, we were given a change of clothing and a hot cup of coffee; it was the best coffee I have ever tasted.

Of the two thousand passengers on the *Santa Elena*, only two engineers, who were at the site of the fatal hit, were killed. An attempt was made to tow the ship to Phillipville, in Africa, but it went down before they were able to get it there.

Later, the Germans came over the radio with a report that they had sunk a number of ships in the Mediterranean, and sent thousands of British and American reserves to a watery grave—but there were no British or Americans in the convoy. It was fortunate for us that this happened in the Mediterranean, as the water was warm, even though it was November. I can well imagine the hardships that the chaps had to put up with, in the Atlantic.

A Trip Down Memory Lane

Warren Shaddock, RCAMC, Seventh Light Field Ambulance

We sailed aboard the S.S. *Monterey* from Liverpool on October 24, 1943, in a convoy which included the *Santa Elena*. As we travelled through the Mediterranean we were attacked by a torpedo-bomber off the coast of Phillipeville, and the *Santa Elena* became the first victim. *Monterey* stopped immediately and stood by to take on survivors. The *Santa Elena* crew abandoned ship and made their way to our port side by rafts, lifeboats, swimming—any way they could. Among them were a hundred nursing sisters from the Fourteenth General Hospital.

I was working in the sick bay that evening with American Corpsman Lawrence Major, of Steubenville, Ohio. Fortunately there were few casualties, and aside from getting a salt water bath, the nurses who congregated on C deck were calm and in exceptionally good spirits.

After landing at Naples we bade farewell to the good ship *Monterey*, but that was not going to be the last I saw of her.

In 1998, some fifty years later, my wife and I booked a trip out of Miami, and it was our pleasure to find ourselves sailing on the S.S. *Britannia*, formerly *Monterey*. What a trip down memory lane! The Greek owners had preserved the sick bay on C deck just the way it was in 1943, when it was full of nurses from the *Santa Elena*.

Professional Coward
Tet Walston, Comox

I flew a sky-blue Spitfire MKXI as a Photo Reconnaissance pilot. I was a professional coward because, with no guns, I could only run if attacked.

One routine trip, which I flew three times weekly, took me to the French border with Spain, then along the south coast of France. I took pictures of enemy activities. I went to Nice, Marseilles and Toulon at a time when the only tourists were in Nazi uniforms. Naturally, I wasn't very welcome—and they let me know it. Then on to Genoa, Italy, to check on La Spencia harbour where two Italian battleships, the *Vittorio* and *Guilio Caesar*, were tied up. They didn't like me there much either! We wanted to know those ships were still there, as they could have caused a lot of trouble had they come out when Sicily was invaded. On to Sardinia for a few shots of the harbour at Cagliari, and after six hours and forty minutes in this high-flying Spitfire gas tank, I returned to base in Tunisia. The aircraft was so full of fuel I even sat on a gas tank, and I've been told you can still see the wrinkles on my backside from the crimping in the top of the tank.

When the American B-17s began their daylight bombing I flew ahead to mark targets, then would take part in the briefing of their crews. Among my memorable experiences was the attack on the fortress island of Pante Llieria, off the coast of Sicily. I went over and got all the pictures for the briefing, then the American Forts dropped their loads. After the invasion the garrison commander told us he was going to surrender anyway, and was just waiting for someone to surrender to. In fact, on that same day, a Spit pilot with engine trouble landed on a nearby island, and the garrison commander surrendered to him.

They Were Just Kids
Guy Trenholm, Cape Breton Highlanders

After basic training in Aldershot, Nova Scotia, I was sent to Debert to train as a Bren gun carrier driver. Then we left Halifax, landed at Liverpool and went on to Aldershot, England.

I was in England for two years before we embarked for Italy. We were on the *Monterey* off Gibraltar when a German bomber came over. It was a near miss but we had one casualty—a nurse fell and broke her back. We were lucky, but the *Santa Elena* was hit. We towed her into Phillipeville but it was a wasted effort; she sank in the harbour. That night we left for Naples.

I first saw action in the battle for Ortona, at the Hitler (Gustav) Line. In the Liri Valley, we took a terrible beating on the Coriani Ridge. Afterwards we got some replacement carriers from the Eighth Army (The Desert Rats) and had to clean about six inches of sand out of the bottom of the carriers. It was no mystery where they had come from.

We were pinned down pretty good; even our Colonel was holed up in an old pig pen. I was bringing up the meals, and when the Germans in the mountain heard the carrier coming they laid a three-inch mortar on me. I lost a bogey wheel, but one of my buddies, who was sitting on the edge of a slit trench putting on his boots, took a load of shrapnel. Cpl. Price went out and brought in our wounded comrade. That took guts!

Sometimes the Germans used a mine that had notches in it, which allowed several vehicles to pass over before it went off. Nothing ahead of me was damaged, and we went over; so did the jeep behind me, but the anti-tank gun it was towing flipped right over top of the jeep and ended up in front of it.

After things quieted down in Italy we were shipped to Marseille, France, then on to Holland. That's where I learned that my brother with the New Brunswick Rangers was killed at Antwerp.

We were at a German U-Boat base when the war ended. It was strange to see them come out in perfect marching order. So many of them were just kids. We held them in an old cheese factory, let them go swimming, gave them regular rations and most of us gave them cigarettes from our own pockets. While we were there we fed everybody with whatever we could spare from rations, and from our own Red Cross parcels.

I signed up for the Pacific but was stranded in England and worked in a nursery, paid ten shillings per day. The war against Japan ended and we finally came home.

I visited my brother's grave in 1990.

Yak, Anyone?
Phillip Redman

You often hear people say that they were born at the wrong time; sometimes I feel that applies to me.

I was born during the First World War in Somerset, England. My parents owned a small farm just outside Bristol, and I had a good childhood; the war didn't affect us much out in the country. I managed to survive the great 'flu epidemic of 1920, but a younger brother didn't. Two other brothers born in 1924 served in the Second World War and both have now passed away.

Things weren't good during the 1920's, so in 1926 we sold up and moved to Littlehampton, in West Sussex. We settled down nicely, but things became worse, culminating in the crash of 1929 and the Great Depression. No longer able to afford to go to school, in 1930, at the age of fourteen, I went job hunting. My first job was pumping gas, but it was short lived. The owner was forced to close down, as no one could afford to buy gas. I managed to get a job at a shop that charged batteries for our radios (no TV then). I had a bicycle with a carrier, and I used to pick up the wet batteries, take them to the shop for charging and then deliver again. It didn't pay much, but it was a job.

Later on, when prospects for the future did not look good, I decided to join the Merchant Navy. Having grown up around Bristol, one of the great seaports, I had always been fascinated by the coming and going of ships from all over the world. When I told my parents, they weren't too keen about my joining up but said that if that was what I wanted, they would not stand in my way. I sent a letter off to Southampton for information, but the reply was not what I expected. Due to the Depression the Merchant Service was not hiring and ships were being laid up and often sold for scrap, many to the Japanese (I will touch on this later). They did suggest, however, if I was eager to go to sea I should try the Royal Navy, as they were still recruiting. My mother wrote to HMS *Victory* in Portsmouth and in July, 1932, we received a letter telling me to report to *Victory* Barracks for an interview. Upon arrival I joined forty other youngsters for medical and written exams.

In September, 1932, I got my letter of acceptance, with instructions to report to HMS *St. Vincent* in Gosport, and to bring my toilet gear and necessary clothes as I would not be home again until Christmas. HMS *St. Vincent* was a boys' training ship and not a bad place to be during the Depression; at least you were assured of three meals a day and a pair of boots!

I remained at *St. Vincent* until July, 1933, when most of our class was sent to HMS *Suffolk*, a County class cruiser heading for the China Station. I spent two and a half years on *Suffolk*, returning to the UK at the end of 1935. We were paid off and the crew went to their various depots. Since I had taken a liking to China, I volunteered for service on gunboats on the Yangste River. While waiting for this, I spent time on a couple of destroyers, one of which was the *Wessex,* taken off reserve and sent to Gibraltar during the Spanish Civil War. We returned to Portsmouth in early 1936. *Wessex* went back to reserve and the crew returned to *Victory*. I remained there until March, 1937, when I got a pier-head jump to the cruiser *Diomede* for passage to China to join the Gunboat HMS *APHIS* at Shanghai. I joined the *APHIS* on April 19, 1937, and spent the next two years sailing up and down the Yangtse river. Then the Japs screwed it up by invading China at the end of 1938. We had one or two narrow escapes; we were in the same area when the USS *Panay* was sunk.

I mentioned earlier about the scrapping of British merchant ships. Supposedly sold for scrap, the Japs used them to transport troops up the river. The British Ports of Registry were still visible on the sterns!

In May, 1939, we headed for Shanghai, and all crew due to return home boarded the trooper *Dorsetshire*. We stopped in Hong Kong to pick up other service personnel, many of them submariners. We then proceeded to Singapore, Aden, Malta and eventually home.

Rumours of war were common as we went through the Suez Canal. We passed a number of Italian ships loaded with troops, heading for their war against Haile Selasse. We arrived home in July, 1939, back to *Victory*, where we were all sent on leave subject to recall, as war seemed imminent.

Normally, joining subs was pretty difficult; you had to wait until someone died or retired. However, with war coming closer every day, they needed all the manpower that could be mustered. After two weeks' leave I was recalled and drafted to HMS *Dolphin*. However, I was not accepted without a non-sub rate, so was sent to *Vernon* to qualify as a seaman torpedo man , returning to *Dolphin* at the beginning of

Redman – identified with 'X' – with crew on H.M.S. United

1940. After sub training I joined the depot ship *Forth* at Holy Loch. By this time I was a L/Seaman, and married. While I was on *Tuna*, my first son was born.

Most of our patrols were carried out in the Bay of Biscay and the South Atlantic. On Christmas Day, 1941, shortly after we had dived off on patrol off the coast of France, our Asdic operator picked up HE. The skipper sighted a transport which he described as a troopship. He fired a salvo of four, sending it to the bottom with two hits. We were depth-charged for a while but without serious damage. This area was used by the U-Boats returning from their Atlantic patrols; we made an attack on one with negative results.

I remained on *Tuna* until September, 1941, when I passed for Petty Officer and rated Acting/PO. I was yanked off *Tuna* into Spare Crew. There I sat until March 1942, when I was drafted to Barrow-on-Furness to join one of the new U- class boats as second cox'n. We commissioned in Apri, 1942, and headed to Scotland for workups. On completion we sailed for the Med to join the Tenth S/M Flotilla, arriving in July, 1942. There was plenty of excitement in the Fighting Tenth, with the bombing of Malta by the German air force and plenty of action on patrol. When we ran out of torpedoes we went over to the African coast and shot up trains and army convoys with our three-inch gun. Often the enemy shot back; then we had to get the hell out of there as it was too shallow to dive.

During my time on the *United,* there were two patrols when we almost had it. The first was in September, 1942, off the Tunisian coast. We received a message to keep a lookout for a ship the RAF believed they had damaged. While surfaced, the Asdic operator had picked up HE, and we headed away on this bearing. Soon the ship was sighted; we closed up action stations and I took over the helm. It was a typical Mediterranean night, the sea flat as a pool table, a full moon. The skipper closed on his target. What he did not know, however, was that it was an ammunition ship with a destroyer alongside. He closed to about eight hundred yards, then fired one torpedo and turned away. At that moment, the earth exploded. We were lifted right out of the water. The bridge was a shambles; water poured into the motor room, short-circuiting everything. Our hull was holed so we couldn't dive, all communication was out, it was dark, and we were a sitting duck on the surface. With a lot of hard work by the crew, the holes were plugged and power was restored so that we could dive. We proceeded back to Malta.

Our next patrol, in January of 1943, was north of Sicily, near Naples.

Nothing exciting had happened the entire patrol, and we were headed south towards home. We had dived all day on January 17. At 1700 hours, diesel HE picked up what he thought were two destroyers. He closed the target, fired four torpedoes, a hit was recorded and the diesel HE stopped. Then the fun began!

Thirty charges were dropped on us in a half hour period. The destroyers were joined by E-Boats from harbours in Sicily, and the depth charging kept up for thirteen hours. Twice, we tried to surface, but the E-Boats were still there. By that time, the air in our boat was pretty nasty. Although oxygen canisters had been released in the boat, oxygen was almost non existent and this was affecting the crew. We had dived all the previous day and night, and were well into the second day. If we could not surface soon, some of the crew would not make it. Finally, at 1830 hours on January 18, the skipper decided to take a chance and go up.

All of the E-Boats were gone. We were able to surface and get fresh air, but nearly all the crew were sick. We started the engines and headed for Malta; they had given up on us as we were reported overdue and presumed lost. But you can't keep good men down, as we used to say when the charges were dropping.

In January of 1944, our skipper, Lt. Haig-Haddow, was posted to the new V-class Visigoth building at Birkinhead. He took me with him as his cox'n as I had recently been made Chief. On December 18, 1944, we set sail for the Far East, stopping at Aden for a week.

I had to take on a lot of stores before we left for Ceylon; dry goods were okay, but fresh meat was at a premium—the only fresh meat I could get was yak. Aden being one of the hot spots of the world, any meat that you wanted had to be killed, brought to the boat in the early hours, cut up and put straight into the freezer. Around four a.m. I got a call from the trot sentry, who said, "There is an awful bloody great animal on deck!" He asked me to come up and collect it.

The chef and I brought the animal down to the fore-ends and proceeded to cut it up. In the meantime I had contacted the outside tiffy to make sure the freezer was ready to receive the yak. When he came to see me in the fore-ends he looked at the animal we were cutting up and said, "What the hell are you going to do with that?"

I explained that that was the food we would be eating on our way to Ceylon. He promptly told the chief tiffy all about it, and that is when the trouble started. *They weren't going to eat that crap, they would go see the skipper first.* By then the meat was all stowed, and when I made out the menus for the trip, the meat would be listed as lamb.

When we arrived in Ceylon, the outside tiffy asked me if I was going to return the meat I had gotten in Aden.

I said, "What meat? There isn't any left. You ate it all; remember the lovely meals of lamb you had?"

I got a real kick out of fooling the tiffy's mess; even the skipper knew about it!

Africa

Life In The Royal Air Force

Edward E.C. Beaven, RAF

On April 9, 1941, I reported to Number One Reception Centre, Penarth, South Wales, to be trained as a radio telephone operator. On July 4, I reported back to Penarth for permanent service, and was kitted out for a uniform. Surprisingly, it fit, although the boots took a little getting used to. In the RAF you received one pair of boots for regular use, and a pair of shoes for "walking out".

At this time I was informed that the WAAF (Women's Auxiliary Air Force) was taking over the telephone duties in the RAF, and that I would have to take a trade and aptitude test to determine where I would be most suited. Being a printer in civvy street appeared not to qualify me for the usual air force trades. So it was decided that I would become a wireless mechanic, as they were short of them.

Our basic training for the next six weeks took place at the seaside resort town of Weston-super-Mare, (Somerset) where we were all placed in civilian homes, at the rate of £1.0s.6d per week, the 6d was for one hot bath per week. It was quite an enjoyable experience. Because the house was so far away from the sea front where we did our marching routines, we took a bag lunch and sat on the beach; if there was enough time we would go for a swim, either in the sea (on this coast the sea goes out about three miles, leaving a large area of wet sand) or in the swimming pool, which was free to the forces in uniform. I must admit that the drill instructors did marvelous things with us raw recruits, even the ones with two left feet. At the passing-out parade—to the strains of military music from an RAF band from the nearest station—I felt proud, not only of my unit, but of myself too.

Then we marched, in full pack, to the nearest RAF camp where we were placed under canvas for a couple of days. From there, those of us who were for radio training were given railway passes to Wolverhampton, in the Midlands. We reported to the Adjutant's office at RAF Cosford. After two days there we were given civilian billets so that we could attend Wolverhampton Technical College for basic radio theory tuition. My civilian home for the duration of this course was in the Whitmore Reams area of the city and, with two other airmen, I was well looked after by an elderly couple. Once again, it was too far to come home for lunch, so we had a sandwich lunch near the college. I chummed up with a couple of the lads in the same class and we spent our lunch periods in the nearby Woolworth's cafeteria, where we made friends with the girls behind the counter. This led to an occasional date, and I had my first serious liaison. The young lady's name was Eva McDonald, from Dudley, about eight miles distant, and we both believed it to be serious enough to think that we were engaged.

The course took about sixteen weeks to complete. It was not all study, of course; we had the regular curriculum of gym exercises, and every Wednesday afternoon was sports day, when you had to play soccer or field hockey, or run. I got into field hockey and tried to play every Wednesday. We didn't bother with shin pads, so we got a few bruises, but it was fun. The course was finished about the middle of December, just in time for two weeks' leave which included Christmas, but not New Year. I finished with a sixty-three percent average—the top mark was sixty-eight percent.

The next course was a more advanced one and took place on the east coast, at Cranwell, (Lincolnshire) at the Number One Signals School. We were now in barracks blocks where we had to tidy our beds military fashion, arrange our lockers in a certain way, keep all our buttons and boots polished and march to classes every day. Church parades were compulsory—even heathens had to parade.

Jewish airmen were classified as OD (Other Denomination) and, unless there was a synagogue nearby, were encouraged to attend the nonconformist churches to allay any suspicions by the Germans if they were captured.

There was little time to visit the surrounding countryside, although a group of us did make it to Grantham one day, not just to see the cathedral there, but to taste an ale or two. At the end of this course, which included hands-on experience with RAF equipment, I was officially an Aircraftman Second Class Wireless Mechanic, otherwise known as an AC-Plonk.

My first posting was to No. 1454 Special Flight, stationed at RAF Charmey Down, not too far from Bath, and close to home. The flight was composed of three Boston A-20's, known as Douglas Havocs in the RAF. They were twin-engine day and night bombers. I was doing maintenance on the Havocs from two p.m. until midnight, seven days a week.

It was not long before I was posted overseas.

The contingent traveled by train to Glasgow, where we boarded SS *Pasteur* for places unknown. The ship was quite a large one, about fifty thousand tons, and was adapted as a troop carrier. There were about six thousand army, two thousand RAF, and a complete Field Hospital Unit, but the nurses were segregated from the rest of us and were in the first-class area of the ship. I did learn the art of chess, poker, and housey-housey (bingo) on board. The games were run by the crew, probably for their own profit.

The voyage was uneventful. Leaving Glasgow, we were accompanied by an aircraft carrier, three cruisers, five destroyers and some corvettes. However, one morning we woke up to find that we only had one destroyer and a couple of corvettes—the fleet had left us to go to Gibraltar. We stopped at Freetown, Sierra Leone, to pick up water and fresh supplies, and had our first experience of bum-boats. You could throw money overboard and the natives would dive and retrieve it before it had gone too far down. You could also buy fresh fruit, which was hauled up in a basket.

Arriving in Durban, South Africa, a lot of us disembarked; the rest were rumored to be going on to the Far East. We were put up at the Clairwood Racecourse, not far from Durban, under canvas. We were told that we would probably be there for three weeks, and to be careful and keep away from the native districts when went into town. Many of us had not seen fresh fruit for a long time, and we could buy sacks of everything from apples to pineapples for a few pennies. There were a lot of us who spent many an hour on one of the toilets that were arranged in a circle in the open air!

We visited Durban several times, and many of the private homes were thrown open to us. The Jewish Services Club provided four-course meals for the equivalent of about 1/6d. A bus trip to the Valley of the Hills, a nature preserve park, was also arranged.

We left Durban by a much smaller ship, seen off by the Lady in White, who had welcomed all arriving and departing ships since the start of the war, with a song amplified by a megaphone. We arrived in Port Said on 25 July, 1942, where we were dispersed to our units. Mine was Number Sixty-three RSU, (Repair and Salvage Unit) based in Ismailia, on the banks of the Suez Canal. This unit went out to collect crashed planes in the desert and specialized in Vickers Wellington bombers. Where practicable, these were rewired, re-engined, and the fuselage repaired by the various technicians on the station.

I spent three days at Number Fifty-eight General Hospital for treatment of dysentery, when they discovered that I had something wrong with my throat. It was a congenital problem—a small hole that occasionally discharged—which they had not noticed when I had volunteered, a year earlier. So I was to go back to hospital for an operation two weeks later. In the meantime, I was sent on a week's leave, which I spent in Cairo where I chummed up with five others who were in the same accommodation. We spent the week seeing the Blue Mosque, the Pyramids, and the Sphinx. I had my fortune told in the sands near the Sphinx. The fortune teller said that I would return safely to England (which was a relief, as I was facing a fairly serious operation) get married to an English girl who would not be from my home town, never be really poor, and have four, maybe five, children. If you count four temporary adoptions, he was right on the button.

The operation was performed successfully. After having two teeth extracted, as the surgeons did not want any chance of infection in a hot dusty climate, I spent six weeks convalescing at El Arish, at the edge of the Sinai Desert. It was not all rest, however. I had to work a couple of days with a donkey and cart, moving stones from one end of the village to the other. I also did guard duty for twenty-four hours on a water tower. With five others armed with rifles, we were supposed to protect the water supply from marauding Arabs, who were not all that friendly towards the British at the time.

I was back in my unit by the first week in December, just in time for the Christmas dinner and show put on by the station members. I had a small job attempting to control the flood-lights that had been rather amateurishly fixed up by the electricians.

On April 20, 1943, I was posted to Number Seventeen SOR, (Sector Operations

Room) which was about thirty miles east of Benghazi, Libya. I managed to catch a supply convoy, and a couple of days later I arrived at the desert. One of the most effective ways of having a brew-up in the desert is to fill a petrol can half-full with sand, pour in some petrol and set fire to it. Instant heat! The Ploesti oil refineries heavy-bomber raid took place on August 1, 1943, while I was on duty. Liberator bombers from the Ninth USAAF, and reinforcements from the Eighth USAAF took part, but the raid, although spectacular, was not a success militarily, as little damage was done and the Americans lost fifty-six planes.

I was at Number Seventeen SOR until 24 July, 1944. Most of my duties entailed the maintenance and tuning up of transmitters to different frequencies. During this period I received my first promotion, to the rank of Aircraftsman First Class (ACI). Also about this time I received a "Dear John" letter telling me that Eva McDonald had met an old school chum, who was in the army, and that they were going steady.

On 25 July, 1944, I was assigned to a special detachment with unspecified duties. We were flown to the Signals Depot in Helwan, near Cairo, and then by train to Nerab Camp, near Aleppo (Syria). No-one knew what it was all about, but when we were fitted out with civilian clothes, passports, and travel documents in Turkish, we knew then what the special duties were. We went by train to Ankara, Izmir and Istanbul, where different groups were put off. I was in the village of Buca with about two hundred others; we were billeted in a very large house. Our job was to train the Turkish forces in the operation of mobile radar and wireless communications.

When Turkey declared war on the side of the Allies, nearly all the special detachment left except for a skeleton crew. Luckily, I got to stay. I left on April 29, 1945.

Arriving at Number Three Signals Depot, Helwan, I was waiting to see where I would be posted next. While I was there, victory in Europe was declared and, as usual in the services, it was an occasion for roast turkey and all the trimmings. This took place on May 8. Sports were arranged by the camp permanent staff and everyone was expected to take part. I enrolled for the one-mile race and the hundred-yard dash. It was 110 degrees in the shade. Of the fifty who entered for the one-mile race, only five finished, and I was not one of them. I only completed about three laps, and I did not even try for the one hundred yards.

My next posting was to AHQ Levant, based in Jerusalem. Once again, I was not at the main unit but accommodated in a small combination of huts in the Palestinian Police Compound on Mount Scopus, next to the Mount of Olives. The work was the same, keeping the transmitters on frequency and in good repair around the clock for general communications between AHQ and other military centres. It was there that I got my final promotion, to LAC, (Leading Aircraftman) in September, 1945.

I took advantage of my stay in Jerusalem to see the Garden of Gethsemane, the Via Dolorosa, Golgotha, and Bethlehem, which I visited on Christmas Eve. It was very cold, and there was carol singing in the Shepherd's Fields, which is believed to be the site of the Nativity. I walked through the underground conduit which was cut through solid rock and built to supply water when Jerusalem was under siege. The water was a foot deep and very cold.

At that time, tension between Arabs and Jews was coming to a head. All British troops were advised to go about in pairs, with one man armed, and to be very wary of provoking either side. It put a bit of a crimp into sightseeing.

The war in the Far East finished in August, but there was little celebration except for a parade of remembrance to the cemeteries of World Wars One and Two. My stint overseas was finished on January 7. I was returned to Newhaven, where I was given four weeks' leave and was told I would be informed by letter about my next posting.

After four weeks' leave with the family (it seemed like ages since I had seen them all, and my brothers and sisters had grown) I received my next posting. It seemed peculiar that I was still in the RAF, with the war over, but England's state of emergency had not yet been lifted by Parliament. Anyway, the government did not want thousands of ex-service men and women looking for jobs all at the same time.

My posting was to RAF Kirkcolm, about ten miles from Stranraer, Scotland, where the boats left for Belfast, in Northern Ireland. With the end of the war, our job was to strip the Short Sunderland flying boats of any useful equipment. Then we towed them to the Army Ordnance Depot on the other side of the loch. We loaded boxes of ammunition onto the flying boats, which were then towed to the Irish Sea by Air/Sea Rescue launches. There, the aircraft, with their load of ammunition, were sunk. It seemed such a waste.

My last few months of service life were spent in the hills and lakes of western Scotland. The weather was beautiful too, making it ideal all round.

On 21 August, 1946, I reported to West Kirby, Lancashire, for discharge. After all my equipment was checked in, I received a suit and was allowed to keep the shoes, plus all underwear and socks, and one uniform. I also got a fawn raincoat, which was recognizable everywhere as a demob one. I was given one hundred days of demobilization leave, with pay, and a small gratuity for the more than five years that I had spent in the RAF. The pay wasn't given all at once; I was issued a Post Office Savings Book, with instructions to draw once a week.

According to my RAF records, I was awarded the 1939 to 1945 Star, the Africa Star and North Africa 1942 to 1943 Clasp, the Defense Medal, and the Victory Medal.

Shoe-Shine Scabbards And Exploding Biffies

Ron Buxton

Early in 1940, I was transferred to a commando unit in Scotland. At first, the emphasis was strictly on training, and not on spit and polish. That changed a few weeks later, when the CO called a parade. We lavished energy on our uniforms, webbing, boots and equipment. Unfortunately, my bayonet scabbard resisted all efforts to bring on a shine, regardless of how much energy I applied. I solved the problem by painting it with black enamel. The result was magnificent, and I went to bed happy.

Next morning, my euphoria vanished when I found the paint was not yet dry. But I still had a great shine. Everything went well as the CO walked along in front, but on his walk back, he stopped behind me and remarked, "My God! Sergeant Major, look at the polish on that scabbard."

The sergeant major clutched the scabbard for a closer inspection and, with an explosive snort, replied, "Sir, it isn't polish, it's bloody paint."

The CO said, " I want to see this man in my office after parade."

I fully expected to be returned to my former unit in dis-

LIEUT. R.E. BUXTON.

68

grace, so was relieved when the CO said, "Buxton, I should punish you for defacing WD property. But because you displayed the type of initiative we require, I propose to take no action at this time. Don't do it again and keep out of sight of the Sergeant Major—he can't get the paint off his hands."

A month later I was promoted to Lance Corporal. Later, after several promotions, I was a Commander in a tank battalion in the African campaign, fighting against Rommel's Afrika Korps. It was hot in a tank in the desert and yet, in the heat of battle, we were so focused that we ran on adrenalin and didn't notice the discomfort until it was over.

Captured by the German Afrika Corps in Libya in early June, 1942, I was transported to Italy, where I was confined in a number of POW camps until the Italians capitulated in September, 1942.

We again found ourselves in the hands of the Germans, who transported us to a very large camp at Moosburg, Bavaria. The camp accommodated 22,000, most of whom were forced labour. The POW's were housed in cages in the main compound. Our cage had, unfortunately, been previously occupied by some Italians, whose unsanitary habits were such that the brick building containing twenty seatless toilets was in such disgusting condition, it was impossible to use. The Senior British Officer complained to the German Commandant who, having inspected the site, arranged for the underground tank (over which the toilets were located) to be pumped out and the building thoroughly hosed down and disinfected.

Feeling it was safe to use, twenty of us took our seats. Cigarettes were lighted and conversation began. Unfortunately, the tank, emptied of its solid contents, was filled with highly flammable methane gas, which ignited when one of the group dropped the lighted stub of his cigarette between his legs. Immediately, ominous rumblings and explosions were heard from below and the building started to violently shake.

The occupants leapt, screaming, off the toilets, followed by long tongues of flame coming up through the bowls. Thinking the building might blow up at any moment there was a mad rush to get outside, resulting in minor bruising caused by too many trying to get through a narrow door at the same time. A number of the men had singed posteriors, and others tripped over pants which were still down around their ankles.

The Germans had the last laugh. They dumped the filthy and odorous contents of the tanker within a short distance of the camp, providing an unpleasant reminder of the incident until the passage of time faded both the smell and the memory.

Bombs And Beer

James (Stocky) Edwards

It was during the Eighth Army's advance from El Alamein. With Rommel's Afrika Korps in full retreat, the Germans abandoned air bases as they ran.

RAF Squadron 260 became the new occupants of the former German base at Derna, south of Benghazi, where we found an HE111 with one engine ready to go, the other partly installed. The German ground crew had not had time to finish the job.

Our RAF mechanics had the aircraft in good working order before long, but they had no twin engine pilots till a search turned up a man at another base who had flown multi-engine. Thus, with our new instructor, we became Heinkel pilots. Given an RAF roundel in place of the swastika, and our squadron letters HS followed by a ? in place of the aircraft letter, we used it for transporting fresh veggies and beer from Cairo. We became the most popular squadron in the desert, with visitors from other outfits inventing excuses to drop in for a cold one.

Everything went well until one day our chief Heinkel pilot, F/L Cundy, an Aussie, was nearly shot down by our own people. A Junkers was reported in our area and a flight from an RAAF squadron nearby had been scrambled. Cundy was on his way in from Cairo when, over his receiver, he heard a broad Australian accent say, "There's the bastard over there."

Four Kittyhawks were closing on him. Cundy waggled his wings, had his crewman shoot off all the flares, pointed at the roundels on his wings and waved frantically. He finally convinced the RAAF boys that he was a friendly, with beer, so they escorted him the rest of the way and stopped in for a few cold ones.

Shortly after that the RAF took the Heinkel away from 260 squadron. I may be the only RCAF veteran who has flown the HE111.

For more information about Stocky Edwards pick up his book, "Kitty Hawk Pilot," at the Nanaimo Library, or write to James F. Edwards, 152 Carthew St. Comox, BC, V9M 1T3.

An Egyptian Cadet's War

Mohammed Sidky

I was a high school student and a police officer cadet in Cairo in 1942, and graduated in 1946. We had blackouts, but, other than a few bombing raids where the Germans were going after bridges and allied army installations, the war never got closer than El Alamein. There were soldiers from all over, on the streets: British, Australians, New Zealanders, Greeks, South Africans, French, Polish, Indians, and more.

One evening, I went to the theatre with a friend. It was a James Cagney movie; my friend was really excited by all the action and started imitating Cagney, shadow-boxing as we walked home in the blackout. All shops were closed and it was very dark. We were just kibitzing along when I saw four legs in front of me, looked up, and there were two big Australian soldiers.

One soldier stopped us and said, "Each of you give me a shilling."

That was equal to five piastres—big money for a couple of Egyptian kids. I could speak a little English, so my friend turned to me and asked, "What does he want?"

The soldier must have thought he was planning to fight back. All I saw was a big fist aimed at my friend. Taking off right between the soldiers, I started running as fast as my legs would carry me. I didn't stop to look back. Next morning my friend showed up in school with his jaw wrapped in a bandage.

In those days, English speakers would call us "Bloody fool." We thought they were complimenting us on our cooking by saying, "Bladdy"—very nice—"Fool"—beans. They are a popular dish in Egypt, but it seemed strange to us that the English liked beans so much.

There was no insignia on my police cadet uniform yet, because I was just a new kid in the outfit. One day I was walking to class when a British soldier stopped me and asked, "What the Hell outfit are you in? Are you military?"

I said, "Police Cadet, Sir."

"So you know how to shoot a gun?"

"Yes, Sir."

"Why the hell should we be here fighting for you?"

I felt sorry for all those men so far away from home.

Egyptian kids ten to twelve years old put together shoe shine kits in wooden boxes and made money off the soldiers, who would stand with one foot on top of the box and get their shoes shined. While the kid was working, he would watch the soldier looking around. When a pretty Egyptian girl walked by and the soldier was distracted, the kid would tie his boot laces together. Then, when the soldier took out his wallet to pay, the kid would grab the wallet and run. The soldier would start to chase him and trip over his tied-together boots.

Eggs Stronger Than Build

Helen Sidky

I was a teenager in Prague on March 15t[...] mans marched in with their tanks and g[...] everybody was in the street with tears rur[...] had loudspeakers in the streets, with Pre[...] we didn't want to see our city destroyed.

Allied bombers started coming in 19[...] living in a hotel when I heard the siren[...] nearby bridge and destroyed it, along with the next building and the one across the road. The church nearby was demolished and all the glass in our hotel was broken; our room was a shambles. But strangely enough, I had a basket of eggs sitting on a table in the middle of the room and not one of those eggs was even cracked.

When the Russians came, the Czechs joined them in fighting against the Germans. At that time we thought the Russians were our life savers.

Russian soldiers were like pigs, very dirty, didn't even know how to sit on a toilet, not very knowledgeable about anything, My husband said he was from Egypt and a Russian soldier asked, " What is Egypt, something you eat?"

There was no Czechoslovakian family untouched by the war.

The Other Side Of The War

Helmut Zittier, West Vancouver

I left my home near Berlin to join the Luftwaffe in April, 1939. In May, 1940, pilots in training were permitted to choose the kind of aircraft they wanted to fly: bombers, fighters, Stuka dive bombers, or transport. As Poland was finished, and everything else was quiet, I thought there would be no more war. I figured on pursuing a peaceful career with Lufthansa, and chose transports. I was laughed at and accused of being a coward. However, it didn't work out anyway, because after twenty three months of training, and with no more schools to go to, I was posted to Geschwader Horst Wessel of ZG 26 to fly twin-engine ME110 fighters with Rommel's Afrika Korps. I figured I was lucky because the alternative would have been Russia.

It wasn't long before things started going badly for us in Africa. Montgomery's Eighth Army was piling up victories after El Alamein, and Eisenhower's Operation Torch had started in Morocco. Our perimeter was closing in on us. One after another, we were losing our landing fields. With Tunisia threatened, my squadron, the Seventh Staffel, was transferred to Sicily on May 7th, 1943.

Shortly after the move, I was called upon to fly to Tunis and bring out the Vichy French Governor and the German Gauleiter (civilian administrator). Being only a corporal pilot I asked my commander, "Why did you choose me? There are so many other pilots more highly qualified."

He answered, "You are much more calm than any of them, and I need someone who won't get too excited."

Given permission to plan my own trip, I flew over at twilight after the Spitfires were down and before the night fighters took off. I stayed overnight and left just before dawn. The Vichy Governor gave me a

Zittier (l) and his Navigator, when Rommel was winning the desert war.

rough time; he didn't want to get into a small plane. He changed his mind when he saw the written order from high command: *These two men are too valuable and they know too much to be captured alive.* I delivered the two men to Trapani, Sicily. That was the trip that earned my Iron Cross First Class.

I was flying every day, from Sicily to Africa and back, with no sign of trouble. We needed some boxes of tools that had been left behind in Tunisia, and two other destroyers were sent out for them. Both were shot down. Like most pilots, they had flown in a straight line to get home fast as possible. I figured that the Spitfires would be patrolling that area, so I flew thirty minutes west, north for sixty minutes, and then east to Trapani. It took me two hours, but I was the only one to complete the mission. Several weeks later, the squadron was sent out to escort thirteen Gigantis (huge six engine transports) which were all shot down. It was my birthday and, as was the custom, I was given the day off. Otherwise I would have been shot down with them. I was the last pilot out of Africa. The day after I left, 260,000 soldiers became prisoners of war.

One morning a mechanic asked me, "What did you do to this airplane?

"I don't know," I replied. "Why"?

My starboard foreflap was not working; no wonder I had such a hard time getting down! Another time I took off with a flat tire and had to crash land with my wheels up. Then there was the time I tried to land at the island of Pantalleria and the runway was out—it had been attacked by allied bombers and I ran into our own anti-aircraft fire. I came down in some wires with my glide slope too high and no runway lights. Nobody could believe I walked away from that one.

In July, 1943, as I was battle-fatigued, I was sent to a fine hotel in Bavaria for a rest.

I was one of thirty pilots there, and I met General Galland. I was also informed that I wouldn't be going back to Rome, as our squadron was coming home to Germany to take part in our defence. That was where the B17G Flying Fortress chin-turret gunner got me. I had not been informed that attacking a Fort head-on was no longer the best way, and with my aircraft in flames, I had to bail out.

The statistics are staggering: on May 24, 1944, there were only sixty-three Destroyers in action; four weeks later forty-one of them were gone. On May 29th, thirty-nine pilots were killed; sixteen of them were from ZG26. On June 27th, the Horst Wessel Wing ceased to exist. In the month of July, our fighters shot down 329 bombers while losing 341 of our own.

The casualties were high, but I was spared. In March, 1944, I was sent to be a flight instructor for the Hungarian Air Force, with the best living standards I had known in the war. That August, in Budapest, I took five trainees out on a tank busting exercise. We played the game with the tanks, but they were prepared for us. As we left for home, I decided to surprise them with another attack. I turned my flight back for another go at the tanks before returning to base.

When we got home, all the runways were severely damaged. I saw a squadron of B17s leaving after dropping a load of cluster bombs. There were a lot of casualties on the ground and we had to go to another base. Had we gone home after the first mock-attack, we would have been caught on the ground when the bombers came over. I believe it was my instinct that made me return to the tanks and made us late. I believe it was my sub-conscious that brought me through the whole war.

I had flown thirty-three different types of aircraft—including the first ME 210—walked away from five crashes, bailed out of one burning aircraft after losing a fight with a B17, had fought in North Africa under Rommel, had been awarded the Iron Cross First Class, and come through World War Two without a scratch. Every Squadron Leader who had signed my pass book had been killed in action, along with several others whose names I can't remember. Since January, 1945, my family had also been lost behind the Russian front line, east of the Oder/Neisse River.

When the war ended I was back in Bavaria, and I was discharged by the Americans. One of my most joyful reunions came in December, 1945, when my mother, who had been missing, and who I believed was dead, came from Berlin to find me.

By that time I had bought some buses from the Americans and leased them out to the post office. Things were looking up. Then the cold war started and I wanted to get as far away as possible.

I arrived in Vancouver in 1953, worked as a mechanic, then started my own repair garage business. Life has been good ever since.

Thank you, Canada.

Italy

Rommel's surprize – The Cauldron (Image courtesy of Vancouver Island Military Museum & Ron Buxton)

Bare-Assed In The Dugout

Gordon Bannerman

I enlisted on July 24, 1940, in Saskatchewan, at age eighteen. My unit was the Sixtieth Field Battery RCA, which formed part of the Seventeenth Field Regiment RCA, Fifth Canadian Armoured Division. Trained in Petawawa, Ontario we sailed overseas on HMT *Oronsay* in November, 1941, for extensive training in England.

After training we sailed for Italy aboard the *John Erickson* in November, 1943. The convoy was heavily bombed by twin-engined Junkers 88's which sank a US destroyer, along with two troopships. Sixteen Canadian General Hospital Nurses who were in the lifeboats borrowed condoms from the troops to protect their watches and rings and came up the scramble nets of rescue ships waving the condoms and yelling, "Yippee, we made it!".

The first action I saw was at San Leonardo, near Ortona, and the Seventeenth Field Regiment RCA was kept very busy from January 8, 1944, until we left Italy to go to France, Belgium, and into action in Holland. We joined up with the First Canadian Army after being attached to the British Eighth Army in Italy.

This move from Italy was by LCT (Landing Craft Tanks) about the middle of February, 1945. I served in action as a Gun Sergeant, then as Troop Sergeant Major, later as Battery Sergeant Major of Seventy-sixth Battery.

In the weeks before VE Day we were on Njimegen Island, where we were shelling in the vicinity of Arnheim and also clearing the remaining German troops on the Allied side of the Rhine. Afterwards, we proceeded through Germany to a place called Otterloo, where we had a bitter battle on April 16 and 17, 1945. There was hand to hand fighting around the guns and two of the batteries were firing over open sights. After Otterloo we carried on in action to a place called Wagenborgen where we shelled the Delfzjil pocket, and also boats leaving Delfzjil harbour across the Ems Estuary. We had a twenty-four hour truce, accepting the garrison surrender at Delfzjil.

During the action in Holland, I was Sergeant-Major of Fox Troop, Seventy-sixth Battery, Seventeenth Field Regiment, RCA. Most times, I saw to my troop's safety as much as possible, as well as trying to set a good example to my fellow gunners, and hoping to stay alive, as I knew it couldn't last too much longer.

A frightening experience was my first time closed in a slit trench in Italy, when the gun position was heavily shelled by the Germans. I heard shells exploding, and splinters striking the boxes of shells and cartridges around me, and thought I was the only survivor. When it was all over, everything was full of holes, but we were all safe, probably because we had good luck and deep holes. I was very fortunate in Italy and Holland, getting only four or five small shell splinters. I still have one in my face, and a couple of stitches on my forehead.

During a violent rainstorm in Italy, my pup tent collapsed into my slit trench and

I awoke with about four inches of water holding me down. I managed to slither out from under, pull out my blankets and scurry naked into the gun position command post. When I arrived, sliding naked under the tarpaulins, I was at the feet of my gun position officer, Lt. Ross.

Lt. Ross was writing to his girl friend in Canada, and said that he now had something to write about as his Sergeant-Major had just slid in bare-assed into his dug-out.

The Battery came back to Canada aboard the *Queen Elizabeth,* together with 12,500 other troops. We returned to the Battery's hometown of Indian Head, Saskatchewan in January 1946.

from *Mines And Bridges*

Bob Cameron, Royal Canadian Engineers

I was one of the D-Day Dodgers with First Division in Italy. We had already experienced a baptism of fire in Italy a year before, and knew what it was like to go into battle. At Ortona, one of the worst battles of the war, we were attacked frequently by the Germans. One day, there were about a dozen of us in a truck when a Luftwaffe bomber, rigged with twenty-millimetre cannon as well as bombs, came in strafing. We all leapt out of the truck and ran for cover. Larry B. was slow getting out of the truck and took a hit in his lower jaw. We put him in an ambulance and he was on his way home.

He was a fine figure of a man, broad shouldered, over six feet tall, good looking and a nice guy. He had five children (among them a toddler he had never seen) back home in Saint John, NB.

I went through the whole war without a scratch, ending up in Holland. A few months after my discharge, I was in a tavern in Montreal. The place was crowded and it was a struggle to catch a waiter's eye. I noticed one soldier in uniform with First Division flashes and RCE on his shoulder, being served promptly. Could he be one of ours? Yes, it was Larry; still tall and burly, but with a face like Frankenstein.

The surgeons had done a great job of rebuilding the lower jaw and he was still undergoing plastic surgery, but they could not replace moving lips or a tongue, and without them Larry could only grunt noises, barely enough to get the attention of a waiter.

I later heard what had become of him. His wife had seen him only with his face all bandaged and when the bandages were removed she freaked out. Apparently, then and there he decided to not go home and let his children see him in that state, and while still in the hospital he killed himself. The war had not ended for him on VE Day.

Forty years after the war I was chatting with my old buddy Ole, and out of the blue he asked: "Do you still have nightmares?" Ole is a much more placid type than I am—always good humoured, not easily scared—so I was surprised at the question.

"You too?"

"Sure, but not lately."

"Same with me; they went away about fifteen years ago."

This narrative is an excerpt from Bob Cameron's book *Mines and Bridges* as dictated to his loving wife/partner of 15 years, Jean Wilder. Bob passed away in July 1999.

Italian Interludes

Sam Deane, RCAF

It was early winter, 1944, and the Italians had capitulated and come over to our side. The situation for the Italian people can only be described as desperate, with epidemics of cholera breaking out all over southern Italy and thousands of people on the move, searching for what little food was available. The British and Americans were faced with the impossible task of trying to provide food and medical aid to a starving population on the move.

In hindsight, it was a poor time to go on leave and travel from our squadron in Brindisi to Catania, and thence to our rest camp in Taormina, Sicily. However, with the confidence of youth, I and my crew started off from the ferry unit at Brindisi to deliver a Coastal Wellington MKXIII to the RAF overhaul facility at Catania. All went well until arrival, when on a downwind BUMFFS it was apparent that our old warhorse had absolutely no brakes. This disconcerting discovery was followed by information from the tower that visibility on final approach was now restricted, as an American B26 Boston had, for no apparent reason, rolled over and gone straight in. Needless to say, our precautionary landing and ground loop at the end of the runway was textbook perfect, with precisely 180 degrees of rotation.

Our leave at the old Timeo Hotel in Taormina (a rest home run by the British Army) was thoroughly enjoyable in spite of the hot tin cup of tea thrust through our mosquito netting every morning at five o'clock, with the admonition, "Drink it all, it's good for you."

The British firmly believed in exporting their customs to every corner of the globe. Of course, the Sicilians also had customs, one of which I discovered almost too late. On two occasions I had the pleasure of the company of a pretty signorina, and was somewhat puzzled that, on both occasions, her married sister was with us—until the sister took me aside and informed me that her little sister was only sixteen, and if I wished to take her out for a third time, her family would formally announce our engagement.

A quick tactical retreat was definitely in order, and we proceeded to Catania airport to catch the regularly scheduled service flight from Cairo to Naples.

With the idyllic Sicilian weather at eighty-five degrees Fahrenheit during the day and down to seventy degrees Fahrenheit at night, no thought had been given to the weather. However, the winter mistral (monsoon) was blowing, there was some doubt about the scheduled arrival. An American C46 did attempt to land, but with the wind gusting, by then, to ninety miles per hour the pilot could not get the tail down into three-point position. After several attempt, and running low on fuel, he landed the Curtis Commando at 200 mph, swung off the runway, locked the brakes, blew both main wheel tires and ended up with the nose of the aircraft twenty feet from the front of the hangar.

We were now forced to switch to surface transportation and, after an overnight stay in Catania, took a day-liner coach to Messina and a ferry across the strait to Reggio, with the intent of catching the train to Naples.

At the Reggio station we learned that Italian civilians had taken over the coach reserved for allied military personnel, and twenty British servicemen and women, plus myself and my crew, were now stranded. Obviously, the situation called for stern measures and the *carbinieri* were called in. The officer in charge, a dapper little General, insisted that he did not understand English (*nienta capicia*) and could do nothing about the situation. He changed his mind in a hurry when our Bomb Aimer, who was of Italian descent, told him I would have him shot if he didn't take immediate action. Upon hearing this news he informed me that another coach would be added immediately.

Our armaments expert/mid-upper gunner, a boy from Franklin, New Jersey, now proceeded to board the passengers. My crew, all combat types, were selected to stand guard with drawn side-arms at the coach door in the event that an attempt was made, by the mob of angry civilians, to eject us.

Upon our arrival at Naples, it was apparent that the tough part of the journey was just beginning. Due to bad weather all flights were grounded and we would once again have to find alternate transportation to Bari. To complicate matters further, in a few hours we would be AWOL. We decided that the best course of action would be to turn ourselves over to the local Provost Marshall. This was a British Army Major who didn't want anything to do with us because, as he said, we were air people and not fugitives. Disappointed by his attitude, we were forced to wait outside his office until precisely 0001 hours. I then knocked on his door and informed him that, since we were now AWOL, I wished to formally surrender myself and crew and place ourselves in his custody, for forwarding to 148 Squadron at Brindisi. I also requested that my CO be informed immediately. This he was willing to do, on one condition—he was short of officers and, as I was an aircraft captain with command experience, he wanted me to take charge of the next train. I reluctantly agreed. To assist myself and crew in maintaining good order and discipline on the journey, I was given a corporal and six Eighth Army Desert Rats.

Due to a cholera epidemic in Naples, and the mass starvation of the inhabitants, thousands of desperate people were fleeing the city. As a result, not only were our carriages packed to twice their capacity, but dozens of men, women and children were riding on top of the passenger cars. To make matters worse, southern Italy was experiencing one of the coldest winters in its history, with temperatures of minus twenty degrees over the Appenines. Fortunately for those who managed to hang on, the British Army had set up a field kitchen halfway through the mountains, with forty-five-gallon drums of bully beef stew. This undoubtedly saved many lives. However, the suffering of the Italians is something no member of my crew will ever forget.

To add to our problem, a large Indian soldier went berserk and attacked his comrades, slashing right and left with a dagger. I didn't know about the *kirpan* and the religious dictate that, once drawn, it was not to be sheathed until it had drawn blood. Using the most commanding voice I could muster, I shouted, "Corporal, get me that man's knife!"

The response was a cheery, "Yes, Sir!"

With one quick movement of the corporal's rifle-butt, the offender was flat on his back and the dagger was passed to me, "unstained but dishonoured."

Without further incident, we proceeded on to Bari. There, I was informed by railway officials that it would now be standard procedure to send an engine with an extra coal car to recover the frozen bodies of people who had fallen off the top of the train and were scattered along the right of way.

An interesting after-note to our journey came about when our adjutant, upon meeting us with transport back to the squadron, told us, "In spite of the difficulties you have experienced, you can consider yourselves fortunate."

An AWOL Australian crew had not turned themselves in, and our CO had had them locked up. He was threatening to court martial them and have them shot at dawn. Of course he had no intention of doing this, but the Aussies didn't know that, and neither did any of the other aircrews. We all got the message.

On VE day I was on a southbound train from Greenock, Scotland, to the RCAF Holding Unit at Bournemouth, on the south coast of England, when the conductor came through to tell us that Germany had surrendered.

My crew and I had completed a nine month operational tour in Halifaxes, with 148 RAF Special Duties Squadron, and had sailed out of Naples, Italy, two weeks earlier, on the 10,000 ton armed merchantman *Prince David*, a former Caribbean cruise ship.

After an overnight stay at Gibraltar, we joined up with a convoy of thirty ships and departed in the morning for what we had been informed would be a three day journey to England. However, on sailing out into the Atlantic, a violent spring storm was encountered and the convoy was forced to slow to a crawl (the speed of the smallest and slowest ship). To make matters more interesting, a German U-Boat wolf pack joined the convoy late in the evening, and a running depth-charge battle ensued. This battle lasted most of the night and we were instructed to stay in our cabins, fully clothed and with life jackets on.

With the rolling and pitching of the ship, and the sound of exploding depth charges reverberating through the ship's hull, sleep was next to impossible. The dawn brought some abatement of the storm but we found ourselves all alone in a rough ocean, as the convoy had been forced to disperse during the night. The submarines were still following us and to avoid interception we would be forced to maintain a westerly heading until the German sub pack either gave up the chase or we reached a point where we would have air cover from Gander. One of our RAF navigators had brought his sextant along and seemed quite confident of his astro-navigation, which showed that we were only six hundred miles off Newfoundland.

The long journey back to England went without incident and we awoke on VE day safely at berth in Greenock harbour. It was late evening when we arrived at Bournemouth, and every pub was full, with crowds of patrons standing outside, waiting to be served. This could only be accomplished by relaying drinks to the rear of the crowd and out to where we were standing on the other side of the street. Unfortunately, by the time a drink reached us, only an inch or two of beer remained in the glass. So, somewhat sadly, we proceeded to our quarters in Russell Court and delayed our celebration until the following day, in London, when we made up for lost time.

Remembering Pozzallo
Harry Greenhough, Seaforth Highlanders

The small seaport town in southern Sicily was a real eye opener to many of us in C Company, Seaforth Highlanders. The stone buildings looked like they would last forever. Beggars crawled along the walks, pleading for handouts. There was also a very tall Guards officer who was the interpreter, and a Catholic priest dressed in his black suit.

Since I was his Bren gunner, Corporal Cromb asked me to go with him and the priest to bring in some Italian soldiers who wanted to surrender. The Corporal and I set off down the road with the priest, expecting to be back shortly. We were in for a surprise. After the first mile, we were dubious about going further. Then we rounded a curve in the road and saw a machine gun set up in a pit, directly facing us. A few hundred feet further, we came across an anti-tank gun facing down the road. It would have been difficult to take this location without many casualties if the enemy troops had stayed and fought.

As we got further along the road, John and I discussed the advisability of proceeding on with the priest, who was insistent that the Italian troops wanted to give themselves up and it would only be a short distance more. We must have gone five or six miles down that lonely road when the priest stopped and shouted something, and up the sloping hillside someone answered. After some chit-chat back and forth, the troops started down the hill towards us. We lined them up and started back to Possallo with John in front, leading the parade, and the priest and myself in the back with my Bren gun.

The original group consisted of ninety prisoners. As we approached the city, small groups of three or four Italians would yell, and our group would stop and wait while they joined the parade. After this happened two or three times, we decided to let them run and catch up if they wanted to join us.

Thus it was that John Cromb led a group of 125 Italian prisoners, one priest, and one Bren gunner back to the city of Pozzallo. The Guards officer was overwhelmed by the numbers.

I was relieved, and I rejoined my section. I had one Italian Berretta pistol and an Italian watch, which I lost to hospital orderlies after being wounded at Leonforte.

Recollections Of Ortona

K J. Gourlay, R.C.E.M.E.

Ortona in 1943 was a picturesque community. Its old section, dating back to the fifteenth century, was huddled around a dilapidated castle on a cliff overlooking Ortona's artificial harbour formed by a pair of stone breakwaters. The great dome of the cathedral of San Tomaso was visible for miles. While the older part of town consisted of tall, narrow houses and dark, cramped streets, the newer section to the south and west was laid out in rectangular blocks. Most streets were very narrow.

There was a deep ravine west of town, and with the cliffs and sea on the other side, there was only one way into Ortona, along Route Sixteen, which turned into the Corso Vittoria Emanuel, the main street. This thoroughfare led to the town square, the Piazza Municipale.

In December, 1943, very few of Ortona's ten thousand residents were still in the town. The Germans had removed large numbers of able-bodied males to work as slave labour in northern Italy or Germany, while others had fled to the mountains.

Two battalions of German paratroopers defended Ortona. They had wrecked the harbour, which was blocked by sunken ships. The side streets were sealed off with rubble in order to channel the Canadian attackers along the Corso Vittoria Emanuele. The main square had been turned into a killing ground, with the surrounding buildings filled with machine guns, anti-tank guns, and mortars carefully sited to lay down a murderous cross fire.

The Canadians began their attack at noon on Monday, the 20th of December, led by the Loyal Edmonton Regiment, and supported by Sherman tanks of the Three Rivers Regiment. Medium machine guns of the Saskatoon Light Infantry moved up to assist, along with the Ninetieth Anti-Tank Battery with seventeen-pounders.

Fierce and savage fighting developed and on the 21st of December, it became house to house combat. On the 22nd of December, 'A' Company of the Seaforth Highlanders was brought in to assist the Loyal Eddies. Fighting reached its peak on December 26th, becoming a fierce struggle from doorway to doorway, courtyard to courtyard, rooftop to rooftop. There were many casualties. It ended on the evening of December 27th when the Number One German Paratroop battalions pulled out. Ortona was ours.

General Volkes later commented, "Everything before Ortona was a nursery tale."

The two infantry battalions of the Second Brigade of the First Canadian Division had borne the brunt of the losses. Loyal Edmonton Regiment had twelve killed or wounded. The Seaforth Highlanders suffered 103 killed or wounded.

Shortly thereafter a sign was erected at the entrance to Ortona which read: THIS IS ORTONA— A WESTERN CANADIAN TOWN

The beautifully sited Ortona-Moro River Cemetery, overlooking Ortona Bay, is the resting place of 1372 Canadians. This is nearly a quarter of all the Canadians who fell in Italy and Sicily. No other cemetery from Agira to Villanova harbours so many Canadian graves.

Some Personal Recollections

During the first week of January 1944, Col. Demaio, CRÈME, First Canadian Division, moved his Second Field Workshop into Ortona to provide maintenance support. This put the workshop in a front line position — an unprecedented move at that time, as Ortona remained under enemy observation and sporadic shellfire. The wet winter conditions that existed created a static warfare of patrol activities and artillery exchanges, and we remained in this location for the next three months.

As a twenty-one year old S/sgt. with the weapons section of the workshop, this new experience proved harrowing at times. Our weapons section was located at the north-western fringe where the railway line entered the town. Our billets were one half-mile south-east and up the street, at the crossroads of route Sixteen and Corso Vittorio, in a large, four-storey stone building.

During our stay in Ortona the enemy seemed to have an uncanny knowledge of our movements in and around town. This fact was established by shelling each day and night at what seemed the most inopportune times—meal time, group activities, vehicle movement. I recall one instance which, although humorous, was not funny at the time. QMS Bill Kingston and I were answering the call of nature one afternoon, and sharing the unit three-holer, when the shelling began. The two of us didn't lose any time, taking off on the double, holding our pants up and heading for the nearest building, while dirt and shrapnel seemed to bounce off everything but us. Now, that's a damn good example of getting caught with your pants down.

We had to walk up the street from our repair section to our billets, for meals. Every day, an Italian woman in her forties would be out on the street near her front entrance, cooking over an open hearth. One day at noon, while she was out there and we were heading up to eat, a shell hit the street opposite where she was. A piece of shrapnel killed her.

During a lull in the weather in late March, we decided to have a friendly game of softball. With the help of a fifteen cwt. truck, a few volunteers and I leveled and filled in an open space between buildings and produced a suitable diamond. Later that afternoon, with all the players in their field positions, in came the shells. Everyone bit the dirt fast. Sgt. Newt Gillespie went down with a cigarette in his mouth and when he got up it was still in his mouth, but bent right up to his nose. The game was postponed. Some of our store platoon vehicles suffered puncture damage from shrapnel. One has to wonder if our activity in the morning had been observed or reported to the enemy.

One afternoon, a truck was hit by shellfire on our street and burned furiously, sending up a column of thick, black smoke—a dead giveaway. S/Sgt. Pat Deveraux, of our recovery platoon, jumped in one of the recovery vehicles, hooked on to the damaged truck and towed it away. This all happened during incoming shellfire. Later Pat was awarded an MID for his cool action.

On our arrival in Ortona there were still many temporary graves, containing both German and Canadian casualties, scattered throughout the town. There were two German graves (with helmets on sticks) just outside the entrance to our weapons section. A week later, the graves commission personnel arrived to relocate the soldiers' bodies to their respective designated graveyards. There were two Italian labourers to do the digging. When they finally uncovered the corpses, one of the labourers doffed his cap and bent over them, saying, *"Bon giorno Tedeschi "* — meaning "Good day, German barbarians." (The word Tedeschi was an Italian term for Germans and it also meant barbarian in Italian.) I was offended by their disrespect for the dead, especially two dead soldiers, and I let it be known, calling him *stupido*. Outside Ortona there are now two beautifully kept Canadian and German graveyards commemorating the supreme sacrifice of the soldiers from both sides.

The experiences I've related here will remain etched in my memory. This, I feel, is a good enough reason for this written account of a time and place in my life when history was made and the greatest adventure of our lives was being played out.

The Ten O'Clock News

Jim Hurford

I joined the First Battalion, Canadian Scottish Regiment, in June, 1940, as the disaster of Dunkirk was happening. In September, 1941, the Regiment went on the *Strath Eden* to train at Aldershot in England. Then I was sent as a reinforcement to the Seaforth Highlanders, and was aboard a ship off Algiers the day Sicily was invaded. We landed at Phillipeville, North Africa and then in the Cork Forest. I finally caught up to the Seaforths in Ortona, Italy.

I became an Educational Corporal and was attached to the Saskatoon Light Infantry, a heavy machine gun and mortar battalion, and remained with them for the rest of the war. I typed the BBC news, given at ten o'clock each day. I distributed copies to the regiment, supplied education courses to anyone who wanted them, sent in their work to Egypt, and distributed reading material.

We got up to the Lamone River, just south of the Po. I carried a correspondence course to an officer east of the HQ Company, and decided to take a short-cut back to my quarters. Walking along, I saw a sign that read: No Vehicles Past This Point.

Continuing on, I saw some Hastings and Prince Edward Highlanders at a *casa*. I asked them if that was the way back to Lamone.

They said, "See that burnt out tank? That is the front line. That road you were on is not to be traveled in daylight."

I got out of there in a hurry.

Our detachment was often shelled. Usually, we managed to have one or two walls between shellfire and us. On one occasion we had two walls, and sheltered in a narrow room. Shells were falling and I looked around. All the men were lying face down on the narrow bed. I thought, who am I to be brave? So I huddled there. Shells were hitting the *casa* next door and landing in the courtyard. When the shelling stopped, the fanlight over the door was blown out and there was a shrapnel hole in the chimney next to me.

In the spring of 1945, the regiment was sent to Leghorn. Whilst waiting for transport, we went to Pisa, where I climbed the Leaning Tower and saw the campanile for the lovely Cathedral. Eventually, we landed at Marseilles, were dosed with a chemical for lice, showered, mounted our vehicles, skirted Paris, and landed at Hougstraten in Belgium. We were just in time to get hit by one of the last V1s, and went around tying up cuts which people had received from flying glass. One good thing about that place was that the people slept in the basement and we enjoyed the soft feather beds.

We continued on through the Hougstraten Forest into Germany, through Cleve, where the buildings were badly damaged. Then we crossed the Rhine, heading west to Daventer and eventually to Rotterdam, passing columns of German prisoners along the way. We were stationed at DeBilt, the meteorological station.

I got my first leave to England to stay with my Uncle Frank's family and to see Granny. I was soon due back and arrived an hour early for my train at Victoria Station. There were so many people, I couldn't get on the train. I spent the night in Dover and got the ferry and train the next day—V E Day. I arrived in DeBilt in time to celebrate by having a glass of stale beer.

I was sent on Canada draft in August and was fortunate enough to go to the Sadler's Wells production on V J Day in London. The *Empress of Scotland* brought me to Quebec after four years in Europe.

Raw Chicken

Lemie Lacouvee

I joined the Eighty-second Battery RCA, which was stationed near my home town at Gaspe, PQ, and trained in Petawawa, Ontario each summer.

In July, 1940, we were mobilized as the Fourth Anti-Tank Regiment, stationed at the Immigration Building in Quebec City. In 1941, the regiment was transferred to Petawawa, and after training we became part of the Fifth Armoured Division. We went overseas in September.

We were moved several times, from our first stop at Aldershot, to Nutley, Brighton, Sheffield Park, Falkenham, Winchester, and Heathfield. In 1943, we left Liverpool for Algiers, then to Zeralda, Phillipville, and the Cork Forest. Our next move took us to Italy, where we joined the First Canadian Corps as part of Montgomery's Eighth Army. We took part in the battles of Ortona, Cassino, the Gustav Line, Hitler Line, and the Gothic Line, with battle honours at Coriano Ridge and the Senio River.

In January, 1945, the Battery was moved from Italy to Toulon, France, thence to Warneton, Belgium, Neimegin, Holland, Cleve, Emerick, Germany, back to Arnhem, Amersforte, Apeldorne, and Groningen. We were in Emden, Germany when the war ended.

During the Italian campaign, after we crossed the Senio River, rations had not kept up with our battery and we were starving. It seemed a stroke of good fortune when we stopped at a little farm and liberated three inhabitants of a chicken coop. With mouths watering we cleaned those birds, built a fire and started cooking. They had barely started boiling, when we were needed in a hurry and had to move forward again. I took the chickens from the pot and we ate on the move.

With the blood oozing out of those raw birds, they were the worst thing I ever tried to eat. I got sick as a dog, and for at least fifty years I was unable to even look at a chicken.

Eating Peacocks

Joe Morton

I was twenty-six years old when I joined as a trooper in the Lord Strathcona Horse, in the Fifth Canadian Division. I was a Sergeant on VE Day, which I celebrated while on leave in Edinburgh.

The Fifth Division had started in North Africa and we had sailed from Liverpool directly to Naples, as an advance party. We were in Naples again when the Italian campaign ended, and we were sent to Belgium.

While we were in Italy, a guy sold us two plucked turkeys. This was in addition to our regular meals and we figured we would keep them to ourselves. We tried to cook them on a camp-stove; they were the toughest old birds we ever tried to chew and we were bloody mad when the seller admitted they were peacocks! Those damn things live for a hundred years, and ours must have been at least that old.

One of our guys started a one-page newsletter for the regiment. Along came the Maple Leaf, a newspaper started for Canadian troops, and they stole Ron Poulton, the newsletter editor, from us.

We were moved to Belgium and took the soft-shelled vehicles—trucks and jeeps—from the British Fifty-first Division, and were refitted with new Sherman tanks. The next time we saw action was in Arnhem, which was the site of the disaster written about in *A Bridge Too Far.* When we went in, the Canadians were bringing German POWs out. Then the Krauts bombed the bridge and killed some of their own.

While in Belgium I went to Passchendale, where so many Canadians were killed in the big battle of World War One. My father's name is on a monument there, along with fifty thousand other Unknown Soldiers. The inscription on the cenotaph reads: "Known only to God."

I never met my father; he went overseas and was killed in action in 1917.

We struck up north, went as far as Groenigen, Holland, and were there ten days before the war ended. The Krauts surrendered there after I went on leave. A while later, the whole German army surrendered. After my leave I returned to Holland and was stuck there until December 15th. That was a hell of a long time to wait to come home.

A Long Walk

Clarence Murphy

I was working in Cape Breton with a Scottish lad named McGuinty, who suggested we join up. I refused, saying, "No way am I going to start wearing a skirt for the Cape Breton Highlanders."

So I went back to Moncton and joined the Carleton & York Regiment. I couldn't get in at first—they didn't have any uniforms—but they were finally able to kit us out and on March 1st, 1940, I was one of one hundred who joined the regiment that day.

Throughout the war, we were identified as members of the One Hundred. (Twenty years later while working on the ferries, a fellow came up to me and said, "You were one of the one hundred.") We trained at Woodstock, then went to Aldershot, NS where one of our lads got scarlet fever. We were put under quarantine for ten days, then another man got it, and before he got out of hospital, there was a third patient. We spent a whole month without being able to leave camp.

While at Woodstock, I was made a member of a Precision Drill Squad and we performed at the Apple Blossom Festival just before we went overseas in May. A few of our guys were sent to Hong Kong; I'm glad I wasn't in that draft.

I was sent to Britain. While we were there, two of us went for a leave on the Isle of Man, rented bicycles and rode to Ramsay; then, being lazy, we put the bikes in the baggage car and rode the train back to Douglas.

The Island was such a homey place and I was amused to see the conductor leaning out the window talking to a woman while she pinned her washing on a clothesline.

"How's Jock?" he asked.

"Got a letter yesterday; he's in Cairo."

"How's the kids?"

And all this time we were just going slowly by.

When we got back to the dock, the last two ferries had left, and we needed reservations for the next morning. We were on the carpet for being AWOL, when we got back, but the Colonel allowed it was a simple mistake. However, Sergeant Major gave me a rough time from then on, till one day he said, "Let's bury the hatchet."

I answered, "Yes, I would like to, right in the back of your head."

We got along okay after that; he was a decent sort.

In Sicily, we marched for the first nine days without unlacing our boots. We all had blisters when we finally did get our boots off, and the heels and toes were gone from our socks. One of the guys sparked some ironic humour when he tried to figure out where all the wool had gone as it couldn't get out of our boots!

I was section leader, with three Bren Gunners in our platoon. I threw my extra Bren barrel down a well because in action, the barrel would get hot, but if you raised your head up to change to the cold one, you became one hell of a target.

One day we had a wounded buddy out in the field of fire. I wanted to go out and help him get back to our position, but our officer made me take a partner. When I asked my friend, young Genette, to go with me he agreed with a nonchalant "Okay."

I had lost my Number Two in an earlier action and knew I'd found the replacement I wanted. He was so cool while we were sneaking around out there, he even felt the cold arm of a dead sergeant and carried on without flinching, whereas I had seen guys freak out when they got close to a dead man. We brought in my friend and from then on we worked together as a team.

We were waiting to cross a bridge. A group of civilians trying to get away from the action came across from the other side. It was a windy day and a gust caught the dress of a young girl, blowing it up over her head. She had nothing on under the dress. My squad made me really proud when they all looked away, and there was no ribald laughter to embarrass the poor girl.

Most of us got desert sores on our exposed flesh. During the night, pus blisters would form; we would squeeze them and go back to sleep. A local doctor told me, "Put piss on your sores and they will go away." I pissed on my handkerchief and daubed the blisters, and he was right—they went away.

Before Ortona, we were involved in the Battle of the Gully. The Germans had dug trenches on the other side, which the artillery blasted all to hell—then we started going down and found they had been concealed under camouflage on our side. It was a hand to hand fight, and we took a lot of casualties.

Before Ortona, we were pulled out of the line for one week of rest in an old three-storey house. A ration truck full of bread was parked outside and one of our lads decided to liberate a loaf for each member of the squad. Then we heard that the bread had been counted and they were hunting for the missing loaves. I was on duty as Corporal of the Guard and while all the others were kept outside, I took all the bread out of their packs and threw it out the window. When the officer came in to inspect he found the loaf I had missed in Smiley's pack, and he was on charge for stealing rations. This was our first and last rest day.

The West Nova Scotia Regiment and the Royal Twenty-Second (VanDoos) were the other two regiments of the brigade. That night, at 0200 hours, the West Novas went on attack and we were all called out to help them, including Smiley. We never heard any more about the stolen rations charge.

I was wounded nine times: in the back, legs, arm, and my kneecap was blown away. That one ended my war.

An Incident in the Bari Opera House

Stan Scislowski, Perth Regiment:

I finally made it to Bari on my first eight-day leave. I was the last in my platoon to get away. I'd been hoping my turn would come when we were at the front, but it came when we were in a rest area a hundred miles behind the lines. After checking in at the newly-constructed Eighth Army Rest Camp, (on the shores of the Adriatic, in southeast Italy) I scooted into town to have a look around. I had no ulterior motive, like hooking up with a local lady of ill-repute or getting drunk. I was just a clean-cut Canadian wanting to see the sights.

I was standing outside an ice-cream parlour when I struck up a conversation with a Yank air force type who was also enjoying an ice-cream. After a while, he asked me if I wanted to go to a play put on by an ENSA concert party at the Opera House. I hesitated, for two reasons. First, I wasn't sure of his motives; and second, being an uncultured klutz, I wasn't keen on sitting through a boring play. But the Yank seemed a nice guy, so I accepted his invitation.

I hadn't realized how many men in the two polyglot armies in Italy went in for 'stuffed shirt' entertainment until we became a part of the milling throng waiting to enter the Opera House, which was a large Baroque structure that looked more like a cathedral than a place of entertainment. By the time the curtains opened for the first Act, it was packed to the rafters. From our choice box-seats on the second tier just off the stage, we had an ideal place from which to watch the show and scan the audience on the floor below.

I felt grossly out of place. There were officers in all the box-seats except the one to our left, which was occupied by five pretty New Zealand Nursing Sisters. Most of the officer crowd was made up of British and Yanks, and only a few of them were below the rank of major. A good many of them were in the company of strikingly attractive ladies wearing fur stoles and stunning evening gowns. Many of the lower-ranked officers were accompanied by their counterparts in the Women's Division.

The first act of "The Merry Widow" was enjoyable, probably because it was somewhat risque. Some of the acts were quite hilarious. At intermission, when the lights came on, the smoking began, along with the usual buzz of conversation. Then, from the uppermost tier of boxes at the rear of the Opera House, an officer took a condom out of his pocket and proceeded to blow it up to the grand and obscene size of four feet. He tied it and released it into the smoky air, where it began a slow descent.

The pale white balloon floated slowly downwards, unnoticed by the audience below. Only the people in the box seats saw its descent. There was a polite murmur of laughter as, on the whims of air currents, the object floated first in one direction and then another. As it approached the level of our second tier, the audience in the seats below became aware of the bloated condom. It was as though someone had suddenly turned on a radio at full volume, just at the part where an audience lets out a loud guffaw at a comedian's punch line.

The condom hesitated briefly in front of our box, then slid sideways and came to rest on the broad railing in front of the New Zealand nurses. Five confused, flustered and red-faced Nursing Sisters tried, without success, to hide their embarrassment. One thrust her hand out and tried to push the offensive beast over the edge.

On her third thrust, the nurse succeeded in knocking the balloon off the rail and it descended rapidly. As soon as it dropped to audience level, it was instantly propelled upwards and bounced back and forth in every direction by a hundred upraised hands. The Opera House echoed with hooting and shouting and uproarious laughter, until the condom disappeared with a loud bang when someone's sharp nail pricked it.

As if on cue, the shouting and the laughter died.

Then all the people who had Sheiks in their pockets took out condoms and began inflating them with great gusto. Thirty seconds later, a hundred or more of the elongated balloons floated in the smoky air, with seven hundred yipping and hooting servicemen flailing away at them. Even the usually restrained senior officers in the upper tiers joined in. Down from the upper reaches of the domed palace floated condoms by the score.

I hadn't laughed so much since I was a kid at a Saturday matinee, watching the zany antics of Laurel and Hardy.

Another hilarious incident took place at the crossroads hamlet of San Giustina, a few miles inland from Rimini. We'd been pulled back from the front for a three-day rest, not out of range of Jerry artillery, but safely out of range of mortars and small-arms fire. The first thing we had to do was to dig a latrine—an eight-foot-long trench about eighteen inches wide and a foot to five feet in depth, depending on the length of the unit's stay in the area. The officers' latrines were different from ours, in that they had burlap screening to shield the officers' bums from the public gaze.

That day, three of us privates were hunkered over the latrine, while ten feet away, three officers crouched over theirs. This time there was no screen to hide the officers' shame. I glanced sideways and noticed, without surprise, that their bums were not much different than ours. A little bulkier, perhaps, but certainly not any prettier.

Far across the stubble-covered farm-land, a hundred yards to our right, I noticed a platoon commander instructing a crowd of newly-arrived troops on the workings of a flame-thrower. Then I saw the officer point the nozzle of the flame-thrower in our direction. A frightening arc of smoky flame came straight at us.

Instinct had us gripping our trousers to make a quick exit, but the three of us privates realized that the flame would fall far short of us, and we relaxed and stayed put. Not so the officers. In trying to jerk their trousers up for a fast getaway, they couldn't get them past their knees, and instead of running, they took off like three scared little bunny-rabbits hippity-hopping across the stubble, their trousers bunched up around their shins. Their faces were as white as the white of their bare behinds.

I laughed so hard, I damn near fell backward into the mess behind me. Across the field, the crowd was rolling on the ground in their glee.

When the officers had recovered their composure, cleansed themselves and adjusted their trousers, the pain of their sorry performance was written in ugly scowls on their faces. Had they reported to the CO the foul deed perpetrated on them by a fellow officer, the CO would likely have split a gut laughing.

Saved By The Cross

Otto Wuerch

I joined the army in Winnipeg, and went overseas with the Fifth Anti-Aircraft Division. It was in the battle for Ortona, in Italy. The German shelling and bombing was terrifying. There was only one place that looked like a shelter, so we ran into the church, right up to the front, and hid behind the cross. The church was completely destroyed, all except where we were. That was when I became a believer.

Brown Boots And Scottish Accents

Hector Young, Cameronian Scottish Rifles

We were resting in an area south of Paterno, in very pleasant conditions, while the attack on Italy was being planned. My buddy Spanks and I went out to the village butcher shop and had some wine, which was awful. An elderly woman tried to sell us more wine, but we had no money left. She told us that for a pair of brown boots, she would provide us with two gallons of the best wine in Sicily.

The only person in our battalion who had brown boots was the padre. We went back to barracks and told another buddy about the deal. He drove the water truck and since no-one ever questioned him, he decided that he would look for the boots.

Next day, he informed us that the deed was done; he would put the boots in the truck and see us at the butcher shop. We contacted the old woman, and the wine was every bit as good as she had said.

At the battalion parade Saturday morning, our RSM announced that the boots were missing, and told us if we returned them all would be forgiven. No one spoke. Just then, across the street, we heard a loud clomp, clomp. There was the old woman, wearing the brown boots. The MP immediately went over and asked her where she got them. She told him she bought them from a soldier. He put her on a jeep and drove her up and down the ranks till she pointed at me. I was arrested and put in the stockade.

The padre came to see me. He said he understood and would not charge me, as we had all been together for a long time. However, I was hit with a minor charge and lost seven days' pay, which was the price the old woman said she paid. The next day we invaded Italy, so all was forgotten. But I can still hear that old woman walking down the street in the padre's brown boots.

The Division was advancing over hilly country, in the middle of which were the towns of Carlentine and Lentini. The enemy guns that were shelling 'A' Company stopped, then started again from a different direction. This time the fire was more accurate, so Captain Kettles went forward to move the company to alternative positions. While he was thus engaged, some of the hay stacks began to move; straw and netting fell away and four German tanks, which had remained concealed all day, advanced on us.

We suffered many casualties. Several of us lay paralyzed. Luckily, a squadron of Kitty Hawks came over from behind the tanks and bombed them, or we would all have been casualties. Our Scottish accents served us well that day—the message relayed was that there were "four tae five" tanks. We were scared and wondering where the rest of the tanks were, but the squadron had heard it as forty-five tanks too, and came in force.

The Edge Of No-Man's Land—The FOP

Roy McKinley, Saskatoon Light Infantry

As a wireless operator, I was a member of a crew of three in a forward observation post. My job was to pass on information about the accuracy of fire from our troops and to pin-point objectives that might assist in further advance. This information was being garnered by the Forward Observation Office. The FOO was the Forward Observation Officer; the FOP was the Forward Observation Post; and the FOOP was the operator.

Our FOP was at a house named Casa Berardi. Our crew consisted of Capt. Torchy Morrison, Private Al Wright, and myself. I was also chore-boy, and sometimes pressed into painful duty as cook. Usually, cooking porridge meant pouring a packet of ready-mix into a mess tin of boiling water. The water was heated over a make-shift stove, which consisted of a discarded stew can half-filled with soil and saturated with gasoline. The top half was punctured with holes, to let in the air. You struck a match and *voila*—a stove.

It was my turn as chef, so I poured two packets of ready-mix into the boiling water. The mixture began to thicken rapidly and I yelled at my partner, Al Wright, to pour in a shot of water. To our amazement, the thinning fluid was not water but gasoline. The gas had reached the spout when Al smelled the fumes and quickly tipped the can back, sending the gas within the spout across our stove, the porridge, and onto the adjacent wall. Everything burst into flames, including the front of Al's tunic. Trying to douse the flames on his tunic with one hand, Al hurled the vessel over the east wall and onto the ground. It exploded with a boom and raised a stream of flame thirty feet into the air.

The ever alert foe began storming us. Luckily, their sights were high—I guess they could only see the tips of the flames—and their mortars landed where Torchy was attending to his morning ablutions. He was astonished to see the blaze in our OP, and assumed that the Jerries had discovered our presence. After the dust had settled,

94

I confessed that I was the instigator. Torchy said, with a grin, "I won't say anything about that, and I'm sure that our friendly neighbours won't mention it—so let's just pack up and get the hell out of here!"

Another incident worth mentioning also happened at a Forward Observation Post. Present with me were Capt. Bill Baker, Sergeant Ernie Thompson, Billy Brand, and Blackie Gallant, Baker's batman. Things were quiet and we were seated around a table playing bridge, with Ernie as kibitzer. Our arms—three rifles, Ernie Thompson's sub-machine gun and my Enfield Thirty-eight—were set neatly in the corner furthest away from us.

Ernie gasped and all eyes swung to where he was looking. Standing in the doorway and squinting in the light was a large, gray-garbed paratrooper, his hand wrapped around the handle of a Schmeizer. While we sat watching in amazement, the paratrooper backed out of the door, closed it softly behind him, and was gone.

We dove for our own armament and raced outside, but the trooper had disappeared into the cloudy, damp night, avoiding the booby-trap safety alarm that arced in a semi-circle around the north side of our Observation Post.

Ernie exclaimed later, "He walked right in as if he was coming home from work!"

We guessed that the trooper knew his way around the OP because we had only ousted them from the position two days earlier. He must have thought that he was still behind his own lines.

And that's how we won the war.

Canada

RCAF radio telephone operator trainees (RCAF photo)

Confined To Barracks

Gelda Bell (Ingalls)

My only claim to fame was nearly getting the whole hut confined to barracks. I had a partner in crime named Mills, who was just across the corridor from me. We both slept in upper bunks, and with an open space at the top of the cubicle partitions, we didn't need a microphone.

One night, Mills and I were doing our running commentary and the whole hut was laughing when a duty sergeant sneaked in. She obviously took her job seriously and she roared, "If there is one more peep out of you, you will all be confined to barracks."

We smothered our laughter in our blankets and that was the end of the Ingalls and Mills routine. After all, if we caused the girls to be confined to quarters we would be as popular as the proverbial skunk at the garden party.

I hope that sergeant feels guilty; she may have ended a brilliant career in the entertainment business.

Marching Band

Gord Bell

In September, 1941, I joined the Toronto Scottish Reserve unit at Fort York Armouries. We paraded one night per week and that August, we went to Camp Niagara on the Lake for two weeks' training.

There were no landing craft available; however, as an assault exercise, Number Three platoon, 'B' Company, marched to a sandy beach on Lake Ontario, where we were supposed to have landed. It must have been about five miles—it seemed like a long walk for this Tuesday night soldier.

I had been playing my three-year-old, made in Germany, Marine Band mouth organ most evenings while in camp, so I was called upon to be the band. The trip didn't seem too bad, with the music, and other teenagers singing.

When we got to the shore, our OC explained the scheme: In the middle of a field, about half a mile away, the stone foundation of an old barn was being used by the enemy as a machine gun nest, and we had to take the position. So up the beach we charged. We got into the hay field and went to ground. Then an umpire watching the assault was picking off the guys that were showing their butts instead of sliding low enough to be hidden in the tall hay. With a "You're dead!" he sent them back to the beach.

I was one of three members of our platoon who slithered all the way. We were congratulated by the umpire for our outstanding skill as soldiers. That made us feel proud. It was almost one o'clock when we got back to the beach. We were hungry, (we had eaten breakfast at six-thirty a.m.) tired, and dirty. All the victims of the battle were either swimming, playing beach ball, or just lying about getting a tan. Not only that, but they were well fed, and the lunch we got was one dry cheese sandwich each, and a drink of water before we started the route march back to camp.

I'd be damned if I was going to be the band on the return trip, and said I was too tired to blow.

I realized then that in the army you had to do a lot of walking and I would rather ride, so that fall I was eighteen and joined the RCAF. I was sent to Lachine Manning Depot, where I spent my first six months in the air force—marching.

Roughing It
Donna Chapman

My husband Ted was the only licensed mechanic in our village, and was the first married-with-children man from Port Elgin to join the Air Force. When he was posted to Fingal, Ontario, I took our three kids—Harry, three years old, Carol, two, and Ted, six months old—and went to be with him.

The only accommodation we could find was a two-room apartment in an old farmhouse, with no running water or hydro. I carried water in pails and washed diapers by hand. I had never experienced such primitive living before. There were four other families there, also living under the same conditions.

In the middle of winter, Ted was posted to Moncton. I spent the whole night packing, with the most trouble being the frozen diapers on the line. I was happy to go back and live in my own home and did not attempt to follow him on any more postings.

One day, while we were at Fingal, Carol slipped down the hole in the backhouse. Harry came running for me. I couldn't stop laughing when I saw her predicament. She was folded, with her knees and forelegs, elbows and neck holding her up out of the mess. I'm sure she would have started crying if I had shown any anxiety.

Dangerous Drill
Helen Henning

The Canadian Women's Army Corp was recruiting for the war in the Pacific. I was nineteen years old when I enlisted at the Hotel Vancouver, on Granville Street. The

100

army sent us by train to London, Ontario for our basic training and then we were selected for specialized courses. I was trained as a dental nurse; that involved developing x-rays, mixing the porcelain and amalgam fillings, chair-side assistance and doing all the office reception work. Nowadays, in the dentist's office, there are three people doing what I had to do. However, I advanced from Lance Corporal to Acting Sergeant in a year. I assisted three dentists, two of whom had just returned from overseas.

My most frightening experience took place while I was assisting one of the dentists and he had an epileptic seizure with the drill in his hand. I shut off the drill, as the soldier patient was still in the chair, and then I called the Sergeant of the Dental Lab that was connected to our office. With him in charge, everyone calmed down.

The Pacific war came to an end and, before being discharged, I was sent to the dental clinic at the Veterans Hospital in London, Ontario. I was relieved and glad that the war was over, but greatly disappointed that I couldn't continue my career in the army. We were all discharged as we were no longer required.

Gelda Bell, pictured while on an Army Admin course in Edmonton

The War Years In Nanaimo

June Jackson

I was twelve years old when the war broke out in England, in 1939. I was sixteen when the Allies returned to France and Germany, so I was too young to be in the services. You may think the war overseas wouldn't affect us over here in Nanaimo, but it did.

First, it had taken my sweetheart (now my husband) away from me, plus my friends' sweethearts, brothers and fathers. I still remember having air-raid practice and at night you had to make sure your blinds were down and had no holes in them. The blinds were made of green canvas and if there was the least little hole in your blind they would knock on your door and tell you to cover it.

That was before 1943, when they were scared of the Japanese. We were also on rations and had coupons for tea, sugar, butter, flour, meat, and so on. If you didn't have sugar, you would trade with someone for tea or butter. My step-dad worked at the CPR ferries and he would come home with his lunch-bucket full of rationed stuff, which he got from bags that had been broken into by one of the workers. There was also gas rationing but we didn't own a car.

We also had a curfew; everyone had to be in by ten p.m., unless they had been given permission to stay out later. A lot of women took over jobs in factories and when the war was over they lost their jobs, as the men were rehired.

We can thank God we never lost our homes to bombs—it sure made us count our blessings.

June Jackson, nee *Forde, in Nanaimo, 1944*

How Ruthie Won The War

Ruth Masters

My RCAF (WD) service commenced in July, 1942, with two months of basic training at Number Six Manning Depot, housed in the old Havergal College on Jarvis St., in the red light district of Toronto. I then spent fifteen months at Number Two Service Flying Training school at Uplands, just outside Ottawa. From December, 1943, until July, 1946, I was stationed at RCAF Overseas Headquarters, Knightsbridge, London, England. That was followed by several months at Patricia Bay, near Victoria, BC, until my final discharge in December, 1946. Being a stenographer, I was assigned to work in Administration.

At Uplands, we lived in a large H-shaped barrack blocks, with about sixty women on each side, and the 'ablutions' in the middle. Uplands was extremely vain about its Cock-of-the-Walk award, and we were continually reminded of the rooster mounted on the top of the flag pole, signifying our superiority. An RCAF officer, known as the Inspector-General, checked the RCAF stations every year, awarding the Cock-of-the-Walk honour to the most efficient station in Canada.

Uplands was the final stage in a pilot's flying training, with a Wings Parade every month, when some fifty pilots graduated. It was the proudest moment in a young man's life when he stepped forward, chest out a mile, for the Commanding Officer to pin on his wings. It was moving for the rest of us, as we knew it would not be long before our boys started showing up on the casualty lists, and in a year or two many of them would be dead.

In the spring of 1943, just before the Inspector-General's visit, Uplands went into a panic of tidiness. Shortly before the inspection, Uplands was surrounded by glorious fields of dandelions. As the time of the visit approached, most of the dandelions had matured into fluffy heads. The general duties airmen were provided with potato sacks and sent out to pick the heads off those fluffy dandelions, so that the great man's view would not be impeded by anything messy. I actually saw fellows out in the fields on their hands and knees, pulling off the dandelion heads. We girls were not ordered out for this chore, but a call came for volunteers. A few girls actually helped. I remember standing in the WD barracks at Uplands, declaring, "The war will be won or lost regardless of the heads on those dandelions, and I won't go."

But that wasn't all. A few days before the inspection, Uplands got landscaped with ornamental trees and hedges. Shortly after the inspection, the new trees started turning brown, whereupon they were hauled away in trucks. They had just been stuck in the ground to look good, without being planted. Such was the military mind.

Looking back I can scarcely believe the hundreds of hours I spent shining my brass buttons and buffing a gleam on my black oxfords. Our NCOs would go into a fit if we appeared on parade with dull buttons or grimy shoes. Sgt. Mark, a tall humourless woman, would stand at the end of our barracks block sighting down the line of bunks to make sure all bed sheets were turned over the right number of inches.

Cameras were strictly forbidden on our station for security reasons—though I am unclear how a picture of me sitting on the wing of a Harvard trainer at Uplands could jeopardize Canada's war effort. I kept my camera right through.

My special friend at Uplands was Lorna Rose, from Olds, Alberta. She had the lower bunk and I had the upper one. An equipment worker, Lorna toiled in a carefully guarded section in one of the hangars. One day, she carefully locked up the equipment premises and went to the loo. As she flushed the toilet, she turned around just in time to see the precious keys swirling down the drain. Dismayed, she returned to confess the loss of the keys to her commanding officer.

Word spread around the station fast. "Hey, Lorna, have they found the keys yet?"

Later, her flight sergeant came into the equipment section waving a newspaper. "Flash!" he shouted. "The keys have been sighted floating on the Yellow River."

Our whole station enjoyed her embarrassment. A few weeks later, a general duties airman cleaning the cistern found the missing keys. Lorna was sent to get them, which she did, bringing them back wrapped in Kleenex.

Our group of WDs reached Halifax for embarkation to the UK on a cold December evening in 1943. Arriving at the barracks, we made a run for the washroom, where our attention focused on long troughs for dozens of men to piddle in at the same time. The barracks were cold, grimy, and uninviting. Talk about a classy send-off.

Because of submarine attacks in the Atlantic, departure date of the *Mauritania* for Britain was the deepest secret. Well, sort of. One WD visited a friend in town who told her when we would be sailing, since her husband had to have the bread on board. Then another WD came back with similar news with respect to the laundry. Their date and time of departure was correct to the minute. I felt a bit uneasy, shuffling up the gangplank for this super-secret sailing, realizing that if anyone in Halifax didn't know our departure time he could have easily found out.

Almost the first announcement on the *Mauritania* was that there were between six and eight thousand people on the ship, and no one had better fall overboard because they would not risk all those lives by turning around to pick us up. Knowing that of the thousands of military personnel, many would not be coming back, it was an emotional experience for us girls lining the rail as Canada faded into a thin blue line on the horizon.

We girls had upstairs accommodation on the ship, while the thousands of soldiers and airmen were squashed below decks. We would grab a few cookies or apples from the dining table to hand to the hungry-eyed guards, who were not being fed as well as we were. The men were not permitted above deck at all.

The *Mauritania* changed course every five or six minutes. This was a little short of the seven minutes a sub required to do its calculations and send off a torpedo to sink us. We sloshed across the Atlantic to Liverpool. Porpoises skimmed along near our ship for much of the way, a comforting escort. Several of our 110 girls were seasick for the whole eight-day crossing.

At Liverpool, an English band was on the dock belting out "The Maple Leaf Forever," trying to help us feel like heroes, I suppose. Some of the girls bawled.

Blacked-out and grimy, London in December, 1943, provided a grim introduction to wartime Britain. The city was crowned with hundreds of barrage balloons to snare enemy aircraft. Our first air raid by German bombers occurred on our second night. The sky was full of planes, searchlights, anti-aircraft fire, flack and exploding bombs. My first thought was, if those guys up there aren't careful, they're going to kill us. Then came the shocked acceptance that that was precisely what they were there to do.

While nobody starved, food rationing took some getting used to. We were allotted one egg a month, and by the time it got to us it was a pretty tired looking egg. A cartoon of the day showed a lady asking her grocer to please slip the cheese ration under the door, if he called when she was out. I have always wondered if the Brits could have made it through the war without fish and chips and vinegar.

I have a lifetime affection for the Salvation Army. Somehow the "Sally Ann" always managed to find food somewhere to provide us service people with a decent meal at an affordable price.

We were billeted all over London so that one bomb wouldn't wipe out the whole RCAF Overseas HQ. One morning, in 1944, I arrived for work at Knightsbridge, where we occupied the top floor of the Harrods building. We had had a sleepless night of bombing, so our boss, Squadron Leader Frank Seidel, asked me, "Masters, were you scared last night in the bombing raid?"

I replied, "Yes sir, I was."

"Well, so was I," he said. "There are only two kinds of people in a bombing raid. You're either scared to death, or you're a bloody liar."

Innocents that we were, we had never heard about homosexuality. One day two airmen, LAC Pink and LAC Pretty, (yes, those were their real names) were paraded through our Orderly Room to face charges in front of F/L "Granny" Black, our superior officer. All eyes were on the offenders.

"What did those guys do?" everyone asked.

Later, one girl found out and quietly told me. I was so uncomfortable and embarrassed that I didn't tell the others, so I don't know if they ever found out.

Like many Londoners, I never went to an air raid shelter during bombing raids. For months, I slept with a pillow over my head and my flashlight in hand. I scrunched into a tight ball whenever I heard a bomb screaming in. I figured if our building was demolished, I would still have a chance. One bomb cleared us and destroyed St. Mary Abbot's Hospital, killing forty-nine people, mostly mothers with new babies.

English humour somehow shone through the eternal wartime shortages, food rationing, blackouts, bombings and dreariness. A tiny pub on High Street, Kensington, near where I lived, carried this sign above the bar: "We stay open during air raids, but in the event of a direct hit, we close at once."

The world's first un-manned self-propelled bombs blasted out acres of London buildings, commencing in June, 1944. These buzz-bombs reminded me of an old Ford car going to beat Hell. They had a lively jet flame spurting out of the rear end. The Germans launched them down slides resembling ski jumps, from the French side of the Channel. As they clattered over London, we could tell they were going to crash and blow when the motor revved up slightly before quitting. Then you heard the scream as they plummeted down, followed by the explosion. Each bomb carried a ton of high explosive, which could wreck a city block, since the blast from these missiles spread out horizontally. In the first month, five thousand people were killed by buzz-bombs in London, and two or three times that number were injured, including fifty people left permanently blind.

Some of our fighter pilots would go after these nasty bombs, attacking them with guns blazing; then they would streak through the flying debris as the missile exploded. Other skilled pilots would fly alongside a buzz-bomb, gently nudging the bomb's wing with their wingtip, effectively turning it around to go back the way it came. Those pilots were incredibly brave guys.

I met one young RCAF pilot in London. "Whatever happened to your face?" I blurted, shocked at the sight of several nicks and cuts.

"I got three buzz-bombs," he proudly replied.

To conserve energy, the Brits introduced double daylight saving time. So in the summer, when we quit work at five p.m., it was really only three p.m., giving us plenty of daylight hours for our softball games near Marble Arch, in London's Hyde Park. In those days, there were thousands of service people, from all over the Empire and the US, stationed in London. Picture Hyde Park in the late afternoon and evening, with its fields covered with people necking—one great battleground of sex. Our outfield ball sometimes bounced off a horizontal couple.

On May 24, 1945, shortly after the end of hostilities in Europe, I rushed over with my camera to the Albert Hall, hoping to catch a glimpse of the Royal Family at the Empire Pageant. I weaseled my way through the dense crowd toward the entrance and was challenged by a tall bobby.

"Official RCAF photographer," I said, and he accepted my statement. As I squeezed up to the entrance of the Albert Hall, there was the real RCAF photographer. He grinned at the sight of my little Kodak "Vigilant." Realizing what I was up to, and being a nice fellow, he told me to crouch in front of him so that he could shoot over my head. I got one shot of King George VI with Queen Elizabeth, and one of the princesses, Elizabeth and Margaret. I particularly remember the lovely complexions and the smiles of the two young girls.

The war in Europe ended on May 7, 1945, with the celebrations taking place the next day. People were squashed in so tightly in front of Buckingham Palace and on the street below Churchill's residence, at Number Ten Downing St., that you could have walked on the sea of heads. After six years of dreary blacked-out, bombed, hungry existence, people went wild.

With the war over, there was an overwhelming rush to get home to Canada. Several hundred of us who were eligible for early return, waived our Repat number and stayed in Britain, permitting the others to go home first. I had an extra fifteen months in London. Because we had let others go first, the Air Force arranged special programmes, courses, and trips for us. I had a week at the Sorbonne University in Paris and a moral leadership course in Stratford–on–Avon. Looking back, I think it was the best year of my life.

We had a short holiday in Switzerland and a quick visit to Amsterdam, where Canadians were treated royally because of their role in the liberation of Holland. This was where I saw my first bidet—green as grass, I washed my feet in it.

My RCAF wartime experiences were the adventure of my life. For us young ladies, it was a nice war—we had free travel, and we didn't have to kill anybody. Service women have come a long way since our pioneering start. Where we marvelled at women being taught welding and truck driving, young ladies now fly helicopters and jet planes.

When friends leave for a holiday in Europe, I suggest they visit at least one Canadian cemetery, perhaps one where a relative is buried. Canadian cemeteries are beautifully kept, scenes of peace and tranquility. You have the impression they were created that way, the dead being interred daily after each battle. Not so at all. Many casualties were hastily interred where they fell, then were dug up after the war and placed in these beautiful graveyards. That must have been one of the most gruesome jobs on earth.

Walking among those acres of graves, each marked with the age of the dead man—the majority of them were between eighteen and thirty-five—the horror of what happened floods over you. All those young men would have given anything for a chance to die of old age in Canada. I like to remind everyone that the freedom we enjoy in Canada today, take for granted and abuse, was bought with oceans of blood.

Paper Balloons
Kay McCaskill (nee Armstrong)

I served in the Women's Division of the RCAF for four years. For part of that time, I worked in the operations room of the fighter control unit at Patricia Bay.

There had been reports of strange objects in the skies over Vancouver Island. At one point the Civilian Observer Corps had called out an aircraft to go chasing after the planet Venus!

One day, a sighting was reported and our unit sent up two Kitty Hawks to see what it was. One of the two pilots got lost in a cloud, and we had to call the radar stations to locate him so we could give him the vector to get back to base. The other pilot was a bit more alert and he managed to fire on what turned out to be a Japanese paper balloon.

The balloon gradually drifted down and landed near the Royal Canadian Engineers base at Sardis, where it was picked up and sent to RCAF Intelligence in Ottawa. Some months later, I was posted to RCAF Intelligence. After I got settled in, I asked the NCO in charge of the Orderly Room if he knew anything about the paper balloon. He did, and he gave me a piece of the balloon, along with a picture of the barometer and charge of dynamite that had been attached to it.

Very little was ever made known about the balloons that were sent from Japan and designed to land on the coast of North America. The intent was that, once the balloon reached the coast and the barometer indicated land, the dynamite would be released, and would set fire to the forests of coastal B.C., Washington and Oregon. The plan did not work.

The officer in charge of the Sappers who rescued the balloon, was ultimately released from the Army to do research on the tar sands of the McKenzie Delta. When I got to Ottawa, I met him and we were married some months later.

In 1984, I was in a hot air balloon over Edmonton when a DC-3, en route from eastern Canada to the Air Show at Abbotsford, circled our group of balloons. I remarked to the pilot of my balloon that I had flown quite often in a DC-3. He asked me when and where, and I told him I had been in the RCAF during the war. He asked if I had ever been at Pat Bay, and I replied, "Yes, I was on duty there when the first paper balloon was shot down."

I thought the man was going to fall out of the balloon! He was writing a book about the paper balloons, and had never met any one who had ever had contact with any of them. He told me what he had found out about them.

The Japanese had started making them in 1931, for the sole purpose of releasing them (on the prevailing winds) towards North America. The only known casualty was a little girl in Oregon who, some years after the war, had gone out to a forested area in Oregon on a Sunday School picnic and was killed when she picked up a charge of dynamite. Apparently, this tragedy was reported in Japan and some Japanese women who had worked in the factory as teenaged girls, heard of it. They wrote to the family to offer their sympathy and apologies for making the "bomb."

It Came Home Alone

Peter Dawson

I recall how my parents feared the German invasion, but as a seven-year-old, I did not understand. Living in a village near London, I witnessed the activity of the enemy aircraft as they bombed the city, and the RAF fighters that went up to shoot them down. After the worst of the Battle of Britain was over, we moved to a village close to Chelmsford, where the Hoffman ball-bearing works and Marconi radio were targeted by the Luftwaffe bombers.

When the Yanks came with their B-17s, I used to lie under a tree and count them as they gathered in formation before heading east for Germany. Later in the day, I counted them coming back.

There were as many as seven hundred airplanes that went out in formation, in groups of twelve. When they came back it was a different scene. They were often all over the sky; some were terribly shot up and barely airborne. Many never came back.

My most unusual experience occurred when I was eating breakfast and I heard the sound of engines throbbing. It wasn't the usual steady rhythm, so I went out to see what it was. There was solid cloud cover and nothing to see, but around and around went the noise. Then all of a sudden a Flying Fortress plunged out of the sky in a vertical dive; she was headed nose first into the village. Just as suddenly, she levelled out and shot skyward in a steep climb, almost to the clouds. Then she stalled, standing on her tail as if taking a last look at the heavens, and dropped back like a falling stone. Beyond the treetops there was a blinding flash—the bomber had crashed in an open field. Several hundred yards beyond the village there was a great, blackened patch with wreckage strewn about, but there were no bodies, or anything to show that there had been life aboard.

I later learned that the American crew had bailed out over the channel, from what they thought was a doomed plane. Abandoned, the Fort must have somehow regained power and, mustering all her strength, decided to go home anyway. Pilotless, she had gotten within a few miles of her base; the B17 was noted for its ability to withstand tremendous punishment and still fly. That one surely lived up to its reputation!

A Time To Question

Ross C. Morton

Although military orders must be obeyed there are times when it is best to ask a few questions first.

I was stationed at Number Six B&G Training School, at Mountain View Airfield. We were completing the gunnery portion of our Wireless Air Gunner course, and one exercise consisted of shooting at a large nylon wind-sock—called a drogue—while it was being towed by another airplane. These activities were undertaken far out over Lake Ontario.

Four or five student air gunners would be flown by a staff pilot in a Bolingbroke aircraft to a predetermined location, and would rendezvous with a Lysander plane towing a drogue. Students were each given a three hundred- round belt of colour-coded ammunition and then had an opportunity to fire the mid-upper turret machine gun. The drogue would be examined later, and the accuracy of the shooting determined by the colour of the smudge around the holes in the nylon.

We sat on the floor of the plane, below the gun-turret, while awaiting our turn. Only the student in the turret had a head-set and was able to communicate with the pilot. We had our parachute harness on, but the actual chute was set to one side. In an emergency, the chute could be quickly affixed to the chest portion of the harness.

We were all startled when the student gunner suddenly made a panic- stricken exit from the turret. He kept yelling that the pilot had said we were going to crash, and we were to jump out. He stumbled as he looked for his chute chest pack, and was restrained by the other students when he tried to open the escape hatch in the floor.

I wasn't about to parachute into the lake without checking with the pilot. I grabbed the head-set that was dangling from the turret and asked the pilot what was happening. There was considerable noise, both from the engines and the static on the intercom, and it was difficult to hold a conversation. The pilot was irritated by my questioning. He said that the drogue plane had not arrived, and rather than waste the flight, he had decided to abort one exercise and implement another. We were going down for a "splash."

A "splash" was a drill where the aircraft was flown just above the surface, and the gun was fired at the water. This allowed the gunner to observe the pattern and location of the bullets on impact. Apparently, the student in the turret had not been aware of this training exercise. In the noisy environment, the word "splash" had sounded like crash, and he had responded accordingly.

The airman received considerable good natured ribbing as a result of this incident.

My First Flight
Everett E. Sponaugle

I was born on December 30, 1925, and raised in Kamloops, BC. When I joined the RCAF to undergo training in an Air Crew category, I was seventeen years, ten months and twenty-two days old, and very green about worldly facts.

In those days, Kamloops had a population of 7,500. As kids, we walked or ran everywhere to make sure we didn't miss anything. Seeing the aircraft which flew overhead once or twice a year, was very exciting. I had to run three miles (which included crossing the Thompson Railway Bridge on the bare ties) in order to get to a grassy field near the Indian reservation to view the plane. Invariably, I would arrive just in time to see the plane disappearing over the trees.

In spite of these brief glimpses, and even though I had never ridden in one, I built a number of model planes from balsa wood and Japanese paper, using rubber bands for power.

I was attested into the RCAF and sent to Edmonton, Alberta for basic training. Then I was posted to Number Three Repair Depot in Vancouver, where I lived off the station. About twelve weeks after this Pre-Initial Training—still without ever having seen an aircraft—I was posted to a Flying Station in McLeod, Alberta, where pilots were trained.

When I arrived at McLeod RCAF Station, I was attached to a sergeant in charge of Works and Bricks. I was given a long-handled stick with a nail on the end, and told to pick up paper and litter and deposit them into a garbage bag, which was carried over the shoulder.

Although there were twin-engine aircraft there, Cessna Cranes and Ansons, we would not be training in them but would be sent to another ITS for training as soon as space became available. I hid my stick and garbage bag out of sight, marched smartly over to the closest hangar and enquired if it was possible to get up for a ride.

I was introduced to a couple of officers who were ready to go and they said, "Sure you can come with us. Just grab one of those parachute harnesses and put it on."

When one of them saw that I had no idea how to put it on, he inquired if I had been up before. I responded that I had not, so he helped me and then handed me a chest-pack parachute by holding both ends of it and pushing it toward me. I grabbed

110

the handle in the centre and promptly dumped the parachute onto the floor, as it started to fall out after I had pulled the rip-cord.

The officer said, "That is going to cost you a dollar. The girls down at the parachute re-packing building sure don't like that happening often. However, since you are new to this, we won't say anything. There is another parachute on the plane. Let's go."

On the way to the aircraft, they informed me that I was in luck because they were both test pilots. They had a few hours off to test one of the Anson twin-engine planes which had just had the main wing spar replaced, and they would need another pair of eyes to monitor the condition of one of the wings to make sure it was strong enough and was not bending or wrinkling. I was to let them know immediately if there was any indication of this; they would be busy checking the other wing and other surfaces.

I said, "Okay," and wondered what I was getting into.

On getting into the aircraft, I was shown how to put on the parachute and given instructions on what to do if I had to jump. If the door was jammed and I couldn't get out, I was to kick out the small round window, crawl through it backwards, then pull out the parachute and snap it on my chest harness. I was to sit on the wing, slide off and count to ten, then pull the rip cord.

Everett Sponaugle , ready for his first flight

I was told to sit on the port-side seat, where there was a small table for Navigator. I managed to figure out which side was port because there was only one seat for me to sit in. I felt better having learned something already. The two pilots certainly seemed in good cheer; they were laughing quite a bit.

We finally took off and headed south. The pilots said they had to make a short trip across the border into the USA to pick up a few items from landing-strip canteen. They flew low, almost hitting small trees. Then they climbed steeply and made turns that were so tight, I could not raise my hands off the small table or move my feet off the floor. As we approached 15,000 feet, they levelled off and said that was as high as this aircraft could go. They would test the main wings, and I was to keep a sharp eye on the wing to see if it moved or wrinkled.

The pilot pointed the nose of the plane sharply down. He seemed to be pulling and pushing the control column. I paid strict attention to the wing, which waved up and down about a foot. The wing surface had long wrinkles which appeared and disappeared. I started shouting as loud as I could to attract the pilots' attention, but they seemed to be talking to each other and couldn't hear me. Each time I tried to get up to them, the pilot levelled off a bit and pulled the nose up, making it impossible for me to get out of my seat.

I looked out of the window again and could see the banks of Old Man River, with trees and bushes rushing past. I finally realized that these two characters were giving me the works and laughing at my antics. Since I couldn't do anything about my predicament I sat back and enjoyed the ride.

The pilot motioned to me to come and sit in his partner's seat. His partner had gone to relieve himself. He handed me a folded chart and asked me to look for a ferry cable in the river below. He didn't want to hit it, he said. I started to unfold the chart when the pilot exclaimed, "There it is!" and pulled the plane straight up two hundred feet. He levelled off and said, "Whew, that was close, wasn't it?"

The co-pilot returned, and the two of them commenced laughing and asked me what I thought of flying. I thanked them profusely for the unforgettable ride and told them I was a bit less naïve now. They then informed me that the Anson Aircraft was built with flexible wings covered by cloth-like canvas which was designed to withstand enormous stresses, and was a very reliable aircraft indeed.

Shortly after that, I was transferred to ITS at Edmonton. After several months, I was posted to the Number One Central Navigation School at Rivers, Manitoba, for flying training. I graduated as a Sergeant Navigator in the spring of 1945, and was told I would be sent to the South Pacific. After thirty days' leave, I received a discharge on May 4, 1945, subject to recall at any time. It was four months after my nineteenth birthday.

Shades of War

A.C. (Fred) Rogers

The year 1939 held grim warnings of what lay ahead. There was no television then; just the radio, but that was enough. Hitler was making constant headlines with the media. We couldn't understand German broadcasts, but the tone of his voice was spellbinding. There was no doubt about his intentions to rule all of Europe, or more. Although we were separated from his threat by the Atlantic, we all had some fear of this mad man.

In 1941, all young men of age 21 were rounded up under penalty of refusal to report to the nearest Army recruiting station. Ours was a thirty-day army training camp at Gordon Head near Victoria in January of that year. The first contingent of 2,000 men boarded a C.P.R. steamship at midnight, and I was on it, wondering what lay ahead. There were no places to sleep that night and no one intended to sleep, for the air was highly charged with tension. It seemed most men were getting drunk and rowdy, and the situation got worse. There was a little canteen aboard that sold cigarettes and other treats. The girl in charge of this soon got alarmed and locked it up. As a result, the rowdies smashed it open with fire-axes. They also hacked a piano to pieces. There was a terrible din of swearing and fighting, and so I went outside to keep clear of the trouble I knew would soon happen.

About two or three hours out from Vancouver, a gang of men wanted to take command of the ship. "To hell with Victoria," they screamed, "Let's take this ship to Seattle." As they charged ahead for the wheelhouse, the officers were ready for them and had firearms ready. Their authority under Maritime law to shoot any mutineers subdued any threat of disaster.

We arrived in Victoria about 7:00am. What a hell of a mess: the ship had broken chairs, mirrors, and assorted fittings. The men were a sad lot, still drunk, or sick. Damages to the C.P.R. vessel were later charged to the Army and the cost deducted from earnings of all who were aboard the ship.

Fred Rogers is on the left in this photo

Camp was a cheap, but a tough place to exist. There were hard cots to sleep on and a wood stove in each hut for heat. Being February, it got cold during the night, for no one was going to get up and keep the stove burning. We had no hot water for washing or shaving, and the food they served was terrible. Breakfast was mostly some sloppy cold eggs, thrown in with a slice of bacon and cold tomatoes. The coffee was little better than dishwater. Even our uniforms were poorly fitting.

The first day was frustrating. Our regimental officer was a dyed-in-the-wool Englishman, blinded with old traditions and class distinctions. He took us marching the roads and back wood trails in all weathers. One day, he had us marching near a slough and we all stopped. "I didn't command you to halt," he bellowed. "Quick march." We were already cold and damp and no one made a move. He was now in a rage and screamed, "You either get marching, or I'll keep you out here till you do." Well, we walked up and down through that damn muddy slough that was almost up to our armpits. But *he* sure as hell didn't. We were all thinking of ways to get revenge on the bastard.

The combination of poor diet, sleeping conditions, and exposure soon began to take their toll. Some men soon fell sick and were unable to train. As time went on, the ranks thinned. More men collapsed on the roads. I was in prime condition when I joined this group, but I was failing too. When the 30 days were up, they had a party of sorts, but it was really a rally to try and get these men to join the active force, for after what we had gone through, nobody was crazy enough to do that.

The recruiting officer gave a speech full of bullshit, saying he was pleased to know we had a fine time at Gordon Head and not to "all rush up at the same time to sign up." He said we'd see plenty of action and get a belly-full of scrap. One man got up and said: "Sir, we don't have to go active to get our bellies full of scrap. We got them filled with worse crap right here!"

It was a happy day for us all when we left that hellhole called Gordon Head camp. My mother and Dad were shocked when I got home. I was too weak and sick to work on my Dad's truck. Mom got our Doctor and he found I had contracted measles. I wasn't surprised, because it had already felled many others in camp.

That dreadful time of army life left its imprint on me. I vowed I would rather go to jail than go through that again. I started working in the shipyards as a welder in 1941. Dad was conscripted by selective service to work in the shipyards in North Vancouver, and sold his truck. I enrolled in a welding school at Main Street. After 120 hours, I went to work in the same shipyard as Dad, doing high priority work, building 10,000-ton freighters for the war effort. Young men employed there were on a six month's deferment from military service. When it expired, it was renewed, and I was welding there until March of 1944.

Now available for military duty, but still intending to avoid the army, I applied for service in the Navy. The Medical Officer examining me suggested I should first try to get into shape. After two months of vigorous exercise, I was accepted. The Navy was a world of difference from the horrible conditions of Gordon Head.

Too Young To Join

Bud Stevens

Staying at home in Halifax during the war was tough, especially with a brother and a brother-in-law overseas in the air force. I turned sixteen just when the war ended. I couldn't lie about my age because I looked even younger, so I found other things to do, in addition to rolling bandages and collecting tinsel, to help the war effort.

Halifax, an east coast Canadian port, was blacked out and held frequent air raid drills. My job, as a messenger for the ARP, was to hightail it on my bike, complete with steel helmet and gas mask, through the blacked-out, cobble-stoned streets, to a control centre. From there I was dispatched with messages to fire, police and ambulance locations if telephone lines were down.

A much tougher job on my trusty, rusty, CCM was delivering specially-handled casualty telegrams. The ones that began "The Department of National Defence regrets . . ." were held until supper time, when at least one other adult could be expected to be home with the addressee. I delivered one on my way home from work, to the corner of Henry and Morris streets, just a couple of blocks from my home. The mother answered my nervous knock, and the daughter started crying as soon as she saw me at the door—pretty hard for a fourteen-year-old to take. Neighbours, who had been peeking through curtains wondering who's house I would stop at, were on their way to the house even before I left. Their cries followed me all the way home, and I remember them to this day.

Cadet duties during school months were a must for boys. I served one year in army cadets and three years in air cadets, which included two summer camps at RCAF Station, Sydney. Most memorable of these were the flights on Catalina flying boats, and seeing the varying shades of the green Atlantic as it blackened into deep water from the foaming white breakers of the shoreline.

All kids saved up quarters for war stamps, which we put in a book and converted into war bonds when we had saved twenty-five dollars' worth. Another job was to run to Green's corner grocery for steaks, to feed the sailors Mother had invited home for Sunday dinner. Mr. Green always had a supply of meat ration coupons to fill Mother's order. CPO Barker from HMS *Hood* visited twice. Long after his ship was sunk by the *Bismarck*, Mum shipped care packages, with carefully sewn cloth wrappings, to Barker's widow.

There was seldom a dull moment: the explosion at the Bedford magazine which blew out all the windows in my girl friend's house in Rockingham; the uncovering of a spy at Mount St. Vincent Academy; putting bobby pins into a screen to count the number of ships in a convoy; investigating various kinds of wreckage along the shores of Point Pleasant Park and Herring Cove; watching Matelots night maneuvers on the grassy slopes of Citadel Hill; and, of course, the infamous VE Day riot.

A Taste of EATS—Empire Air Training Scheme

H. L. Symon

After a year's ground training with the RAF, February, 1944, saw me waiting at an embarkation camp near Manchester. We knew that we were being sent either to Canada or to South Africa to train as Navigators, but where we were going was a complete secret. At that time the German U-Boats were hunting the Atlantic in packs, and any troop ship, tanker, cargo ship, or ship of any kind, stood a good chance of being torpedoed. To the Germans, the easiest marks were the slow moving convoys of merchant ships. Conversely, the speedy zigzagging troop ships were the most difficult to sink, as the U-Boats simply could not keep pace with them.

Under sealed orders, we boarded a troop train early in March, and travelled all that night. The next day found us on the Clyde, where we boarded barges which conveyed us to a four-funnelled troop ship standing about a mile off shore. She was the former passenger steamship, *Aquitania*, once the proud owner of the Blue Riband race across the Atlantic. Some of the magnificence of the old *Aquitania* remained, but for us enlisted men, it was two meals a day in the hold, and a twenty-four-hour a day guard on all the water-tight doors. We appeared to head south by west, and did much zigzagging. The sea was rough and many of us were seasick.

After five days the temperature became much warmer, and life was pleasant again. The canteen candy shop opened, and although no sweets were available, one could get sweetened condensed milk—a real luxury to enjoy while relaxing on a wooden bench in the sun.

Then we seemed to change directions again, and got into some bad weather. About eight days out, a U.S. Navy blimp appeared to escort us into New York harbour, and we rushed to the side to see what the New World looked like.

We didn't have long to wait.

The following morning we disembarked at New York, to the merry lilt of the bagpipes, our piper being a Scottish lad from Perth. Kind American ladies fed us coffee and doughnuts on the pier, and then we loaded our gear on a train.

We journeyed west and north all that day, seeing the upper reaches of the Hudson River and farming settlements. It was early March, and there was snow on the high ground. At ten p.m., a porter in a white uniform came around and made up the beds. We travelled all that night and most of the next day, now going north by east. We were in either Quebec or New Brunswick. After three days on the train we arrived at Moncton, New Brunswick, RCAF Station.

My rank at that time was Leading Aircraftsman, and my pay was two dollars a day.

In Moncton, we got inoculations, and three weeks later we were on a special train carrying airmen west to Ontario, Manitoba, Saskatchewan, and points west. Our destination proved to be Malton, Number One Air Observer School, a small town twenty-five miles from downtown Toronto.

When we arrived at Malton, we were issued tropical kit. Though it was only April, it was already much hotter than in Britain. For most of our stay we wore open-necked khaki shirts and drill trousers. The pace was fast and furious. We were told the war could not be won without adequate flying crews, and this was the last stage of our training. At the end of seven months we would be given wings and promoted to either Sergeant or Pilot Officer. We were here to work and not to play. Consequently, illness or truancy were not encouraged. Our days consisted of ground classes, day air-navigation trips, and night air-navigation trips. In addition, we had to take two hundred ground star shots, and one hundred night shots with a sextant.

It became hotter through May and June. One morning I was handed a telegram which said that my elder brother John had been killed in the invasion of Normandy. John was twenty-two years old and a Lieutenant in the Royal Engineers. His speciality was blowing up enemy mines. Apparently, he had landed at zero hour on a Normandy beach and was killed instantly by either mortar fire or a high explosive shell. It was a bad blow to my morale, as John had always been the leader and I, the follower. He was well above average at school and had the gift of all things mechanical. Even at the age of fifteen he knew it was the army for him.

It was now mid-June and the only time it cooled off was between one and four-thirty a.m. We slept without blankets and dreamed of swimming. We spent our time off in Toronto. I met three friendly Canadian families and was welcomed into their homes. We were given five days off half-way through the course and I used it to hitch-hike all the way from Toronto to New York. It was my first experience of American hospitality and I was overwhelmed by my royal treatment.

The last ten weeks of the course went by quickly, and in early September we wrote our final exams. I had some difficulty taking Morse at twelve words a minute, but otherwise did well. Our wings were pinned to our tunic breasts on September 7, 1944. It was my twenty-first birthday. Seven months of vigorous ground and air training had come to an end.

From that day, I was Pilot Officer H. L. Symon, qualified to fly vast distances over land and sea in any part of the world. It was a sobering thought because we well knew that many multi-engine planes were lost because of poor navigation.

Our Graduation Day called for a celebration, and this we had in hearty Canadian fashion at the best hotel in Toronto, The Royal York. I have few memories of the occasion—after twenty-two weeks' abstinence, the Canadian spirits proved too much for me. A Canadian friend kindly offered me a bed for the night. I sent a wire home to my parents: "Wings and commission received on my birthday—am now heading home."

A Friend For Life

Shirley Williamson

I joined CWAC in 1942 and was posted to Gordon Head (University of Victoria) and worked in the officers' training mess. The men who had been working there had all left, so we were very short-staffed. Our hours were five a.m. to eight p.m., with one hour off.

I was transferred to basic training in Alberta. Vermilion was a nice agricultural college and I did well at marching and map reading. Then I was told I could go on to Quebec for

Vermillion, Alberta, September 1942, we graduated basic training.

officer's training, or go back to Gordon Head. Ken and I had become engaged and were to be married on November 6th, so I had to go to Gordon Head. They gave me a job at the Post Office. We had to be in barracks by ten p.m., except for weekends. Our times off didn't jive, so Ken wanted me to leave.

I think the CWAC was very good for me. A lot of the girls said it was the first time they had had new clothes and three meals a day.

We were two girls to a room, in bunk beds, and I made a friend for life. Eleanor Creasey was her name. We kept in touch until she died.

Winnie's Cigars

Lorraine (Wilkinson) Bonar, by Marilyn Assaf, Island Life Magazine

I was born in Nanaimo to a mining family. My father was four years old when his father was killed in a mine explosion in 1884. Because of that, my father stayed away completely from the mines and worked in the hotel business.

I received all my education in Nanaimo, including my commercial course at St. Anne's convent and it seemed I would always remain a home town girl. However, that was not to be. From January 1943 to February 1945, I worked for the Department of National Defence, RCAF, Western Air Command in Victoria and later in Vancouver. I ended up working as a secretary to Air Commodore Doug Smith, Chief Staff Officer, Western Air Command. During this time, I met Jim Bonar, a Wireless Air Gunner, a member of the Air Crew Assessment Board. Little did I know he would become my future husband.

In February 1945 I worked in Quebec for Col. Frank. W. Clarke, Honorary Colonel of the Royal Rifles Regiment, and former assistant to the Adjutant General of Canada. He was one of the $1.00 per year men who donated their management skills to our nation when we were so in need. Very little has been written about these industrialists and the part they played in our successful war effort on the home front.

Frank Clarke was a close friend of Sir Winston Churchill, and the British Bulldog accepted an invitation to take a holiday in the Clarke's winter home at Miami Beach, Florida. Col. Clarke's staff spruced up the grounds, had the rooms painted in the house, and purchased extra linens. I rounded up a typewriter and got to know the bank manager and airline people to ensure everything went smoothly during Churchill's visit.

The staff was ready for action when "Winnie" arrived with Mrs. Churchill, daughter Sarah, a Scotland Yard man, a maid, a valet, and a secretary, "Jo" Sturdee. I was turned over to his staff for the duration of their stay. I worked with Jo, typing letters, preparing for meetings, and so on. Jo and I roomed together, got along really well and became good friends.

Along with my other treasured mementos, I still have a letter I received from Mrs. Churchill, an autographed photo from them, my copy of the speech I typed which he presented to the University of Miami, and two of his private brand

118

Cuban cigars with his name on the cigar band labels. I liberated them one day when he wasn't around.

I went back to my old job in Quebec for a few months and then returned home to Nanaimo because my father was dying. Then I returned to the RCAF in Vancouver as secretary for Air Vice Marshal John Plant, Air Officer Commanding Western Air Command.

That's when I began dating Jim. We were married in 1947 and remained in Vancouver until Jim was transferred to Nanaimo in November, 1948. We raised our son Leigh, and I returned to work for another twenty years as a secretary. I retired from the purchasing Department at Nanaimo Regional General Hospital in December 1981, but continued to work part-time until 1986.

Jo Sturdee and I still correspond. She lives on her estate, "Sturdee Freelands," Oxfordshire, and is known as Dowager Countess of Onslow, but still signs her letters to me "Jo, Lady Onslow."

---

n.b. In the book *Never Despair* by Winnie's biographer Martin Gilbert, two pages refer to Lorraine (Wilkinson) Bonar's important contribution during the three months she spent attached to Churchill's staff.

Battle of Britain

Everything That Goes Up Must Come Down

Peter Cornfoot

I was living at my grandparents' house in Kingston-on-Thames. I was nine years old and my father had just come home on leave from the Navy. It was the 27th of December. Eighteen German bombers came over about nine o'clock in the evening. The whole block was destroyed. Mom's fourteen year old sister had been talking over the fence with a neighbour boy when the bomb struck; they were both buried alive and died in the rubble. Grandmother suffered the rest of her life after a splinter of wood went in under her left ear and stuck out under her eye. When they came to, walls were gone, one floor—with a bed still made—was hanging from one wall, and the bathtub was standing up on the pipes. We were covered with pieces of wood and parts of a gas stove from the house next door.

I've been asked, "Why didn't people go to the shelters?"

We had become rather blasé about it, but the Anderson shelter in our back yard was always full of water. We had a budgie that came through okay but lost its tail feathers and had a hell of a time keeping its balance on the perch till the feathers grew in again. The thing that scared us most was the shrapnel bouncing off the road. We had so many anti-aircraft guns around us, and everything that goes up must come down.

Fire Watch

Marjorie Miller

I was a schoolgirl when the war broke out. I became a teenager during the hostilities, and was anxious to wear a uniform. I marked time making guns at BSA, in Worcestershire. We had our own Fire Service with two fire engines, one or two regular firemen, and a volunteer crew. I was accepted and I had a lot of fun owing to the fact that I was young and dainty. I got to be "saved" a lot.

One Saturday night I was on fire watch duty when I was told to report, next day, to the field at the back of the factory, for practice. There was a small stream running through the field. The practice assignment was to dam the stream, dig a pond, and put our hoses in. All other water outlets were to be used only in emergencies.

I was not keen on digging a pond, since I had gone on watch straight from our Saturday night hop at the Scout Hut. However, during the night, a kind German airman dropped a bomb smack on the spot where we were to have dug. So there we had it: our instant pond.

Bomb Raid

Gary Noland

I was with a parts supply unit of the Ordinance Corps, stationed at Little Hampton. It was a Saturday afternoon, and I was lying on my bunk in the old convent, which had been converted to barracks for the duration, when I heard the anti-aircraft guns. I jumped up and looked out just as a German bomber went past the window, about a hundred feet off the ground, firing his machine guns at something up ahead. Then he let the bomb go.

The bomb went right through a stone wall and didn't explode till it hit the school, three hundred feet away. There was an awful roar, the building shook, and there was a huge cloud of smoke and debris. When it cleared up, the school was gone.

The bomber must have been doing about 250 mph. He continued flying out to sea, and was gone over the horizon.

I didn't have time to get scared, but I sure was glad he decided to go past the barracks. Nobody got hurt, but it would have been terrible had it been a school day.

National Fire Service in Hull, UK

Irene Duff

I spent my teenage years in wartime England. The town I lived in was in East York-shire, near the coast. It was a prime area for Hitler's planned invasion and suffered over eight hundred air raids.

At the time, like most very young people, we thought that our lives were full of activity and excitement. We didn't understand the consequences, or the serious nature, of war.

When I look back, I think I must have had nine lives, like a cat. There was the night when my mother, my sister, and myself were huddled in a cupboard under the stairs. That was a favourite place, before bomb shelters were built. We would be reading by candlelight, trying not to hear the planes droning overhead and the bombs dropping. That night the sounds came closer; there was a thud and the ground shook. After that, there was silence. Then came men's voices, shouting: "Is anyone there? Everybody out!".

We came out and were hustled away, clad only in our nightgowns, and taken to a community centre about a mile down the road. It was an unexploded bomb that had lodged between the gas-pipes, which were underneath the cupboard we had been in. It was some weeks before we were allowed back into our home. I remember being concerned about my school clothes and personal things, never realizing at the time how lucky we were.

There were two nights in May, 1941, when the town of Hull was heavily bombed—always after known as the Blitz. I went with my friends to the cinema. It was a rare treat to be allowed out in the evening. About eight p.m. the sirens went and the raid started. The cinema was evacuated and we were told to seek shelter. I was claustrophobic and didn't want to go down in the shelter.

We started to walk home. A policeman cautioned us to look for cover. After walking two blocks, we looked back at the city centre. The sky was lit up and we saw a land mine floating down on a parachute. When it hit, a large area was covered by the blast. We were badly shaken but not hurt, except for a few cuts and bruises. The blast had killed all the people in the shelter.

We walked home ankle-deep in broken glass, stopping to help people with children. It was six a.m. when I reached home; my mother had been dreading the worst all night. All the windows in our house were blown out and we were homeless again. The policeman we had talked to that night was never found; only his helmet was discovered, and was used to identify him.

Not long after that I was evacuated with my school, the Hull College of Arts, to a seaside resort call Scarborough. My mother and sister were able to go with me, so life was easier there. It wasn't such a target for the bombers.

At seventeen years old, girls were called up to do war work. Because my mother was widowed, and my older brother was away in the services, I was allowed to stay home and was given several choices. I opted for the National Fire Service. I returned to Hull, where I worked the switchboards at the Civil Defence Headquarters. We were bang in the middle of the city, but underground. Twenty-four hours on and twenty-four off were our shifts, but when we were busy down there we couldn't see or hear the bombs dropping. We always knew what was going on, though, by the number of call-outs for the fire engines. When I came up out of there, I wondered who and what was left, after yet another raid.

When I was eighteen, I met my future husband, James A.. Duff. He was in the RAF, stationed at Leconfield, about six miles outside the town of Hull. Not long after we met, he was injured whilst on a mission with Bomber Command—just one of the close calls he had, during his five years in the wartime RAF.

A friend, who was going out with the pilot in the same crew, called and asked me, "Would you go to the hospital with me? James is asking for you."

The boys were covered with bandages and feeling sorry for themselves. Our friendship blossomed. Then we fell in love and were married about six months later.

I gave up my chance to go to the London Art School, and he gave up medical school in Scotland, but we have never had time for regrets. We are grateful to have survived when so many others didn't. We took a chance on each other, and it worked for us. We are still together after fifty-four happy years.

Hurricanes In The Defence Of London

Doug Haynes

I joined Seventeenth Squadron, RAF, in 1939. Stationed in East Anglia, I flew Hurricanes in the defence of London. During the Battle of Britain I chased German bombers. I was shot up in late 1940, and my leg was crushed. Unable to fly, I was grounded and remustered to radio operator mechanic.

I was in Farnborough when an American B17 arrived in England, to be evaluated prior to purchase by the RAF. I worked on the B17s till I was sent to a base in Bengal, where I was reacquainted with them in 1942.

An American group of seven Forts and one B24 Liberator was sent to our airfield. They were to use it as an advance base for bombing the Japanese fleet. The Yanks had brought no ground crew, so I was one of sixteen ex-RAF air crew at the station who were put to work because we knew how to service the planes.

A sad footnote: the only B24 crashed on take-off.

Our Avenue: 1939 to 1946

Iris Heywood

When England and France declared war against Germany in 1939, I was a twelve-year- old school girl. Together with my parents and four brothers—the boys were older than me by ten, seven and three years, and the baby was eight years my junior—I lived in a brick semi-detached three bedroom house in Wembley, Middlesex, a half-hour trip by bus or tube train from London's West End. September 3rd was a sunny morning. Outdoors on our avenue, children were dressed in their Sunday best when the sound of the air raid siren frightened the younger ones, excited the older ones, and all rushed to their homes. Indoors, everyone listened to Prime Minister Chamberlain's radio broadcast: we were at war with Germany, and for the duration of hostilities church bells would be rung only to warn of an attempted invasion by sea.

Home changed rapidly, that first year of the war. Blackout curtains were made for every window. Food ration books, clothing coupon books, identity cards, and gas masks were issued. Parents were advised to evacuate their children, and so Frank and I spent some homesick months in South Wales. Luckily, I went home for Christmas and was allowed to remain, and Frank returned the following spring.

The conscription age was seventeen and a half years, but the only uniforms seen locally were worn by servicemen on leave; Wembley had no area suitable for barracks and training grounds. My oldest brother, who was classified as being on essential

126

war work, remained a civilian. He married and moved to his own flat. George enlisted in the Fleet Air Arm, and Dennis joined the Royal Marines later.

The house was very quiet without the boys. All three had brought their friends home, as well as dirty football uniforms, every Saturday during the season. My parents were both age forty-seven then. My father's working hours increased to twelve-hour shifts, thirteen days out of fourteen—plus he volunteered for fire watch patrol some nights. Every house had a bucket of sand on the front entry step, to be used should an incendiary bomb land.

Dad also heeded the pleas of the government to "Dig for Victory," and so we lost our lawn to Brussels sprouts and other vegetables. He erected an Anderson shelter at the bottom of the garden—the farthest point from debris, should the house be hit. When the raids began on a nightly basis, we slept in the shelter, but only for a short time after winter arrived. We had few daylight raids in Wembley, and the shrapnel from the ack-ack shells was the most lethal. A stray bomb did fall two streets away one evening.

We became accustomed to the air raid siren sounding at dusk every day, and were fortunate that the planes that droned overhead were on their way to bomb London's East End dockyards and industries. I clearly remember looking at the sky late one evening; it blazed a brilliant red, like an exceptionally vivid sunset, but unlike a sunset the radiance grew stronger. Dad said it was the flames from the fires in London.

Another incident stands out. A German plane was shot down, and one of the crew landed in our avenue. When my father came home with this news, I asked, "What did he look like?" and "Where is he now?"

Dad said, "He looked like a frightened kid, that's all. Mrs. Wallace was making him a cup of tea while waiting for the police to arrive."

Through these times, my mother coped with clothing coupons, (never enough for two growing children) food rationing, and shortages of everything except queues. The coal ration only allowed fires to be lit in the late afternoon and the house was cold during the winter days. Every time the gas mains were damaged during air raids, she had to cook the evening meal on a fireplace meant for warmth only. The raids were in progress well before my father came home from work, but his meal was always warm when he arrived.

Nothing was wasted in those days. Bins were placed on residential street corners, and all suitable left-over scraps of food were placed in the "Pig Bin." Meat bones (few of those) went into a second bin, to be made into glue. The civilian suits left behind by George and Dennis were altered by a tailor into skirts and jackets for me. Mum dyed the kitchen curtains each year to make them appear fresher.

I remember slogans in the tube stations: "Be Like Dad, Keep Mum" and "Coughs And Sneezes Spread Diseases." Lord Haw-Haw was scorned mightily, but the BBC Home Service was listened to with reverence. Spirits would rise and fall to such reports as "All of our aircraft returned safely" or "A number of our aircraft are missing."

Winston Churchill's speeches always had the power to move and motivate us. We felt such pride in our retreating army, patiently lining up on the beaches of Dunkirk. We were proud, too, of the Royal Navy, which rescued so many of our soldiers, aided valiantly by civilian sailors in small craft of all types. (So proud that Churchill had to remind us we had suffered a defeat, not a victory.) We were proud of the young Spitfire pilots who won the Battle of Britain.

D-Day, June 6, 1944, was ten days before my seventeenth birthday. A quietness descended upon England that day. It was dispelled when V2s began dropping around England's capital, and the war became personal. Just two days after my birthday, a V2 fell a block away from my home. My friend Joan and I were more than a mile away when it fell, yet the effects of the concussion were earth shaking. For the first time, I felt afraid. We ran home.

Our avenue had just nine houses on each side of a road bordered by a grass verge and a sidewalk. Each house had yew hedges around its lot, with a front garden gate. As we turned the corner, we could see the damage. Gates, roof tiles, and shattered glass littered the avenue.

 My house was the eighth down, four doors past Joan's. The front door had been blown off its hinges and had fallen sideways on the stairs, which were covered with debris from bedroom ceilings. Windows were broken. But my family was safe, as was Joan's. Our dog was the only minor casualty, sporting a small lump on his head. I remember how angry I was because our home had been damaged and my family could have been hurt. Mum and I were picking up shards of glass when an Air Raid Warden arrived, checking on casualties. His manner was so calm and gentle: he said to my mother, "Have you put the kettle on?"

So Frank and I were evacuated again, but this time Mum and Joan joined us. We were to stay with relatives in Bristol, where Dad felt we would be safe because Bristol had suffered much damage previously. Youth rebounds quickly. I can still smile when I recall Joan and I standing behind Mum and Frank, lining up to have addresses changed on our rations books. Two sailors noticed us, promptly got in the queue behind us, and started talking to us—not realizing my mother was with us. They were very young too; Mother saw the humour in the situation.

Bristol was teeming with American GIs. Some were casualties who were recuperating in local military hospitals on the Downs, and most were waiting to be moved out to France. It was still only fifteen days after D-Day.

We returned home for Christmas and decided to stay. Joan's sister had been a WAAF for two years, and Joan and I longed to be old enough to join the WRENS. We saw an advertisement stating that switchboard operators were needed immediately at American Army Headquarters. Feeling that this would be the next best thing, we applied for the jobs and were accepted.

UK Base was housed in the annex of Selfridges, off Bond Street, London. The room, with a long row of huge switchboards, was in the basement, and had English supervisors. We worked two shifts: eight a.m. to three p.m., and eleven a.m. to eight p.m. While the room itself was gloomy, we felt great handling incoming and outgoing calls to bases in England and France.

Coming back from lunch one day, we were waiting to show our passes at the entry. The guard was busy talking to two American soldiers, who had just arrived in London and were asking for directions. The guard wondered if we could help them. Their names were Hollis and Bob and they were in London on seven days' leave from France. They asked if they could meet us after work, but we said, "No, we're working until eight p.m."

We found them waiting for us after our shift was finished. They seemed like nice fellows, and as my mother would be expecting me home for a late dinner, I took them home with me. Somehow, Mum found rations to make them a meal too, after which they accepted an offer of coffee, while we had tea. Later, I found Mum very red-faced and embarrassed in the kitchen. She was holding a bottle of HP Sauce and had just realized she had mistaken it for the bottle of Camp Coffee. Mum apologized for her mistake and asked why they had not queried the taste. Hollis politely replied that they thought that was how the English liked their coffee.

VE Day was celebrated in May, and my mother felt Joan and I should return to our normal secretarial jobs. Few uniforms were seen in Wembley, so Joan and I were surprised to see two soldiers at a local fairground one evening.

In London, one saw uniforms of all nations, but this was the first time I had seen Canadians. We found that a Canadian Forces Postal Depot had been set up nearby, hence the arrival of a few Canadians who worked there, but were billeted with civilians. One of the soldiers was named Roy. He came from Grimsby, Ontario, and had trained at Niagara-on-the-Lake before being shipped to Nova Scotia, and eventually to Italy in 1943. He had recently been posted to the UK. I was not yet eighteen and Roy had celebrated his twentieth birthday in March, 1945.

It is odd how a simple decision to spend an evening at a local fair can change one's life. Roy and I were married in March, 1946, and I became a war bride, arriving in Canada in October. Our son was born in May, 1947.

Roy and I moved to beautiful Vancouver Island in June, 1986, when he retired. It was a move Roy had wanted to make for years. I became a widow in 1994.

The Plymouth Blitz

Bob Williams

My wife Margaret lived in Plymouth, England, and endured the blitz for months on end. She lost three homes due to the bombing. The first home to be bombed had a small Anderson shelter, six feet by ten feet, in the back garden; it was about twenty-four feet from the back wall of the house.

During one raid, a bomb landed and exploded in their front garden. The family were all huddled and screaming at the terrible noise and ground shock of the explosion. When they were able to get into the house, they found all the windows blasted out, the roof completely gone, and a deep pit where their front garden had once been. In Margaret's bedroom they found a huge kerbstone had landed on her bed and had depressed the bed-springs to the floor. Margaret had a lucky escape that night.

The blitz went on every night and eventually Margaret and her siblings were evacuated to the countryside. But Margaret's mother remained to provide what home she could, for her children to return to now and again.

It was my ninth birthday and I visited my dear grandmother, Sarah Ann Croft, a lovely lady. She said to me, " I wish I could give you an orange, Robert, but so many hundreds of men are dying at sea to give us bare food to live on. God bless them!"

In January, 1942, we learned that my cousin, Michael Harlick, was a prisoner of war in Japanese hands. He was nineteen years old. Michael returned home in wretched condition, as did thousands of others. The three-and-three-quarter years he spent as a POW in Changi prison, on the Death Railway, and working on the docks during the American bombing, together with malnutrition, beriberi, malaria, and the constant fear of violent punishment or even decapitation, had taken its toll on Michael. He suffered anguish and pain the rest of his life. When he died, he left a legacy to be used for the betterment of children.

On the street where I lived, everybody came from somewhere else, just like in Canada. We were a close knit community and we were always ready to help each other. Most of the young men were in the armed forces, and we all dreaded the approach of an officer—it invariably meant bad news for a family that had a loved one in the forces.

In December, 1941, the Philips, Bird and O'Brien families each lost a son when HMS *Repulse* and the *Prince Of Wales* were sunk by the Japs off the coast of Malaya. Everyone did what they could for the grieving families.

Sometime later, Mrs. Philips won one hundred pounds and she gave every family on the street ten pounds each. Such generosity was not uncommon in those days.

We shared her grief and her good fortune.

England

Boffins And Doodle-Bugs

Maria Bowering

It was 1944, and all leave had been cancelled in preparation for the Second Front on June 6th. I was serving as a driver in the Women's ATS, in the British army. I was posted to Britain's Experimental Rocket Establishment, which was in a very quiet and secluded spot in Wales—very hush-hush.

The serving forces were outnumbered by the civilians who worked there. They were scruffy looking figures, many of them in baggy cord trousers, tweed jackets, and beards. These were the scientists—we called them "Boffins." We had vehicles and weapons, painted in camouflage colours, that had been captured on the various fighting fronts. These were examined and experimented on to discover their strengths and weaknesses.

Our job was to load rockets onto the backs of queer looking vehicles that were nicknamed "Dilly." This vehicle had a very small cab, with an exhaust pipe that ran up the front, and a long, low truck bed on which the rockets were loaded. We would drive the Dillys up to a high headland, and the rockets were fired out into Cardigan Bay.

One day, our Commanding Officer gave me orders to take a van and collect a load from an address near London. I knew it had to be some kind of explosive object, but I was thrilled to go to London. I was the only Londoner in the unit .

In those days, before the motorways, it was a long and tedious drive to London, so I had to take another driver along too. My instructions were to go to a house called Bentley Priory, near High Wycombe. I had official papers for the Police, so they would guard the load if we had to stop for meals.

We drove into London at ten p.m., in the blackout, and in the middle of an air-raid. We could see Flying Bombs overhead, heading in the same direction we were—to the East End, where we were to stay overnight with my family.

Early next morning we arrived at Bentley Priory, a magnificent old house. It was only years later that I realized this was the headquarters of Fighter Command. I showed my papers and was told that Sq. Ldr. Blank would come out to see me. He was a short, pompous little man with a large F/0 Kite moustache. He gave us a haughty look and asked where we were from. When we told him Wales, we could see he was thinking: a couple of hicks from the sticks. He took us into a hangar and showed us the load we had to collect. There was a long, metal pipe about a foot in diameter, some broken off wings, and a radiator. Knowing the sort of things our unit dealt with, I asked, "Is it one of those Flying Bombs"?

He gave me a contemptuous look and said, "We call it a doodle-bug."

We loaded up our doodle-bug and headed back to Wales. We later discovered that this was the first doodle-bug that had crashed and not exploded. It was gathered up and rendered safe so the boffins could discover its secrets.

Military Police

Henry J. Gagne, Queen's Own Cameron Highlanders, Canadian Provost Corps

I was born on a farm near Jack Fish Lake, Saskatchewan. At age seventeen I could not wait to join the army. No sooner had I received my uniform than we hit the Parade Square for foot drill and marching. I got most of my basic training in Saskatoon. A few days later, I was asked to go on a Canadian Victory Bond tour. With a four-member honour guard, I proudly carried a Commando dagger on a cushion.

Bonds sold like hot cakes, since this was after the raid on Dieppe, France. We had posters of the raid showing how many lives were lost. We were trying to outdo the other groups, and with only an hour to go, a nice Jewish man said, "I'll take $3,000 worth."

That put us in the lead, giving us the next day off for a free supper and a movie.

A few of us were selected for Remembrance Day parades at North Battleford, Sask. The rest of the winter was light duties and much more drill and marching. On May 28, 1943, I was eighteen years old. I requested a move to Regina for more basic training, and then on to Shilo, Manitoba for advance training.

One day in August, 1943, the Sgt. Major called a kit inspection and we received a second pair of boots, shirt, mess tins, and one blanket. We were advised to stay in camp, as we would be moving out in the morning. At five o'clock the following morning, our corporal shouted, "Hit the deck!"

By six-thirty we were in the mess hall, followed by roll call on the parade square at seven-fifteen a.m. There was a line of trucks waiting to take us to the train, where we met other troops. An hour later we were on our way to Halifax. When we arrived there, we stopped just long enough to drop our packs and were off on a run. In my mind was the question: how are they going to get all these troops on board a ship?

I had never seen a ship before I marched on to the gangplank of the *Queen Mary*. There were truckloads of troops waiting, and the loading went on all afternoon and evening. I went to sleep and woke up at sea. There were 23,000 troops on board that ship as we zigzagged across the Atlantic.

On the morning of the fifth day, we sailed into a bay in Scotland. It took hours to unload us all onto tugboats, after which we were on the train headed for a camp near Guildford, Surrey. A month later, eighty of us were transferred to The Queen's Own Cameron Highlanders of Winnipeg, an infantry regiment stationed in Worthing, Sussex.

After a couple of months of hard training and sleeping outside in the fog and the rain, I came down with pneumonia and pleurisy and landed in Number Three Canadian General Hospital at Taplow, Buckinghamshire. I came out in the spring of 1944, and went to a convalescent unit near Guildford. I was told by the Medical Officer that I would not be going back to my regiment.

"You have a big scar on your left lung due to the pleurisy," he said.

I was being re-classified to P-3.

A few days later I went for a walk and saw massed planes in the sky: Bombers, Spitfires, Hurricanes, anything that could fly. I got back to the barracks and men were clustered around the radio. When I asked what was going on, I was told that it was D-Day and that they were landing in Normandy.

For days we mapped the course of advancement, and received daily reports of our regiments. The Cameron Highlanders, South Saskatchewan Regiment, and Fusiliers Mount Royal were cut down at Caen, Dieppe, and the Falaise area. There were reports of hundreds of dead and wounded; the news was often bad, but there was progress.

A couple of days later, I was transferred to an OTC as Military Police. I checked traffic in and out of camp, and guarded the ammunition dump and storage—thirty-five tons of mortar shells, twenty-five-pound shells, and more. We had an area about two hundred yards square, surrounded by barbed wire and a minefield on three sides.

Early one morning I was on guard when I saw a man cross the fence and start across the mine-field. I yelled at him to turn back, but he kept coming. I called out the guards and expected to see him blown into the sky any minute. Despite my yelling, he kept on coming until he stood beside me.

The man said, "What's all the fuss Guv'nor? All I done was cross your lawn!"

It was an old Englishman, drunk as a lord; we got the Orderly Officer, who handed him over to British authorities.

One foggy morning we were on the parade square for roll-call, but it was such a miserable day that the officer called off the drill session and told us to go to the hall for lectures. We had just left, when a couple of German planes came over and machine-gunned the square and dining hall. No men were killed, but a few received cuts from the glass and wood splinters.

Lord Haw-Haw, the English traitor, whose broadcasts of anti-British propaganda were well known throughout the war, did a news-cast that same evening which said, "You Canadian boys were lucky this morning and got off the parade square in time. Your clock was five minutes slow."

He was referring to the big clock at Bordon, which was close by. He seemed to know our routine better than we did.

My most frightening experience whilst in England was in late 1944. The Germans had come out with an awful weapon, the V-2, a pilot-less plane that carried a 500 lb. bomb and was pre-set to fly across the Channel and go inland. The engine would then cut out, and this weapon could go left, right, or straight down.

A lady friend and I had been to the movies, and were walking across a park. We saw the plane, and then heard the engine stop; it came towards us, passed over us and landed about two hundred yards away.

The V-2 exploded on impact, and we were showered with flying tree branches and rocks. There was an enormous hole where it had hit, but apart from being really shocked, we were unhurt. We were very glad it had gone past us as far as it had.

I was transferred to Number Three Canadian Military Prison and Detention Centre, near Aldershot. One of my duties was to look after a German general by the name of Kurt Meyers. He was charged with murdering thirty-six Canadians, and had been sentenced to life in prison. In March, 1946, we escorted him to Canada.

My Commanding Officer informed me that I had been selected to escort a shipload of soldiers under sentence back to Canada. These were our bad boys, doing from two to twenty years for crimes ranging from robberies to rape. Some were in handcuffs, others in leg-irons, and they were loaded into trucks and taken to Glasgow, King Five docks, Scotland. There they were put aboard HMS *Trumper*, an old aircraft carrier.

The *Trumper* had sixty-nine planes aboard, that were being returned to the US by the British, having been part of a lend-lease deal. This ship was no *Queen Mary*. We had gales, snow, rain, and very strong winds, which meant the planes had to be checked every couple of hours, in case they broke loose.

The ship steered north towards Iceland. We were in ice four inches thick. My bunk was right by the side of the ship, and I could hear the crunch of the ice against the ship. Twenty-two days later we sailed into Halifax, and then travelled by train to New Brunswick to unload a few prisoners at Dorchester prison. Another dozen were unloaded in Quebec, and a dozen at Kingston Penitentiary. The last eight or ten were to be delivered to Prince Albert and then my work would be finished.

I was met at the station in Regina by an officer who gave me a hundred dollars and said, "Go home and see your people; we will see you in Regina in a month's time."

I returned a couple of days late, and expected to get told off. Instead, the Commanding Officer said, "I have a job for you as a drill sergeant and PT instructor, for six months, at Dundern Detention Centre."

I agreed. Six months later I went back to Regina and the same officer asked me, "Are you ready for civilian life yet?"

I told him, "I think I have had enough of the army for now," and received my honourable discharge.

A week later I was working at the mental hospital in Battleford.

After forty years of working in Military Police, gaols, correctional centres, and courts, and as a probation officer, I retired at age sixty. I often think back to the army days when I was on duty twenty-four hours a day, and every day was full.

You're Not In Canada Now

Dick Jackson

I joined the Army in Vancouver and went back East for basic training in the Tank Corps. After basic training, I was transferred to the Infantry.

We were on our way across the Atlantic, to Britain. One morning, around daybreak, we were awakened by the sound of empty anti-aircraft artillery cartridges dropping on the steel deck. When we inquired, we were told it was just a routine practice. We arrived in England around three a.m. and were all standing around complaining about being cold and wet, when a thundering voice split the night air.

"Smarten up! You're not in Canada now."

After training around the South Downs, we were shipped to Belgium, where we were assigned to the Canadian Scottish and put into holding units. We were outside of Aurich, Germany, ready to go in on the morning of V E Day; we ended up marching in, instead of fighting our way in. We guarded German prisoners for a couple of weeks after that.

Some of us volunteered for the South Pacific and were shipped back to England for a week's leave. That ended abruptly when we were recalled and shipped to Greenwich, Scotland, where we sat in the harbour, on the *Queen Mary*, for a week. Later, we learned that it was to get us away from the riot in Aldershot.

Dick Jackson & friend on leave in London after hostilities ceased.

When we returned to BC, we were given one month's leave. The Japanese surrendered while we were on leave, but we were shipped to Shilo, Manitoba. Six weeks later we were sent home. I ended up at Nanaimo Military Hospital as part of the rear party, and helped to close it down.

Love In The Water Tank

E. Ted Leeson

Many cities in Britain had large water tanks which were level with the street. If bombs damaged the mains, there would be water to douse the fires. A fence was erected around these water tanks as a precaution against falling in.

I was on a weekend pass to the wicked city of Leeds, with a fellow airman. We met two girls and after an evening in a pub, we were all in good spirits. As we walked the girls home through the twisting streets, a bomber's moon made it bright as daylight. My lady and I, walking along slowly and chatting, had fallen behind. When we rounded a bend in the street, we saw our friends standing against the fence. As we drew nearer, it was obvious this was not a simple embrace, but passionate love-making.

Alas, the fence broke, depositing the pair into the tank. We pulled them out; their ardour cooled. We took them home and dried them out. My friend, who lives in Toronto, still gets reminded of this escapade.

American Hospitality

Sid Philp, RCAF, 419 & 426 Squadrons

Most of the Number Six Canadian Bomber Group airfields were located in the Vale of York where, during the winter months, it was not uncommon for fog to descend during the early morning hours and obscure the whole countryside. If that occurred when bombers were returning from a night mission, they had to be diverted to airfields in the south.

One such morning we had to land at Bury St. Edmonds, an American bomber station. What an eye-opener! What generosity! I had been in England for about a year-and-a-half and had become accustomed to good, but not great, RAF food, with its rationed amount of rabbit stew or sawdust sausages, and Brussels sprouts or powdered eggs.

The first thing I noticed when I entered their dining hall was a sign saying: "Take all you want, but eat all you take." The first meal served was frankfurters and sauerkraut. For me, that was a delicacy! But the best was yet to come. For dessert, we had fresh fruit salad with ice cream.

Later, we were sitting around the officers' mess, shooting the breeze. The Americans wondered why we did not patronize the bar. When they discovered that we were penniless because we were not allowed to take cash with us on our operations, they told us we could have whatever we wanted from the bar, for as long as we wanted. We were glad that the weather kept us there for three days.

A Knockout, An Unhappy CO, And A Toe

Bill Pineo

I joined The Canadian Scottish in Port Alberni, and got into the boxing team to get out of route marches and drill. I stayed with it until I got to England and realized that being knocked about was tiresome, especially after my last bout.

The Championships were being held at Camp Borden, in Hampshire, and I was number five on the card. They told me one of the other guys was ill and I had to take his place.

One look at my opponent, and I realized why the other guy got sick. He was a big, ugly heavyweight. The outcome was inevitable; I was put away in the first round. While I was doing fancy footwork and feinting with my left jab, as I had been taught, he came at me like an out of control freight train. When I came to, and climbed out of the ring, I met the scowling Commanding Officer. He had wanted a winner.

That was the end of my boxing career. I was transferred to the Signal Corps as a dispatch rider.

Tony Hornby and I, along with a guy called Zeke, were on our motorcycles, escorting an army truck convoy somewhere in the south of England. Our job on escort was to block traffic at crossroads, to allow the convoy through. One of us was always in the lead, one stayed at the rear, and one travelled along the length of the convoy.

Hornby was at the rear. He pulled out to take the lead, and collided into Zeke, who was coming back. No one was hurt, or so it seemed, at the time.

Back in camp, we were preparing for our showers when Tony let out a yell. A part of his toe was missing. He started groping around inside his bloody sock, looking for the missing digit, while teaching us a whole new vocabulary.

Tony had a choice of returning home, but decided to tough it out. He stayed with us to the end.

A Day To Remember

Gordon Quinn, Royal Canadian Engineers

It was a sunny day, and I was standing across the square from Westminster Abbey, waiting for my friend. We were to go on a hike in the South Downs forest. As I was early, I decided to take a look at the Abbey.

Inside the door, an old clergyman was leading a tour group. I tagged along. We stopped at tombs of royalty, which had stone statues reposing on stone slabs high on the wall. Then there were stone slabs in the floor of the aisle where we trod. Our guide referred to these as "Honourable gentlemen."

We paused at Poets' Corner, among statues of famous bards, including one of William Wordsworth. There, a short curved stone bench invited me to rest and think. However, it was time to leave, so I took an aisle leading to the west door and walked upon names of ancient men who lay buried there.

Near the west rotunda, a shaft of sunlight shone on a group of old men in worn clothing, standing with their heads bowed and their hands behind their backs, or leaning on canes, looking as if they were praying. I felt compelled to join them, and stood at attention with cap in hand and head bowed.

The sun shone on a stone slab with a row of red poppies carved around the border. There was a large stone cross on top of the slab, and at the foot of the cross were carved the words, "He who is known to God alone . . . Lest we forget."

I hurried to the west door, but walked around this slab, not daring to step on it. I walked out into the brilliant sunshine and the embrace of my lovely friend.

Big Ben, across the river, struck eleven. And then I remembered: the eleventh hour, the eleventh day, the eleventh month.

We boarded double-decker bus Number Twenty-seven to Hayward Heath, where we hiked forest trails, kicked at piles of fallen leaves, and walked arm in arm, as I'd often done with my girl back in Canada.

"Damned war," I muttered. "I want to go home."

My friend said, "Come, let's enjoy tea and a dance at the pub."

It was so relaxing to sit at a table set with real china, look out at the rose garden, and danc, on the tiny floor, to music by three grey-haired ladies playing cello, violin and piano. With no soldiers there, the war seemed a long way off.

After dinner, we gathered around the piano to hoist a pint and sing till the barman called, "Time, gentlemen, please!"

The maid had warmed the bed and turned down the covers. Those white sheets and pillows were so appealing. An embrace, and two sets of clothing fell to the floor.

On the morrow, she would return to her position in charge of the assembly line producing tank radios, and I would go back to Army life. But this was our night.

Target Practice

Georgina Rosewall

I was stationed at a Civilian Rehabilitation Unit on the grounds of a beautiful country estate. We were in the oldest part of the Manor house, built in 1503. It had a billiard room with a full sized table, and a church with marble tombs which were topped by statues of knights and their ladies, dating from the Crusades.

We also had a ghost. Luckily, I never saw her.

This unit was for men who had been Japanese captives and who had just returned home. All barriers between ranks were dispensed with. In the dining room, the tables were laid with place settings such as you would find in a nice restaurant. We even had our own lake, complete with swans, to swim in. Idyllic place.

A much-coveted permanent pass

I came back to reality when I was posted to the 144th Heavy Artillery Regiment in Washington Co., Durham. With a few hundred of us in camp, it was a lively place. Not far from Newcastle and a good NAAFI, there were lots of pubs, and dances.

There were three Batteries: 297, 298 & 301. Periodically, we were sent on a cadre course down to Weybourne, on the coast of Norfolk, and would be loaded into trucks full of equipment, for the journey. At Weybourne we lived in Nissen Huts, which must be the coldest places known to man.

A nearby air force base provided us with a plane towing a drogue for target practice. The 279 performed well and were proud of themselves. One evening, in the village pub, a Battery from another regiment suggested a competition. This ended with someone shooting the lines at the tail of the plane, where the drone was attached!

Target practice resumed a couple of days later, when they got another pilot and plane. In the village pub, there was much discussion about which Battery had made the mistake.

While we were waiting for the new plane to arrive, we played on a lovely beach south of where some German POWs, who were attached to our base, were clearing mines. One day, four of us went for a swim, and I was the first one in. The water was cold enough that you had to walk in steadily. I was not moving very fast, which was lucky, because as I looked down I saw a large metal object, about the size and shape of a curling stone, between my feet.

All of us froze in place. Then the guys edged forward, and reached out their hands for me. I backed up very slowly and gently.

I was told later, by a friend, that it had probably been an anti–tank mine, which would not have been activated by my size and weight.

These memories added to the joy of dancing on both VE and VJ days.

London Adventures

Margaret Ruston, CWAC

I was among the first of the CWAC to be trained for service overseas. We came from every province in Canada, and trained in Ottawa and at MacDonald College, near Montreal.

We were to sail on the *Queen Elizabeth* out of Halifax harbour. Her great speed meant that we were to travel without the protection of a naval escort to Scotland.

Once on board the *Queen Elizabeth*, CWAC were directed to a mustering area where we were counted, instructed on basic behaviour at sea and made aware of areas prohibited to us. Then we were assigned to our cabins. Twelve bodies were packed into an eighteen-by-twelve-foot inside cabin, but we had a three-piece bathroom. Our beds were four rows of three-tier bunks made from chicken-wire netting and two-by-four lumber, with so little headroom that we could barely sit upright. I was assigned a bottom berth.

We assembled twice each day for meals: breakfast at eight a.m., dinner at five p.m. There was no shortage of food, and we had plenty of crusty rolls, which we sandwiched with cheese and wrapped in napkins as take-aways.

We were barred from the open decks during daylight hours, except for boat station drills, which were frequent and unexpected. These were unnerving at night. When the klaxons blared their warning, we collected our shoes, life jackets, and emergency bags, struggled into our clothes and exited our stateroom. The dim corridors would be filled with pushing, shoving bodies. From time to time we heard anti-submarine depth charges being tossed overboard. Some of us lost our ability to sleep at night.

I recall time spent in crowded lounges reading, gossiping and playing cards. There was no mingling of the sexes during daylight hours, with the exception of boat drills. But after dinner we were allowed out on deck. Fresh air, exercise and fun, with several thousand young men, and less than one hundred women.

Officers, male and female, were on perpetual patrol. For the most part, everyone behaved, but I recall giggling coming from beneath the canvas covers of the lifeboats.

On the second night, one of our patrolling officers, father of one of my civilian friends, stopped to say hello and invited me to a game of cribbage in the Officers' Mess. I spent the evening sitting on the hard floor of a crowded room, drinking warm fizzy drinks and losing game after game. We listened to a short- wave radio broadcast from Berlin by the English traitor, Lord Haw Haw, who announced that five submarines were about to pounce on us. It did nothing to improve my evening.

The following evening, I was on deck when a soldier lit a cigarette lighter and held the flame high above his head. If he was signalling the enemy, it was short-lived. The men nearest to him threw him to the deck and would have killed him if he had not been rescued by some of the ship's crew.

Our Atlantic crossing eventually came to an end. Steaming north of Ireland, we turned southeast to anchor at Greenock, in Scotland, in the early morning hours. We emerged into a world of pelting rain, skirling bagpipes and squishy mud. We stepped aboard a large barge and were transported across the river to the rail line. Hot, wet and steamy, we lined up to be counted, then dragged ourselves along the train tracks to a long open-sided custom shed, where we sheltered from the rain.

British trains were different from the CPR and CNR trains. Instead of Pullman coaches, there were small compartments seating five or six passengers. Our compartment had green plush seats, a bracket vase, a bevelled mirror below the luggage rack, and a private wc with a fold-up hand basin, hidden behind a tiny door.

I slept through the lowlands of Scotland and woke up at Carlisle station, in Cumberland. It was the town where my mother was born. The local women welcomed us with hot mugs of coffee and delicious boxed brunches to enjoy, as we rattled on our way. We arrived at Kings' Cross station late that night.

One weekday morning, not long after our arrival, I was travelling down Edgeware Road on a bus crowded with busy shoppers. On the aisle seat beside me sat a large woman with a snuffling dog on her lap; her basket took up most of the space intended for my feet. Suddenly the bus pulled over to the curb, and the driver bounded from his seat, yelling, "Buzz bomb overhead! Under the seats, everyone."

I looked around and saw bottoms, dogs, and heads, all struggling to disappear into impossible spaces. Fortunately, the bomb landed far away.

On another chilly Sunday morning, I decided to stay in barracks instead of venturing forth to lunch with Aunt Grace. As the phone in the barracks seemed in perpetual use, I walked part way down the hill to a phone kiosk. Two British naval ratings waited patiently as I apologized to Aunt Grace. Then I heard a buzz-bomb. Thinking that the sound was coming over the telephone, I urged my aunt to rush to her shelter. Before I had time to hang up, I was pulled from the kiosk and thrown to the ground. A naval rating threw himself upon me, and my tin helmet went rolling down the hill.

The blast had blown the second seaman onto the top of the nearby static water tank; its rusted mesh cover was unable to bear his weight and he was almost submerged in the murky water. As my vision cleared, I saw him emerge from the depths, coughing and sputtering. At the same time a London bobby arrived, carrying my helmet and exclaiming, "I 'alf expected to see an 'ead following the 'elmet down the hill!"

Santa Wore Blue

Ken Stofer, RAF

It was Christmas, 1942, in London, England. I was a Canadian in the Royal Air Force and was about to enter St. Andrews Hospital, in London's East End. At the main entrance, I hesitated briefly to check my appearance: brass buttons shining on my best blue, razor sharp crease in my trousers, shoes polished to an ebony gloss. I was there because of a letter I had written to my mother, asking for chocolate to give to the many English kids who thought we Canuck servicemen had an endless supply.

Mom belonged to the Time Klock Klub of radio station KIRO, in Seattle. They had 20,000 members who listened in every morning. It was a fun program, but their

Ken Stofer in India.

main purpose was to help the unfortunate.

Mom sent my letter to the radio station and it was read over the air. I became their representative and sent in reports from the front. Little did I realize the catalytic effect my letters would have. The big North American heart and pocket-book opened wide. Cases of toys, candy and clothing, began arriving in England.

I took a deep breath and entered the hospital. A nurse, who had obviously been designated as the lookout for someone in Royal Air Force blue with Canada patches on his shoulder, came forward and asked, "Are you Mr. Stofer?"

She introduced me to the head matron, and the three of us walked over to a large ward. Down both sides of the room were long tables, around which sat scores of children. They were having a tea party with sweets and cakes. Strung across the ward, among brightly coloured Christmas decorations, were several British flags; a large American flag hung in the centre of the room. At the far end were tables piled with toys and clothing.

I had never felt so proud in my life; to think I was partially responsible for it all. Then it was my turn to be Santa. It mattered little that I was clean-shaven and in air-force blue, instead of white-whiskered and wearing traditional red and white. Over 120 excited children filed by, and I gave each a present of their choice and a handful of candy. One little boy kept returning to shake my hand.

Later, I went on a tour of every ward in the hospital, accompanied by nurses pushing hospital carts overflowing with toys and candy. We visited kiddies who were unable to leave their beds.

After my role as Santa was completed, the staff told me of their experiences during the air-raids. I was shown over the hospital, and taken up to the roof, where it was evident many incendiary-bomb fires had been fought.

In every direction there was rubble and partial remains of buildings, crumbling masonry walls, exposed plumbing, and lone, sentinel-like chimneys. Some of the orphaned children to whom I had just given a toy had once lived in those houses.

Of all the wonderful Christmases I have had over the years, that was the most memorable.

Ten years ago, after a chat on the radio about this story, I received a phone call from a lady who lived less than four miles from my home. She was one of the little girls to whom I had handed a toy that Christmas.

Memories
Iris Francis Nichol, W.A.A.F.

I joined the W.A.A.F. in the latter part of 1942; prior to this, I spent two years in the Cadets. My dream was to work on one of the many planes that flew over our house, but when I joined up, they weren't allowing women to work on the aircraft.

I then became a waitress at #10 Officer training unit until finally I was able to re-muster and take a course as a safety equipment worker. I was sent to Wyton, as an L.A.C.W. to work in #8 group with the Pathfinder Squadron. My dream finally came true. I installed dinghies in Lancaster bombers and Mosquito bombers. I also worked with the Canadian #109 Squadron Meteorological Reconnaissance Flight.

Once I was working in a Mosquito in which they had installed radar. It took me longer to work around this equipment and the plane had to be towed out to flight deck, but with me in it! That was the only time I had a trip in one of their planes.

I loved my job, and on V.E. Day we worked with a different feeling. We had a great time in camp that night, celebrating the Victory, so well deserved.

VE Day in Milford Haven, Wales
Roy Hinder, OS/RR LST

I was an Ordinary Seaman on an L.S.T (Landing Ship Tank). I often think of the joy I saw on VE Day. We knew the end was near for the German war machine, so my ship was sent to refuel, then anchor in Milford Haven, Wales to await further orders.

I had not had any lengthy leave in over four months and my chum, a leading cook, invited me to his home in Pontypool, where his father was Mayor. So with seven days leave, we were away.

Pontypool was a small town of friendly people where the Welshmen would sit in the pubs at night and love to sing. It was the second day of my leave and my chum and

VE-Day in Pontypool.

I were walking down a typical street of row housing. Doors began to fly open and people began shouting "It's over, It's over." It took a couple of seconds to sink in—the war had ended.

The street suddenly filled with people hugging and kissing, and so we joined in also. Then the party atmosphere really took off. Tables appeared almost magically, upon which local residents rushed to place bottles of beer and wine for anybody to help themselves to. I had never witnessed an instantaneous party like that in my life and I doubt I ever will again.

My thoughts at that time were varied - my first was "Thank God, it's over!" I then thought it would be great to have the street lights on again, so that I wouldn't get lost trying to get back to my ship. I also thought of my married shipmates who would be re-united with their spouses and families for good. I thought also about the children of England, some of whom I had personally witnessed become paralyzed with fear during the Battle of Britain, and their parents or other grown-ups who would pick them up and carry them off to an air raid shelter.

That evening, the pubs threw open their doors and remained open till 4.00 and 5:00 A.M. Bobbies came in, took off their helmets, and joined the locals in the celebration. Nothing was mentioned about closing time.

On returning to my ship, I found we were to leave for Plymouth, our home port, to decommission the ship. The H.O's. (Hostilities Only) volunteers were being de-mobbed and sent home. This took away two thirds of our ship's company. I was then drafted to a minesweeper to clear the central European coast. The Navy still had plenty to do, but at least now it would be without danger of air attacks or torpedoes.

Eleven Plus One
Hilda (Ingalls) Whitehead, RCAF

A few relatives and close neighbours had gathered in our small Maritime town to bid me *Bon Voyage*. After everyone had left, Mom and I sat in front of the fire, each of us loath to say goodnight. As we sat talking, the noise and tumult of Europe were far away, but tomorrow would bring it all closer when I boarded the train for Halifax to wait for my ship.

As I went to my room and stood in front of the mirror, I examined my features and wondered if Bill would find me much changed from the girl he left three years ago to go overseas with one of the first contingents of soldiers. Bill and I had met in a Northern Ontario mining town where I had been attending a Business College. After he had joined the Army, I had gone to Toronto and worked as a Secretary for two years, before joining the Air Force.

146

I awoke the next morning and realized this was the day I was to leave for Halifax and my ship. What was the war really like in Europe? I wondered, as I dressed to greet my family for breakfast. As I made my goodbyes to my family, I felt a sudden desire to weep, for although I would miss my family and homeland, my vast sadness was for the whole human race.

When I settled down in my seat in the train, my thoughts returned to that first wartime summer in Toronto—lady riveters, war bonds, and all the excitement of the precious V-mail letters. For most people, the news of war in distant lands was urgent and personal; there was heartbreak for many, and every aspect of life was coloured in some way by the fact of a wartime crisis.

I used to go over to the YMCA to help entertain the service men, play ping pong, Chinese checkers, or just listen to their talk of their homes and their girl friends. We were all caught up in the events of the times; most of the girls waited every week for letters from their sweethearts, and the boys couldn't wait to get overseas and finish things off. As I talked to Norwegian Airmen, New Zealand and Australian service men and our own Canadian flyers, soldiers or sailors, I was filled with a state of disenchantment with myself and everyone around me. I couldn't wait to be in the thick of things myself. So when my thoughts returned to the fact that I was on my way overseas, it seemed it was like living a dream.

One could never really comprehend the feeling of being lost by war's parting until one experienced it oneself. As the blacked-out ship slowly crept out from home port, with no flags flying, no bands playing, and no one upon the dock to say farewell, we wondered if ever this ship would return again and how many of these service men would be coming back. I was feeling the full poignancy of leave-taking as never before—a new strange life ahead. We were all experiencing it for the first time, but in different ways, some with bravado, some with sadness, some with gayness, but all were hiding their true feelings as never before.

It was an uneventful crossing: five beautiful sunny June days on the Atlantic and like a dream come true, an ocean voyage that I had always longed for. The *Louis Pasteur* was crowded, crammed with servicemen from our three forces, plus others from foreign countries who had taken their training in Canada. Needless to say, the few girls aboard did not lack for attention. For most, it was a flirtatious time, a time for us enjoy, before getting down to the business of war. It was a time to be kind to all, for many wouldn't be coming back.

So as we lazed upon the sunny deck, even the sighting of a sub didn't seem to excite too many of us, or pull us out of our lethargy. However, we did look forward with gusto to our meals, as the sea air made us ravenous. Although not consisting of a stunning array of delicacies that might have been served on an ocean cruise, the meals were of good wholesome foods.

We docked in Liverpool. For many it was the parting of the ways. The Airwomen all went to Bournemouth, the trip on the boat train being long, hot and dusty.

When the stewards came around to serve us a meal, they had huge pots of mashed potatoes of which we each received a large mound. After waiting about a half hour for something to go with it, we all dug in, thinking, "if this is what the meals are like in war-ravaged England, who are we to complain?" But the humorous part of it was, that after we were all finished, along came the same stewards with two pots of mutton stew to go with the potatoes. I guess they thought, "Those blooming Canucks are an impatient lot."

When we arrived in Bournemouth for training, and were given our quarters, we experienced a few changes to our accustomed way of Canadian living. The mattresses on our beds consisted of three sections, called biscuits and our pillows were hard bolsters. We had to carry our gas masks and helmets with us everywhere we went and when we experienced a real air raid, we all had to run for shelter.

The day arrived when we were finally given our postings. Mine was to a Northern England base. As we settled in, we christened our Nissan hut the 'Canned Crabs.' We started our long shifts in the signal section, located in a Castle called Allerton Hall, and soon began to realize what the war was all about.

We had to get used to the blackouts, carrying a torch with us, back and forth to the Castle or to town; we had to get used to mutton stew and canned meat, powdered eggs, and stewed dried fruit. There was thick fog at night and early mornings, when we used to shiver even in our heavy uniforms.

It was not until after we were all settled into the routine of things that we were at last given our much longed for leave. My girl friend and I went to Folkstone; she to see her grandparents and I to meet Bill, who was stationed near enough to come visit me. After three and a half years, he looked tall and handsome in his soldier's uniform and a little more grown up than he had when we had last met in Canada. We had a perfect week, we took long walks along the beach in Folkstone; we rode the bus to Dover and saw the much sung about 'White Cliffs.' We visited London and saw all the historic landmarks of which I had read. We rode subway trains all the while trying to catch up on the three years we had been apart.

Finally, we had to say goodbye. Bill stood with his arms about me, as I buried my face against his kaki tunic. "Don't cry Heidi," he said. "The war is not going to last forever. I'll be back and we'll get married. Let's set a wedding date."

"How can we do that?" I replied. "Wars don't wait for weddings." But knowing that he was being shipped out, he suggested we made it a year from then. Little did we know that it would be over two years before we met again. There should have been something more to say, but time seemed to stand still, and I just stood with my hand in his, waiting for his train to carry him away.

Returning to Camp, we learned to work hard and try to keep a tight rein on our emotions, especially when we would receive the casualty lists after a night of operations. We dreaded reading about missing or dead flyers, as many a time, they were friends, fiancés, or relatives. We grew up fast in those days and learned the horror of war was no child's game.

After an evening shift, we would, like thieves in the night, creep home from our Castle to our Nissan Hut. We would undress quietly in the dark, so as not to disturb the early risers. It was also a time for quiet meditation as we unwound from a night of busy operations and lie in our beds. Listening to the rain step cautiously on the roof, as if it, too, had to tread softly in the blackout.

My letters to Bill touched on the mundane things of life and were all about my leaves to various parts of the country, such as Edinburgh, London, Torquay, and even Ireland. Once, a girlfriend and I were sent down to London to a Battle of Britain service, in Westminster Abbey, where we saw some of the Royal family, along with leading figures and high ranking officers who were controlling our destiny. I also wrote about learning to ride a bicycle or the movies I had seen. We both knew that sometimes our letters were received in batches and I grew self-conscious about their contents. How many ways are there to express what is nearest to your heart?

He wrote about his life in the Army, his buddies, the card games. Each letter could have been from almost anyone, except of course, when he mentioned our plans for the future, and even this was rare, as if he wasn't sure he would be one of the lucky ones that would be coming back.

In the latter part of 1943, Roosevelt, Churchill, and Stalin met for the first time at Teheran to name the representatives who would sit in London on the all-important European Advisory Commission. Then in January 1944, General Dwight D. Eisenhower was appointed Supreme Commander, to arrive in London to take over his post. We learned of these things and other important missions, but were all sworn to secrecy. This made one feel a sense of being only an infinitesimal part of something vast and overwhelming that had to be carried out.

So as the winter of 1944 progressed and the Russians began sweeping through Eastern Europe, we watched the Halifax Bombers and RAF Fighters go out on their missions. We also saw Buzz Bombs fall over London, and took Top Secret signals to the Ops room. Of course, none of these things could be talked about off base or discussed in our letters home; instead, we touched lightly on historic landmarks and the different picturesque places we had visited in an attempt to assure our families that all was well.

At the time of the liberation of various occupied countries, people began to realize the end of the war in Europe was near. Bill and I then started to dream again and plan our wedding, hardly believing that it would actually take place. After numerous letters back and forth and a lot of red tape, Bill returned, and we were married in a little church in Worthing, for which an old friend of ours, Aunt Nellie had made all the plans. It was a wonderful wedding, with both of us in uniform. Maureen, my best friend was my bridesmaid, Bill's buddy the best man, and Bill's brother-in-law gave me away. A number of the townsfolk turned out to help it seem more of a celebration. To us it was the wedding of the year.

As the signal for cease-fire began all along the front, we were enjoying our honeymoon. Looking about at all the people in London celebrating VE Day, we considered we really had something to rejoice about. To be two of the lucky ones to escape unscathed, when so many had suffered so much. Now it was just a matter of a few months until we would be back in Canada and back to the business of living.

When my time came to go back to Canada and I marched into the drill hall at Lachine, Quebec, the band was playing "O Canada"; there wasn't a dry eye among us. That's when I finally realized the war was really over.

Lucky Escape

Stan Walpole

While I can't claim to have been in the thick of any fighting during my six years in the RAF, I did have a few scary moments, especially when the German Airforce was dropping bombs "willy, nilly" early in the war. Newly married in 1940 and stationed at No. 6 Flying Training School in Little Rissington, Gloucestershire, I had managed to wangle a living-out pass, as my wife was from London where heavy air raids were expected at any time. I then found "digs" in a village called Lower Slaughter (quite a name), not too far from the camp.

While waiting for the result of my application for air crew (observer), I was assigned general duties. When the Germans started bombing Air Force stations—if they could find them—all G.D. types had to do guard duty on a 24 hour basis. One night when I was on night duty, I left my wife nicely tucked up in bed and cycled my way to the camp, taking a shortcut across some fields. Half way across, I heard an aircraft overhead that was looking for our station. I knew it was not one of our planes. Then, as I was crossing the field, I heard a "plop," but thought nothing of it. Next day, I found out that a bomb had dropped, not many yards from the footpath on which I'd been walking. Fortunately, it turned out to be a dud, otherwise I rather doubt I would be relating this tale.

My Story

Harold A. Tomlinson, R.A.F.

In the late 1930's and early 1940's Capt. Henry Seymour-Biggs of Victoria, B.C., was instrumental in assisting young Canadian lads join the Royal Air Force. Harold

A. Tomlinson, one of those Biggs' boys, who now resides in Fallbrook, California, tells his story:

Al Martin and myself had been friends for several years and during that time, had both held somewhat low level jobs. However, we spent many evenings in Al's basement workshop where we built small radio receivers and experimented with many other electronic gadgets. We both felt the need for more education before we could try for a job in electronics, and looked initially to the RCAF as a source of training.

The educational requirements for the RCAF at that time were too much for us, since neither of us had attended high school and when Al heard about Capt. Biggs and the RAF, we decided to give it a try.

Having made an appointment, we were interviewed by Capt. Biggs and introduced to his pet parrot, which he told us he had rescued from the ocean after his ship was sunk in the Battle of Jutland. After a most interesting interview, we saw a local doctor for a preliminary health check and we were on our way.

We went by Greyhound Bus from Vancouver to New York where we stayed for two days at the Times Square Hotel. We then made our way to the docks and the *S.S. Ausonia*, a Cunard Liner - sister ship to the *Athenia* which had been sunk early in the war. Our trip lasted six and a half days, spanning Christmas Day, and due to rough weather, there were only three of us who sat down to Christmas dinner - everyone else was sick in their cabins.

We were met at Victoria Station, London, by a representative of the RAF and inducted into the Air Force on January 4th, 1939—my twenty-first birthday.

We spent the next ten weeks at Cardington in Bedfordshire doing basic training. One day, our Flight sergeant - a crusty old gent said to us, "You guys think you're here for a nice free ride at taxpayers expense, but think again; you're here to help fight the war with Germany that's coming a lot sooner than you think." About that time we began to wonder whether the first major decision of our lives was about to become a disaster.

The next six months were spent at No.2 Electrical and Wireless school near London, where we finally got a bit of the education we were looking for.

A considerable portion of our schooling was dedicated to learning the Morse code and how to use it practically. It often causes me to wonder why the Morse Code stays as fresh in my mind although it is fifty years since the war, and I have not used it since. I guess it's like learning to ride a bike - once learned, never forgotten.

During our last week at wireless school, war was declared. The old flight sergeant's promise had come to pass and I can remember watching a solid stream of cars full of kids go past our camp. Tied on top were mattresses, furniture and all sorts of belongings. The people were leaving London because they felt sure it would be bombed at any moment.

From wireless school I was sent to Bicester in Oxfordshire, attached to 13 O.T.U.

where I got my first flying time - my first experience with air attacks, which scared the living daylights out of me. Here I saw my first air crash, a Blenheim bomber which crashed into an ammunition dump, killing all on board.

During the time at Bicester, we spent several seven day passes in London and, although London had been severely battered by massive German air attacks during the Battle of Britain, the morale of the people was simply amazing.

While at Bicester, we were once bombed and strafed by a Hampden bomber with RAF markings on it. We had to assume it had been captured in France and was piloted by a German, although it was never explained to us. They eventually constructed a dummy airstrip about five miles from our base in the hope that the Germans would waste some of their bombs there instead of on our runway. It worked some of the time as we found out — the hard way. One day I was sent out along with another operator. We were carrying a radio transmitter-receiver and two big heavy batteries. We were told to meet a Flight Lieutenant from Abingdon, a nearby base, and to establish contact with an aircraft that was sent from there to observe the dummy flare path and to instruct us as to any needed changes. We met the F/Lieutenant and carried our gear out into the field near the flare path, where we set it up and started to work with the aircraft. We had barely got started when nearby sirens started. We could hear the German bombers coming closer. One of them dropped a string of bombs right down the flare path with each one closer to us than the last one. Our brave F/Lieutenant made a run for the nearest bomb shelter and when we started to do the same, he turned and shouted, "Stay there. Keep in contact," as he dived for the shelter. We stayed and got through all right, but I thought, "What a fine example he set for us."

A couple of weeks after that, I was back in H.Q. Signals on night watch when a message came through describing a raid on the base at Abingdon and the only casualty was an injury to a F/Lieutenant (same guy) who was struck in the buttocks by shrapnel. I had to assume he was diving for cover at the time. Some kind of justice.

During some of our stays in London, we were treated to several displays of Hitler's VI missiles, or as they were called, BUZZ BOMBS, which were frightening to say the least. They were designed with a small propeller on the front, which, after a pre-determined number of revolutions, put the bomb into a power dive into the ground. However, they didn't work quite as they should have. When the nose was flipped down, it threw the remaining fuel to the top of the tank and the engine stopped. Then the silly thing would glide around crazily and finally would hit something and explode. You always knew you were okay as long as you could hear the engine, which sounded like an old Harley Davidson motor bike. When the engine stopped, you dived for cover. While I was staying in London with a chap from Newfoundland, there were several hits close enough that our window blinds were blown out into the room, but by that time, we were so used to it we didn't even get out of bed.

After almost two years at that base, I was looking for a change and being in HQ

Signals I got first look at all the incoming information. I noted that they were wanting a Cpl. Wireless/Op for an over-seas draft. I noticed that the draft number was C619 and wondered if I could be lucky enough that it could mean "C" for Canada, since they were into the Commonwealth Air Training Program at the time. I took a chance and asked our Signals officer, a real old "spit and polish" regular force F/Lieutenant named Groom, if I could go. He approved it so readily I wondered if he was maybe glad to get rid of me.

We left there and were put on a troop ship, the *Louis Pasteur*, and headed out in a southerly direction accompanied by an aircraft carrier, a cruiser and two destroyers. We felt pretty important until the next morning when we discovered we were all alone – with no escort and zigzagging in a westerly direction.

I was one of eight airmen selected to man the six inch gun on the stern, along with one Navy man who was supposed to train us in the operation of the gun. I was so grateful that we didn't have to use it, because I'm sure we would have blown the blunt end right off that boat.

We landed at Halifax after a terribly rough crossing and I went from there to a personnel depot at Moncton, N.B. and then on to Charlottetown P.E.I., where I was stationed as an aircrew operator with an observer training squadron.

We flew in old Avro-Ansons with pilots who had done their limit of combat missions and who were supposed to be taking it easy. They sure were a crazy bunch. We would spend hours flying at wave-top level over the Atlantic, or else with one wing over land and the other over water. Other times they'd be dive-bombing the fishing boats around the Magdalen Islands. We had the sickest observers in the air force. Many contributions were made to the "spew fund" which we collected for cleaning up the mess. When we had collected enough we would use it to pay for a night out so that we could drink too much and get sick.

I got leave from there and travelled across Canada to Victoria, where I made the smartest move of my life - I married Florence Hornsby. We had dated for years before I left, and had promised to be married as soon as we could. After I went back to P.E.I., I applied for posting at Pat Bay airfield near Victoria, B.C. I never dreamed I would get it, but a couple of months later, I was on my way to the West Coast. It sure was great to be only twenty miles from home.

After a couple of months, I was operating a direction finding station away out in a field, all by myself, where I didn't even have to check in or out at the gate.

I did that for quite a few months and I guess I got a bit sloppy, because one day I was on watch and had neither shaved nor polished my brass, when the door opened and there stood my old signals officer from Bicester, now Group Captain Groom. We talked for a few minutes and then he said, "It looks to me Tomlinson, like you've been out here too long."

Three weeks later I was on a draft back to jolly old England, and just when I had figured I was there for the duration, back I went across Canada and on to the

Empress of Scotland, which was also converted into a troopship. This time we crossed very slowly in the middle of a large convoy, complete with Naval escort. We made it without major incident. When we landed, I was attached to HQ at Lyneham in Wiltshire for a few months, during which time I was finally able to get my transfer to the RCAF, after working at it for several years.

After my transfer was completed, I was sent to Linton-on-Ouse in Yorkshire, where I was on the maintenance crew in a transmitting station in use by an operational bomber squadron. This was late in the war when things were going badly for the Axis countries and the bombing of England had diminished to practically nothing. We were far enough north that we enjoyed a quiet and peaceful few months before I was sent back to Canada. After my fourth trip across the Atlantic and my sixth trip across Canada from coast to coast, I was discharged at Vancouver on Valentines Day, February 14, 1945.

VE Day in Trafalgar Square

Hugh Noakes

The week before VE Day, I was stationed in Yorkshire, putting in time awaiting transfer back to Canada. On VE day, I was in London, England in Trafalgar Square watching the celebrations.

My most enjoyable times were traveling by train throughout Britain on a pass given to me by the Air Force. The most favourite spot was Aberdeen, Scotland where I met a girl who taught me how to ballroom dance and relax between bombing trips over Germany.

The most frightening sight occurred when I was flying over Germany in the stream of aircraft, watching a Lancaster being incinerated by a load of bombs dropped by a friendly aircraft above.

I have retained a letter written VE Day eve, posted in London to my mother. She saved over 100 letters that I mailed to her during my 2-1/2 years that I served in the Air Force.

Dear Mum:-   May 7th, 1945.
                    Monday, V.E. Day Eve.,
                                London.
        It certainly looks as though I have
a very good chance of going home. I found
out my marks for the instructors' course,
I got 77%, 80% is supposed to be a pass.
My assessment was "Tried very hard but
hasn't got enough control over the class."
I consider that a good recommendation to go
home on. I hardly know anybody on the
station as all the old fellows have gone home.
I have to wait for a posting and got tired
of hanging around the station so got some leave.
I could have as much as I wanted so took
ten days. I sold my bicycle and radio. I
decided to come down here to London so left
yesterday morning. I arrived here last night
and am staying at the Canadian Legion Club.
After lunch to-day I went to see Hyde
Park. I didn't realize it was so big. The sun
was shining so I sat in the park for awhile.
I then walked down to Buckingham Palace.
There were a lot of people there and movie
cameras. I then walked through St James
Park to Whitehall where I saw Big Ben,
Houses of Parliament, Westminster Abbey &
Downing Street. There were a lot of people
outside the War Office waiting to hear
Churchill but he didn't come. I then went

to Trafalgar Square & was given a theatre ticket so saw a play until 9 o'clock. I then went to Picadilly where there were hundreds of people yelling. The traffic was blocked. One of the cinemas in Leicester Square was all lit up. There are hundreds of Canadians in town & everybody is singing & dancing. You would almost think to day is VE day. Some people are singing in the Underground trains.

ARMED FORCES
AIR LETTER

AIR MAIL

If anything is enclosed in this letter it will be sent by ordinary mail.

FROM:
(Sender's full name and address)

K261763
F/Sgt. Noakes, H.A.
R.C.A.F.
Overseas

TO: Mrs A.O. Noakes,
627 Falkland Rd,
Victoria, B.C.,
CANADA

F.P.O. S.C.
MY 10
45

F.P.O. S
POSTAGE
REVENUE

Well its nearly midnight so I guess I had better go to bed. I might not stay here for ten days as I might get a posting before. I'll write at the end of this week and let you know what I do here.
Much love,
Hugh.

My Life as an Army Nurse

Terry Gallacher (Vidal), Nurse, RCAM

I joined the R.C.A.M. Corps on June 21, 1943, and was stationed at Curry Barracks, Calgary, Alberta. I worked in the hospital there from June, 1943 to January, 1944. My sister, Barbara Vidal, had joined a few months before me and was stationed at Suffield, near Medicine Hat. We were both put on draft for overseas in early December 1943 and joined No. 4 Canadian General Hospital in Sherbrooke, Quebec, where the unit was mobilized. We spent six weeks there awaiting a ship and other units who were to go overseas at the same time. But luckily, we were billeted in private homes.

We spent our time listening to lectures from the doctors, attending church parades, and playing a lot of bridge to pass the time. Near the end of February, we were put on draft and sailed on the *Empress of Scotland*, formerly the *Empress of Japan*. This was, indeed, an experience. We were fourteen in a cabin which, in peace time, would have accommodated only two people. (We slept in three-decker bunks.)

We traveled far to the North Atlantic under convoy to escape the German U-boats, which were sinking a number of ships at that time. After five or six days, we docked at Liverpool, and traveled south to Farnborough, near Aldershot, Surrey. It was a lovely trip through the English countryside, during which we stopped at train stations where we were given K- rations with NAAFI coffee or tea.

We then set up our hospital with 600 personnel of all ranks: doctors, nursing sisters, lab and pharmacy personnel, cooks, and staff for laundry and maintenance, etc. The nurses lived five in a unit in duplexes near the hospital, which had previously been used as married quarters for the permanent Aldershot army personnel.

I worked in the operating room. Because we were near the coast of England, we were to be a casualty clearing station after the invasion and until the C.C.S's. were able to move into France. We had a busy life, tending to sixty cases a day. The wounded arrived directly from the battlefield as the allies pushed forward. This condition lasted a month or so, and then we became a base hospital.

Our life at the hospital was hectic, working twelve hour shifts. It was also enjoyable with its busy social life. We were often invited to dances and dinners at Aldershot, and also went to London as often as we could, since it was only an hour away by train. We once had a great leave in Londonderry, Northern Ireland, when we were guests of an elderly lady who had given hospitality to some 650 Allied personnel.

In July, 1945, along with fifty nursing sisters who had overseas experience, my sister and I were picked to go to American hospitals in the Pacific war zone. While we were on the high seas, returning to Canada on the *Niew Amsterdam*, the bomb was dropped on Japan and the war was over. I finally received my discharge June 11, 1946.

It was a great experience to have been involved as a nurse during this period in my life.

War Bride
Pat Dunlop, WLA

After surviving the London Blitz and having our house blasted inside out by a landmine, I was feeling very 'cheezed off' with the factory job that the Labour Exchange had sent me to. So I decided to get out of the factory and join the Women's Land Army. The day I went off to a farm in Lincolnshire, my Dad thought it was all a joke and said, "I'll be seeing you very soon. You're a city girl and won't last long on a farm." Maybe he knew that was all it would take to make me stick with it. And if that was the case, it worked. For the next few weeks, when I could hardly drag myself out of bed in the mornings and I ached in every muscle God gave me, I would hear Dad's words and so went off to lift more spuds and get more blisters.

About that time, five young men in the R.C.E were leaving Work Point Barracks in Esquimalt. They left Canada several times in convoy and a few times thought they had reached England, but they were back at Halifax again. However, they eventually did reach England where they were all dispatched to different units. The man I have shared my life with for the past fifty-four years was one of those men and he was sent to the town where I had been born twenty years before. I often wonder if that was an omen.

That same year, I moved to Slough in Buckinghamshire and Sgt. G Dunlop (my future husband) was in the same area, working on the construction of a new hospital and the hauling of equipment from the ships on the southwest coast. This went on for a long time, but still we never met. However, my friend in the W.L.A had met one of the lads from Esquimalt and they were planning to be married and live in Canada. I thought she was a little crazy to go to Canada. "I wouldn't," I protested. But when a couple is in love, it takes more than a war to stop them.

158

I really didn't want to go to that wedding at the village of Bamfurlong, just four miles in from Wigan. Train journeys to Lancashire were not my idea of fun at that time, but they persuaded me. The groom-to-be had quite a time finding George Dunlop to be his Best Man, for at that time George was hauling from Scotland and when he was located, he said he was not at all interested in being a Best Man at anyone's wedding. But again, fate stepped in and he was also persuaded to go to Wigan in cold miserable weather in February 1944. And that's where we eventually met.

In the next few months, we were another couple heading for the altar and war or no war, my Mother insisted it should be done properly. When a big wedding was arranged, family and friends were looking forward to the celebration. With only one week away, the 'powers that be' decided that June 6th would be the day that France would be invaded. My poor mother's plans had to be shelved, as ours did too!

On D-Day, my Lancashire friend and I were standing on ladders, picking apples at Datchet, near Windsor. The sky was almost black with so many planes. First the bombers, then the fighter planes. It wasn't hard for us to guess what was happening. Later, we were counting the groups returning from France and felt very sad when they were short in numbers. A day we shall never forget.

We continued working on that market garden farm, sending the fruits of our labour off to Covent Garden in London. My Dad was right, it was very hard work and the Women's Land Army was never recognized as a service, but I enjoyed working outdoors and met some very interesting people.

In March 1945, George was able to get nine days leave. So for Mother, it was "action stations" again. After a few days of marriage, however, it was back to Holland for George, who didn't return to London until August 1945.

After a glorious month's leave, he left for home in Esquimalt, arriving in time for Thanksgiving. I'm sure his Mother was glad of that, as her husband and two sons were all in the R.C.E. It took another six month's waiting before I received notice to report to a collection point in London, and next day we were off to Liverpool to board the *Scythia*. I remember looking at that ship and saying "Not very big—only one funnel—I doubt that will get us to Canada." And I wasn't far wrong. Two days out and we had oil line trouble and had to drop anchor while a crew was brought out from Belfast to make repairs. We made front-page headlines: "War Brides Stranded at Sea." That was in February 1946, and the weather was as bad as when my husband and I had first met!

I arrived in Victoria at 7:00 am. I looked around and wondered, "What on earth am I in for?" It was so quiet and different to anything I had been used to. That was just one week before our first wedding anniversary, and we have been happily married ever since. We're proud of our fine family, two sons, three grandsons and one granddaughter. In November 1999 we welcomed our first great-grandson.

I have never regretted coming to Canada, although the homesickness was hard to take at times. I was able to take my young sons back to meet my English family in

1958. My Dad died before we left here, so he never had the pleasure of meeting our sons. It has been quite a life, and I wouldn't have wanted it any other way. We lived in Victoria until George's retirement, before moving to French Creek, where we've lived for ten years.

On reflection, my Father-in-law served for 32 years in the R.C.E. and my husband for 23 years. We all did our share towards making a better world, but I must admit that today I look around and wonder.

.A Sweet Memory

Edith Measure, WAAF

I was 17 years old when I joined up. One day in 1942, I was ordered to drive to a Canadian airfield unit, some 75 miles north, to pick up aircraft parts for our own bomber station #4 Command. On completing my duties, I noticed that the aircraft were prepared to take off on daylight operations. I delayed booking out at the guardroom in order to watch them go up, and drove to the perimeter track where I parked my small van.

During the take-off, one bomber blew a tire, and carrying 1000 lb. bombs, that "kite" as we called them, was no more. The horrible explosion knocked my van over on its side. Other than suffering some shock, I remained unhurt. I can't recall how long I was there in that position, but after some time, my van was righted on its four wheels. In the next instant, a Canadian airman asked, "You OK Honey?" After reassuring him that I was, he gave me a packet of Sweet Caporal cigarettes and also a mug of tea, before disappearing on his bicycle.

Ten years later in 1952, having arrived from England only two weeks earlier, I was walking through the village of Ridgeway which is twenty miles from Niagara Falls. Knowing no one there, I was surprised to find myself being picked up and swung around by a tall handsome gentleman. In a most kind manner he asked, "How are you Honey. What brings you here?" I replied that he had made a mistake—I didn't know who he was and we had never met before. "Oh but we have, I'm sure" he said, and proceeded to recall our 1942 meeting, along with the tea and cigarettes he had given me. Needless to say, I was astounded.

He and his lovely wife became very good friends to my husband and me, until sadly, he passed away while only in his forties. As well as a wonderful gentleman, he was also Police Chief of Welland, Ontario. Don McArter will always remain in my memory.

Flying Fortresses

Vic Childs, South Alberta Regiment

We were stationed on the south coast of England in the spring of '44 and were very familiar with air raids, both our own and of course, those of the Luftwaffe.

Although I had nothing to do with the American Air Force, I had heard of the Flying Fortresses' ruggedness and seen thousands of them pass overhead, but this one on this particular day I will never forget.

It was a bright sunny day and we were lined up for the noon meal parade. We were swinging our mess-tins and chatting when a flight of B17s flew over, obviously returning from a raid on Germany. One of them was labouring, only about 100 feet above us, and gradually sinking lower and lower. But the fantastic thing was that three of its props were feathered and it was flying on one engine. There were holes the size of barn doors in this kite, but it laboured on, still fighting to get home.

I cannot imagine the charnel-house that must have been inside, or the brave man who had brought it back over the channel. Some of us wept while some of us removed our berets and cheered. Talk about a "wing and a prayer." I still remember those gallant men and the crippled "Fort."

An Aged Kid

Vic Childs

I was sixteen when I joined up. Most kids my age were turned away, but I guess I looked older or something; and I somehow managed to keep my secret.

The South Albertas was formed with about 1200 men from five militia units and by the end of the war, some 3000 passed in and out of the regiment. Hundreds were wounded in battle and over one hundred of my chums were killed. We were the only Canadian regiment to win the Cross of Normandy and the only Canadian armoured regiment to win a Victoria Cross.

I was badly wounded and spent five months in a hospital in England, before being invalided home in 1944. I was 20 years old chronologically, but more like 120 years in wear and tear on the body.

BRITISH RED CROSS SOCIETY AND ORDER OF ST. JOHN

PERSONAL PARCELS CENTRE.

to :

Service No. *190520*   Rank   *LIEUT*

Name   *R. E. BUXTON*

Prisoner of War No.   Red Cross Ref. No. *A.O. 2920*

Camp Address   *P. G. 21, P.M. 3300   ITALY*

CONTENTS

No.	Item	No.	Item
1	SHIRT	1	SHAVING SOAP
1	PULLOVER	8	RAZOR BLADES
1	PANTS	1	SHOE POLISH
1	TOWEL	12	CHOCOLATE (H)
1	SLEEPING BAG	1 TIN	BRILLIANTINE
1	GLOVES	2 PRS	SHOE LACES
2 PAIR	SOCKS	1 BLACK	MENDING WOOL
1	TREASURE BAG	1 PKT	NEEDLES
2	SOAP	1	FACE FLANNEL
1	TOOTH BRUSH	1 KAKI	MENDING WOOL
		1	TIE
1	TOOTH PASTE	2	COLLARS
		3	HANDKERCHIEFS

[P.T.O.

Image courtesy of Vancouver Island Military Museum & Ron Buxton

Dieppe

A Survivor of S.S. *Lancastria*

J. F. (Joe) Sweeney

The date was June 17,1940 and the S.S. *Lancastria* had been hastily mobilized for active service, first for the evacuation from Norway and then from France. I had been unaware of her existence until a few hours earlier. Now I made myself comfortable in what had once been a luxurious small salon. My sole companion was a soldier of a British regiment, whose name I never knew. An air-raid warning was in effect, but we were both immune to sirens by this time, just simply war-weary, and didn't care a damn.

Unexpectedly, there came the unmistakable sound of a Stuka dive-bomber—the whine, the whiz, the wail to which soldiers and civilians alike had become accustomed throughout Holland, Belgium, Luxembourg, and France, throughout the preceding weeks. Then came the nerve-wracking whistling of the bomb, followed by a leaden thud. The ship shuddered. We could not believe that our ship had been hit. "It must have been a near miss," I said to my nameless comrade. "I think it would be a good idea to close the portholes and clamp down those metal covers." We did this leisurely, unaware that throughout the ship were several thousand souls, mainly from the United Kingdom, most being members of the British Expeditionary Force to France. Without really comprehending why, we were on our way back to 'Blighty'.

Tugs, trawlers, and tenders, small craft of all sizes and shapes had been ferrying exhausted service men from the harbour of St. Nazaire. A motley assembly of evacuation vessels, each crammed to the hilt, headed for the larger vessels that were anchored about ten nautical miles off-shore in the Bay of Biscay. Earlier that

Lancastria rolled over with 900 doomed men clinging to the bottom of the ship before going under.

morning, together with some two hundred other servicemen, we had been hastily off-loaded from a tug onto the Lancastria. True to merchant navy tradition, everything was well organized. We were handed a card, which told us where to eat and sleep.

The ship had exuded an atmosphere of serenity and security. I enjoyed my first hot meal in days. After having a bath and shave, I slept until my dreams were interrupted. Dragging myself on deck, I spotted a plane banking sharply, just as its bomb-load exploded on the *Oronsay*, which was a short distance off our stern. Debris from the *Oronsa* flew in all directions.

Three hours later, there was a repeat bombing attack by the Luftwaffe. This time, the whole ship shuddered. It was ominous and unnerving. The ship gave a violent lurch to port and we almost slipped to the floor. My comrade and I were unaware that the ship had been mortally wounded and was doomed to disappear within twenty minutes, but we rushed to the door and found the companionways and stairways blocked with troops, many of whom were still carrying packs and rifles.

I vividly recall one demented soldier, swinging his rifle round and round above his head, cursing and swearing. One poor soul came within its orbit and was felled, his crazed aggressor then cleverly rugby tackled and dropped. The shouts and screams were deafening and worsened as the lights went out. Only a dismal light from the top of the stairwell silhouetted the chaotic scene.

In fiction we read of miraculous happenings; in real life we sometimes see them occur. The liner gave another lurch, this time to starboard. Within seconds, a trickle of water rippled down the companionway, its sight intensifying the struggle to get up on the port side. As soon as the starboard side was deserted, I seized the chance and bolted up the staircase. I must have shouted as others began to follow. At the first landing, I met a multitude coming from elsewhere in the ship. With mild jostling, semi-serious banter, everyone moved to the lowest deck open to the sky.

I do not know how long I stood and dolefully contemplated the sight. I felt uneasy because I could not swim. Trying to console myself, I told myself that a ship that size would take a long time to sink, and that there were so many ships around that we would all be rescued quickly. "Joe," I kept repeating to myself, "There's no need to worry."

Everything wooden was being thrown over the rail to there would be ample floating objects, should the unthinkable happen. Then people in the water began pleading to desist throwing anything more overboard as objects were striking many of the hundreds bobbing in the water. Some who had been struck never rose again.

The sounds of hissing steam from fractured pipes and boilers, the clanging of bells, the rat-tat-tat of pom-poms and screams and moans of injured men could be heard, until incredibly, the unearthly fracas eased into an eerie atmosphere. The ship was sinking quickly at the bow while rising majestically at the stern.

There are times when one searches for a meaning to life and answers to philosophical questions. For me, this was one of those moments. I wondered, and asked myself why innocent men, women, and children had to endure the privations and sufferings of total war. I then questioned if this was to be my last day on earth. Strangely, I felt no fear—only regret that I was young and would never realize my ambitions. I felt resigned and although I prayed, I never asked God to save me.

Exactly how long I stood there, I don't know, but as I returned to reality, I realized that the chances of survival were becoming slimmer. I avoided the idea as long as I could, but I knew I had to get into that water and as far as possible from that sinking hull. I did not want to be sucked under when she made her final plunge. I watched men jump, I watched men sink, yet still I hesitated . . . and I wasn't the only one. To brace morale, many, including me, began singing popular military songs.

Sadly, singing and procrastinating could not help. I took off my battledress jacket and footwear. I had been raised in a community where nudity was deemed to be immodest, so I never removed my trousers, although I did empty the pockets, stuffing what I could into my boots and jacket and hiding the lot behind a ventilator, hoping to retrieve them later if the boat didn't sink.

I returned to the rail, staring and still vacillating. Finally, I made up my mind, backed up as far as I could, and took a half-running leap over the rail. My geometry was adrift; I had not appreciated the angle of tilt. Instead of landing in the water I hit the starboard side plates, slithering down onto the shaft casing, which at that point, was about forty feet out of the water. Luckily my pants had preserved the lower portion of my anatomy, but everything else was covered in rust, paint, and slime, and my back was bruised and scratched.

I recovered my breath and realized I had company, a motley lot of equally bedraggled men, some fully clothed, some bare as babies. Some were arguing that clothes would sink you; another individual kept insisting that clothes would keep you warm.

One wag suggested that a 'fag' was what was needed, and one 'old sweat' handed cigarettes all round. Some still had matches and lighters, and soon that entire assorted bunch was puffing away. Destiny did not, however, allow us to enjoy that soothing effect. The doomed ship yielded to another downward thrust and there was no longer any choice. I wavered, took a final puff, and threw away the cigarette. Yelling "modesty be damned," I tore off my trousers, trusted to luck, and leaped.

I seemed to go down into the water for what seemed like an eternity. I extended my arms upward, holding my breath until it seemed my lungs would burst. I finally popped up, jerking my arms like paddles. I tried floating on my back but just as I had acquired the knack, a voice close by screeched, " I can't swim." I screamed back in equal terror, "Neither can I." But too late. The terror-stricken soul grabbed me around the neck and dragged me back under. I couldn't undo his death-grip and I felt finished. Together we seemed to go down and down, but with one last ounce of strength, I flung one of his arms away from my neck, the other slackened and then went limp. I had only sufficient consciousness left to point my arms upward, finally reaching the surface, coughing and spluttering, spitting out water.

It took an age to regain my breath and I knew I had to get hold of something, or I would not last. Looking around, I saw a plank with four men already clinging to it. In distance it was not far, but in time it was. Eventually reaching that plank, I clung to it, clutching it more tightly than I had ever clutched anything before.

One man was prostrate across one end and though continuously urged by the others to lower himself into the water, he steadfastly refused, thereby making the task of keeping an even keel extremely difficult. During the seven hours we clung to that piece of wood, he never stopped ranting and raving with language that would have made a hardened trooper blush.

A second man was holding on with one only hand. He was supporting a third person who was obviously in great pain and unable, without assistance, to stay afloat. The fourth only stayed until a rescue vessel seemed near at hand. With a cheerful, "Cheerio" and "I'm a good swimmer," he calmly swam off in the direction of HMS *Highlander*.

Life on the plank was monotonous, conversation being restricted. At one stage, two German planes flew very low above us. The pilots were clearly visible and I could have sworn that one gave us the "V" sign. The mere sight of them sent our 'ranter' into fresh hysterics, casting doubt on the legitimacy of all Germans, past, present, and future. There were other times when we saw more planes, heard the furious rattle of machine guns, and the answering ack-ack pom-poms. We were covered with the thick black oil from the ship, but it kept us warm and calmed what otherwise might have been a choppy sea.

We drifted along helplessly, coming close to live men without life jackets, struggling to stay alive, whilst dead men with life jackets bobbed along and passed us by. They gave me a haunting impression that through exhaustion they had gone to sleep. We subsequently learned that several, in their haste to escape, had jumped from the upper decks and had not held down their life jackets. The force of the impact had wrenched their necks upward, causing instant death.

It seemed like an eternity as we floated where the currents took us, not knowing the extent of the rescue mission. We could see many rescue vessels, but they were so busy with survivors that they were unable to spot us. The number two man who was supporting the injured man was very exhausted and I edged my way carefully around the plank to take his place; throughout the hours, we changed places several times.

At that latitude, twilight is long, and the two of us, still fairly capable of speech, began to express our doubts about our ability to last the night. The oil had thinned, and the waves grew larger. One moment we were in a trough and the next we were able to see for miles. The coldness of the water chilled our bones, arms and shoulders; our legs and thighs ached and our lower trunks were numb.

In that creeping darkness, we could only see one tiny boat. We had almost given up hope of being spotted. It took time before we realized that this insignificant boat was getting nearer and nearer, until miraculously, we found ourselves alongside and two sailors were throwing down ropes. It was one of the two *Lancastria* lifeboats that had not capsized. With great difficulty we placed ropes under the arms of the injured man and of our cantankerous comrade so that they could be hauled upwards and lowered into the lifeboat. My agile friend, however, needed very little help and almost leaped aboard. As for me, when I tried to jump, I couldn't even grasp the side of the boat, but with help from the crew, I slid like a sack of potatoes into the boat. Even though I had not asked God to save me, I whispered a grateful "Thank you."

Two surviving crewmembers, supported by two volunteers, manned the small craft. These volunteers were expecting court-martial for having disobeyed Royal Navy orders by jumping into the lifeboat from the destroyer *Highlander*. For many hectic hours, the four had been busy plucking souls out of the sea and, as soon as their boat was filled to overflowing, had transferred them to roomier craft. They would then rush back to resume their relentless search for more survivors.

The four 'fishers of men' were down to their last ounces of energy, and the just-rescued men, being incompetent landlubbers, were unable to help. Two men urgently needed medical treatment; the third made a tenacious effort to row solo, while the fourth, myself, was in no fit state to help. Accordingly, the boat was left to drift with the currents, the two sailors taking turns at the tiller trying to hold it steady.

For the next hour or more, conversation diminished to a minimum and we sat passively. Yet, even though there was no ship in sight, there was little evidence of concern. At that time of year, the night sky never really goes black, so the uninjured ones searched the horizon, and eventually our patience was rewarded with the sighting of a tiny speck in the distance. We were confident that if it kept on the present course, it would see us. When it was near enough, we were happy to recognize its French Tricolor, for up to then, we had been only guessing at its nationality.

The crew gave no indication that they had spotted us and it came within hailing distance before slackening speed. Panic was rising, and in desperation we were shouting and bawling. Suddenly, the smack changed course and came charging down on us, racing to within a few feet. Just as it skimmed our prow, we heard the sailors shouting and saw them scurrying to throw lines into our boat. Expertly, one of the seaman, revitalized, seized the ropes and lashed them to the holdfasts. Within seconds, our boat quivered and we knew we were under tow back to St. Nazaire, the evacuation port from which we had sailed the day before.

As we reached the outer harbour, the smack hardly slowed down. It steered directly to a small jetty, suddenly veering with its crew yelling to us to cast off. Our salvage vessel then disappeared into the night, no doubt to look for more survivors. The sailors rowed the last few feet, civilian volunteers pulling us in and securing us to bollards.

A voice crying out *"Allons-y! Vous deux! Sautez"* (come on, you two, Out!) startled me out of my reverie. Hastily, the two of us who were uninjured bade our "Adieu" to the others and jumped ashore. My companion, more agile than I, rushed up the stone steps, whilst I was still steadying my shivering body. Gingerly I clambered up.

Without deciding on a plan, I just set off blindly. Walking barefoot was not easy, but I struggled over the cobblestones toward a town I hardly knew. Even though I had spent two days there avoiding bombs, I had not been sightseeing. In the distance, pandemonium still reigned—gunfire flashes, the drone of bombers, the clatter of ineffectual ack-ack, and the sound of bursting bombs. My main obsession was to find a speedy cure for my hypothermia, before I became too feckless to care about anything.

Since leaving the landing, I had not seen a soul, but some instinct made me aware of an estaminet across the street. Sensing that there were people there, despite it being past closing time, I crossed the street and pushed open the door. I was unprepared for what I saw: The saloon looked like the anteroom to Hades. The bar and eating areas were packed with troops, most standing, packs on backs, and rifles slung. Some were singing, some were screeching, some swearing. All were drinking, drowning their sorrows and cursing their fate, knowing that tomorrow would seal it—either home to Britain, or else to Lagers in Deutschland.

I knew I would get no special treatment and would have to serve myself. I tried to avoid having my feet squashed by army boots. A naked indigent like me had to duck to avoid a swinging rifle as the owner swayed uncertainly. Luck was on my side, however, when I noticed a hatch door below the counter had been left unbolted. I slid downwards, scrambled through and sneaked into the unlit back room.

In spite of the lack of light, I made out rows and rows of shelves and many, many bottles. I wasn't sure which bottle would cure my shivering and boost my spirits, but as I hesitated, all hell broke loose close by. The owner's wife, " La Patronne," pounded the wall and in a strange, invective-filled patois, she screamed and screeched, while my shivers increased in tempo.

I had the feeling that I would be ground to mincemeat ready for the stockpot, but fortunately she hesitated before felling me. I snatched the chance to pour out my pleas and tell the story of the *Lancastria*. Statue-like, she stood totally unimpressed. I even tried to invoke the sacred sentiments of French nationalism. Alas! It was in vain; she was Bretonne.

Suddenly she announced in a less stern tone, "Wait here!" And I meekly obeyed. In a moment, she was back. "Take this!" she muttered roughly, thrusting a half-full bottle of Brandy into one hand and "Gauloise" cigarettes and matches into the other.

It was then that I realized she had previously not noticed my nudity. But now used to the darkness, she appreciated my plight and knew I had been telling the truth. "Go on! Get out! Now!" she swore using language more becoming of a trooper than a lady as she opened a back door. Then her voice softened and she whispered, *"Bon chance, Gamin"* (Good Luck, Rascal). *"Pareillement, Madame!, Bon Chance! Et merci infiniment,"* I exclaimed, wishing her good luck and thanking her for her thoughtfulness.

Once more I ventured into the darkness, this time more confident with my shivering hands clutching those items so vital to my survival. I rounded a building, crossed the road and I sat down with my legs dangling over the raised sidewalk. I took a sip of the *"Eau de Vie"* and felt warmer. I smoked one cigarette after another. With a growing feeling of euphoria, I began to mull over plans to escape overland to Spain. "If only I could get some civvies," I convinced myself that I would stand a good chance.

While I fantasized, a girl in her teens turned up from nowhere. Politely I rose to greet her; in reply she asked firmly, "Are you injured?" "No," I answered, "I am alright, just frozen stiff." We sat down. She was eager to learn of the *Lancastria* and I told her what I could. Suddenly, a flare lit up the sky overhead. Screaming in shocked amazement, she jumped up, "Good Lord! You've got no clothes on." She hesitated, then added, "Poor man." She then left to bring me some of her brother's clothing.

In a few moments, she was back with some riding breeches and a flannel shirt. I tried, then she tried, then we both tried to get me into those breeches, but they were too obstinate. In the end, we ripped the outer seams as far as the thighs before forcing them on. The shyest part of my nudity was now hidden and I felt less embarrassed. There was a further struggle with the shirt, but we widened the neck opening and tore the sleeves open and I managed to get inside. Despite the slits I felt much warmer. The thoughtful Nightingale had also brought along a small bottle of cognac, cigarettes and matches. So with supplies replenished, the Good Samaritan and the Ragged Rascal gossiped a little more, before she left to search for more wounded servicemen.

The next person I saw was an immaculately dressed Royal Navy Officer. He asked me if I was from the *Lancastria*. "Of course I am," I replied. He told me I had two choices. "There should be an ambulance along within a few minutes. You can go in to the Hospital, under cover of the Red Cross or . . . you can take your chance of getting away on a ship. But I warn you that the possibilities are slim."

"I'll take a chance . . . but which docks do I head for?" I replied. He pointed in the direction of the reverberations. Then an ambulance came. The medical orderly opened the rear door, shouting "Come on! Jump in! Hurry!" Four stretchers were occupied by seven serious cases; other casualties and shipwreck survivors huddled together, filling the remaining space. My bottles were passed around, purely for medicinal purposes.

The ambulance stopped and everyone who could move was ordered out into another ambulance alongside. The first vehicle headed towards the Hospital, with its occupants destined for treatment by French surgeons before a long trek to a *kriegsgefangenerlager*, a POW camp. When ours moved off, we could only guess where.

The next stop turned out to be the last. The rear doors opened alongside a gangplank. Quietly and quickly, we left the ambulance, descended the plank and found ourselves on a collier. Yet the cargo was not coal; it was human. Every available inch was packed with escapees; it was "standing room only," with not much room to stand. I inched my way to a staircase where some kind soul gave up his spot. I curled up and was soon lost to this world. I remember vaguely hearing, "Like some tea?" and I must have indicated I would, because a mug of steaming, sweet and thick tea, army-style was placed beside me. And I enjoyed it.

Later, I heard panicked shouting. Some soldiers were loading rifles and others steadied theirs against their shoulders. There was a submarine on the surface ahead, but the word soon spread that it was not a German U-boat. In fact, it was the French *Surcouf*, at that time the largest submarine in the world.

Too cold to stay on deck underneath the staircase, I gained a narrow corridor that led to the Officer's Quarters, which had been designated for women and children survivors. I slept standing up.

The next day, we sighted Plymouth. As the quay grew bigger and bigger, the excitement reached riot levels. Along the docks were ambulances and lines of tables with food and soft drinks. We were greeted by crowds of cheering civilians and the band of the Royal Marines lustily playing popular tunes.

First the stretcher cases were taken ashore. Then came the call for "walking wounded and shipwreck survivors." As I headed down the gangplank, I felt ridiculous in my tight, torn and ragged attire. But quite unexpectedly, a terrific cheer went up and everyone started laughing and clapping. I looked around to see what was so funny. It soon dawned on me that I was the cause of the hilarity and I blushed for the second time in a few minutes. As the laughter subsided, my mood became serious. I whispered to myself, "Out of the depths you have come. And when you reach the bottom of that gang plank, you will once more be marching into the unknown, Joe Sweeney!" Then I looked upwards and uttered a fervent "Thank You" to the Lord above.

Along with about 1600 other survivors, Joe Sweeney was sent to Ludgershall, where they were all told that to mention the *Lancastria* and its fate was an offence under King's Regulations (The Military Secrets Act). This was later reinforced to Joe by his own unit (Ordnance Corps). He never mentioned the loss, even to his own family, until much later in life.

The Warren Twins: Gemini Flight

Doug "Duke" Warren, RAF

What more could a fellow ask for than to have his twin brother as his wingman? When we were growing up, our friends started calling us both "Dupes," a contraction of the word "Duplicates." This being somewhat unflattering, it later was changed to Duke. My brother Bruce and I were separated for the first time, when he left Halifax on a draft and I had to wait for another boat.

We weren't the only identical twins in the service, but we were the only ones doing the same thing in the same outfit, and after we were sent to Royal Air Force 165 Squadron, flying Spitfire fighters, problems developed. After being instructed to fix P/O Warren's aircraft, mechanics complained to the C/O, saying, "We waste a lot of time trying to find out which a/c is the one that needs something fixed, because we can't tell them apart." Naming Bruce 'Duke 1' solved this problem, and since I had arrived on the squadron about 3 weeks later than Bruce, I became 'Duke 2.' And our names were printed, thus, on our aircraft.

In August, 1942, 165 Squadron was moved south to be part of the Biggin Hill Wing. We had just turned 20 years old and were on our first operational tour, when

My brother Bruce, Duke I, on left beside my Spitfire.

on the evening of the 18th of August, we were briefed for a special operation to take place on the 19th. We were told it was to be a "reconnaissance in force" largely of Canadian soldiers. This was of special interest to us for many of the friends we had grown up with in Wetaskawin, Alberta had joined the Canadian Army. We pilots were also told that there was a small airfield on the outskirts of Dieppe that the army planned to capture and that we might land there if in difficulty, but only up to 14:00 hrs., for after that the army planned to withdraw.

The squadron of 12 aircraft took off early in the morning and patrolled over the beaches of Dieppe. Although flying at altitudes of 18 to 20,000 feet, it was obvious from the flashes of the guns and smoke on shore, as well as shot falling in the sea around the landing craft, that a large battle was in progress below. On our first sortie, the squadron was not engaged and there seemed to be no Luftwaffe activity. Our next sortie, however, was very different. The Luftwaffe launched a heavy attack with bombers escorted by fighters. Our section of four, a Scot, an American in the RAF, my twin and I, destroyed an enemy bomber, which was attacking our troops. Many dogfights were taking place and the sky was a madhouse of circling fighters. The final sortie in which we took part was relatively quiet, with little Luftwaffe opposition. During the day the RAF launched approx 3000 sorties and the Luftwaffe about 1000.

It has been described, and rightly so, as the biggest air battle of the war. All this action took place over an area the about the size of Halifax, or Nanaimo. The Canadian Army casualties have been explained in many history books, and historians with their hindsight have their opinions about the value of the operation. However, I am firmly convinced that for every man we lost at Dieppe, fifteen or twenty men were saved on D Day.

My twin and I continued operational flying, and there were many close calls. One of them occurred when we were diving on a target near Calais, France. I heard a loud bang, and it felt like someone had hit my legs with a baseball bat. I could see daylight where a piece of shrapnel had put a big hole in the floor.

In March 1945, we were withdrawn from operations, having completed two tours as fighter pilots. We were sent home in late April, and were at home with our parents on VE Day. We felt rather guilty, for we wished we were with our squadron mates who had survived the war. At the same time, our parents were deliriously happy that we were home safe with them.

Read more about the Warren twins in *Gemini Flight*.
If not in your library, order direct from:
Duke Warren,
2069 Beaton Ave.
Comox, B.C. V9M 1V1

Operation Jubilee (Dieppe Raid) & the Essex Scottish

Roy A. Jardine, Essex Scottish

When we landed at Dieppe, we had a certain role that we were to perform and within about fifteen minutes, it was pretty obvious we weren't going to perform anything. We were right out on a bare open beach with no place to hide and no place to take cover. My platoon commander told me to go and find Colonel Jasperson and tell him that we were pinned down and then ask him what he wanted us to do. So I took off to find Colonel Jasperson. But I never did find Colonel Jasperson. I never found Battalion Headquarters. I never found much of anything, except a lot of dead people. So I went back to where I had last seen Lt. Kent, but I couldn't find him or anybody else. In the meantime, we were getting pretty heavily shelled and people were dying all around me. I then came to the conclusion that this was no place to be and I needed to find someplace to take cover.

There was a tank landing craft sort of sitting at an angle, which had been set on fire and burned out. So I thought that if I could get behind it, if they were going to hit me, they were going to have to come at me from the ocean. I waded out into the water to the landing craft. The beach shelved very sharply there, so I was up to my neck in water in about nothing flat, and it was quite comfortable there.

Then I heard a voice, which said "Steady the boat!" I looked up and there was a British naval officer with a rowboat hanging, nose down on a rope. I don't know where the hell he found it. I could just reach up and touch the point of this boat. He had an axe in his hand, so he cut the rope. Down came the boat and I hung on to it. He then bailed off the top of the LST with an oar in his hand and splashed into the water beside me. When we got the boat sort of righted, he asked me if I had ever sculled, and I replied, "No." "Well, you are about to learn," he said. So I got in and we went around the stern of the landing craft.

I thought, "Boy, we are getting away from the beach." But no—instead he went up to the beach and dragged about four or five guys into the boat ... one of them was a guy from my unit, Alex Lorimer. Then we took off. Eventually we got far enough out to sea where we were picked up by what is called a T.S.F.L. [Troop Support Flack Landing] which is a mobile gun platform sitting on a magazine, and not the greatest thing in world to be on when there are Stukas flying all over the place. An interesting thing was that as we were rowing away from the beach, near the entrance to the harbour we reached a huge buoy on which two British sailors sat with their thumbs out, hitchhiking. So they bailed into the water, one on each side of the boat, and we made better time after that. The T.S.F.L. picked us up with banging and firing all around. Of course with the Brits, everything can be handled with a cup of tea. There was a fellow there and he had a great pot full of tea, which he served in huge white mugs. They had us propped up against the bulkheads and

THE RAID ON DIEPPE
19 August 1942

No 4 COMMANDO

COASTAL BATTERY

SOUTH SASKATCHEWAN REGIMENT
CAMERON HIGHLANDERS OF CANADA

RADAR STATION

ROYAL HAMILTON LIGHT INFANTRY,
ESSEX SCOTTISH, FUSILIERS MONT-ROYAL,
ROYAL MARINE "A" COMMANDO
CALGARY REGIMENT (TANK)

ROYAL REGIMENT OF CANADA

AERODROME

COASTAL BATTERY

HEAVY A.A.

PLANNED OUTPOST

FIELD BATTERY

DIEPPE AREA GARRISONED
BY 571ST INFANTRY REGT
WITH ELEMENTS OF DIV
ARTILLERY AND ENGINEERS

Puys

No 3 COMMANDO

COASTAL BATTERY

H.Q. 302ND INFANTRY DIV
AT ENVERMEU, 1¾ MILES EAST

Vesterival

Low WATER MARK

Varengeville-sur-Mer

Pouivi

Dieppe

Offranville

Onville-la-Rivière

Saane

Arques-la-Bat

the first thing he did was check and make sure nobody had a stomach wound [because he knew, and we all knew too, that you never give someone with a stomach wound anything to drink]. Just then, they knocked a German plane down—I guess it was a Stuka, because that is mostly what was flying over us. So he rushed over to a blackboard where he was keeping score, and he chalked up another Stuka and then came back to pouring tea again. We thought, "this is the middle of a war, and this guy is pouring tea and keeping score!" But that's the way the Brits are.

Eventually, a large ship picked us up. It seemed it was a different type of tank landing craft with scramble nets down its side. Although we weren't in any position to do much scrambling, the old Brits came boiling over the side and helped push us right up on to the deck. They put us in a huge room where we stayed for about 7 or 8 hours, until we got back to England and ended up in Newhaven. They put us on a hospital train and sent us to a hospital in the Midlands. A padre also came along who wanted to know if we had anybody that we wanted notified about us. My Dad was in England at the time and I knew where he was, so I told that to the padre. When we got to the hospital just outside of Birmingham, my Dad was already there, waiting for me.

Meeting Queen Elizabeth, now the Queen Mother
Roy A. Jardine

Charlie Dixon and I were in London just after the blitz had started; it had been going on for maybe six weeks or two months by this time. There was a very famous restaurant in London called *Gattis,* right on the Strand, and it was one of the premier restaurants in the whole of Britain. It had been turned into a serviceman's club and you could go there and have lunch.

Charlie and I were only up in London for the day and we had gone in there for lunch. Just as we were leaving, one of the hostesses said "'you can't leave now because the King and Queen are coming." So they lined us up in the main entrance to this place—there were about 20 of us. We were all just standing there and in walked the King and Queen, with equerries and other people running all over. After they had checked out the place and were starting towards the door to leave the building, the Queen suddenly spotted Dixon and me. She then turned and made a bee-line for us, saying, "I must talk to my Canadians." When somebody told her that they had to be at such and such a place, she said, "ver-y well, we will be there, but in the meantime, I am going to talk to my Canadians." It was the most unique thing you could ever imagine—like talking to your dear old auntie over the back fence somewhere. She asked where we were from and I told her I was from Regina. I then said to her, "I remember when your train was coming into Regina, I was up on the roof of the hotel where I worked, and I could see your train long before you ever got to Regina." "Yes," she replied, "I can understand that; it's terribly flat isn't it." Then she asked about a few other things, and asked Charlie where he was from. He said "Windsor" and the Queen knew all about Windsor and how close it was to Detroit. After about 10 minutes, though it seemed much longer, people were looking at their watches and getting all excited, but she ignored them. She finally said, "I'm sorry that you have to see our poor old London in this shape, but we must thank you and all you Canadians for coming over here to help us when we need help. And I wish you the best of luck and, with good fortune, you will survive this terrible thing that we are in." And away she went. It was an experience I will never forget.

Sniper

Bill "Boots" Bettridge, Queen's Own Rifles of Canada

Over the four years we were in England, as well as guarding the shores, we were kept busy training, and for most of that time I was shooting. Each company always had two snipers.

The food wasn't very good in England, and our company Commander would give the two of us a lunch, a truck, and a full case of ammunition, and tell us to go out and get some food. We were in the "White Cliffs of Dover" country where it's all white rock up in the hills, and we got in a lot of good target practice. We would pick out a rock and estimate how far away it was, draw a diagram of the area, the rocks, trees, and bushes, etc. and just wait until some food came along. With a sniper sight, and decent light, you can get a pretty good idea of what to shoot at. As long as we kept taking the stuff to our O/C, he would send us back repeatedly. So we did an awful lot of shooting.

One of the reforestation areas we liked was on a little hill. We'd lie down at the bottom and with the light behind us, we could get a good bead on pheasants and rabbits. We supplied a lot of meat as well as keeping a bit for ourselves. Actually I wore out a rifle from shooting so much. When the bullets start coming out a little wonky you know the rifle is no good.

Prior to D-Day we were locked up in a camp in the South of England, with British guards making sure no one got out. The Intelligence people took us into a room one platoon at a time. Inside there was a big sand table model of our sector and each one, right down to individual privates, was given a role. According to the instructors, we were going in at a little resort area with cottages close to the water. They told us things like "there's two feet of concrete in the walls of this house, and this house has two or three machine guns." They went through everything and made it sound so good that I thought "boy this is going to be a snap."

I was with the first wave of assault boats that landed on "Juno Beach," but we were taken off course by the high wind and rough water and when we went in on the attack, we weren't where we were supposed to have landed anyway.

There was so much going on and so much noise and confusion, that it is difficult to clearly recall. It was quite a mix-up. Speaking of intelligence, we were told we would need ladders to get over the sea wall. Well three guys were carrying a ladder and the guy in the middle stepped on a mine and just became a piece of raw meat; I could hear him screaming for several minutes afterwards; it took him such an awful long time to die and we didn't even need a ladder, for the wall was only about three feet high and it just took one jump to get over.

I would have to say that with all the supposed "covering fire" from the battle-ships off-shore and from the big guns, there were no shell holes on the beach at all. We had no help from the artillery and big battleships. The tanks were all water-proofed with rubber skirts to make them float and they had little pieces of tin attached to the treads to help propel them in water. To turn up mines and break through barbed wire were flails made of great big logging chains thrashing around on a wheel. These tanks were to have landed ahead of us, but because we were ahead of them, we had no help from them either. By the time they landed, they were down low on a slope, and couldn't bring their guns down to bear on any-thing. Every shot they fired went over the tops of the buildings, till they caught up with us.

As I recall, we took cover behind a kind of a sand dune between the wall and a railroad track, and every once in a while, one of us jumped up and made a dash over the track, only to face great rolls of concertina wire the Germans had installed.

There were five of us over the tracks on our own, pinned down by enemy fire with all this barbed wire to go through, and to get to where we were supposed to be. Bert Sheppard, a real character, was lying to my left when the Sergeant Major hollered, "Boots, I'm tossing you my wire cutters and when you get them, throw them to Shep, and tell him to cut a hole through that wire and we'll all go to-gether." Shep heard him, and with his undiminished sense of humour hollered back some very kind words about his parentage, which included the suggestion "you go first, you're getting more money than me." To this day I can't tell you who cut the wire; however, all five of us made a dash for the hole. We then got into a minefield, but some mines had been in the ground so long that they didn't go off right away. One of us—I don't know who—stepped on one and it didn't go off until after we had passed. We all got a few little pieces of shrapnel from it, but the explo-sion was quite weak and no one was seriously hurt. I was lucky as it landed on my helmet and got caught up in the field dressing bandage I was carrying under the helmet netting.

After a couple of months in France, the Regiment was down to one sniper. Then our Commanding Officer formed a "Sniper/Scout" platoon, with me as Sergeant,

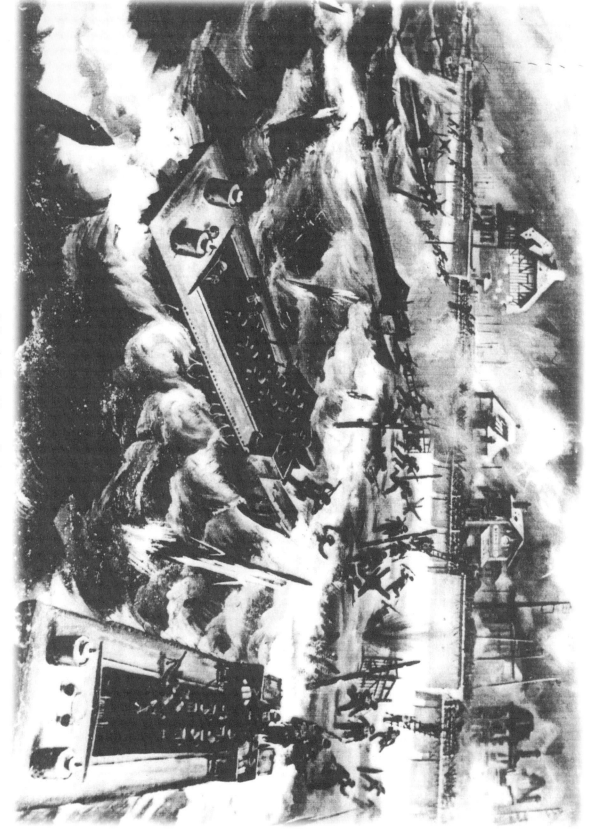

D-Day landing, Normandie, June 6, 1944

because I was the only one with any experience. We got volunteers from trained soldiers in rest areas, and wound up with ten snipers and twenty scouts working as a Headquarters Company Support platoon for any unit that would call us to go on a patrol, do some shooting or observe. We acted the same as the Bren Gun Carrier and Anti-Tank gun; if anybody called on us we would come and help.

In schools many kids ask "How many Germans did you kill?" But I could never count how many I even shot at, and as far as killing them is concerned, when you're shooting at somebody three or four hundred yards out front and he falls down, you're not going to run up to see if he's dead. That's no way to live through a war! We got more credit for doing our scouting, camouflage, observing, that sort of thing, because every time the regiment stopped and dug in, we would set up an observation post, manned twenty four hours a day with two men on duty at all times. The purpose was that in the daytime, if you saw something going on out there, you would take your compass, get a bearing on it, and record the angle and the time. The time was very important because if somebody else down the line, say in the next regiment to the left or right, spotted something at the same time, then the two co ordinates would cross and that would tell you where the enemy was. No one can ever tell how many people were killed as a result of skilled observation.

At night, we would track a gun flash, take a bearing on it and if some other regiment had seen a flash at the same time, then those bearings showed us where the gun was. We would track guns firing, rockets taking off, and anything that was happening out there.

In Lacappell, I was up in the steeple of the little church (something I learned not to do because you'd get return fire pretty quickly). But we were there for a few days and I was checking a small forest three or four hundred yards out front. I had a phone rigged up to the artillery and as I was scouting along the edge of this bush, I noticed a tree in the middle of it that just didn't look right. I put down my field glasses and picked up the telescope for a better look and saw enemy troops moving around. That tree turned out to be the barrel of a big 88 gun attached to a tank. When a scout knew he had a target, he would take the map reference and draw a line from the number at the top and another line from the side number and where the lines would cross, he would give that to the artillery, way back behind the lines. As they were not near enough to see the enemy, he would ask artillery to fire only one smoke round. As soon as the enemy knew they were spotted, they would start moving, but I was able to give the gunners a range correction, probably something like 200 yards, but too long ago to remember. There was a bunch of tanks coming out of that bush, so as it was only a few days after D-Day, it was logical to assume they were getting ready for a big counter attack. It turned out to be a good shoot, and I was congratulated by the Brigadier for all the gun emplacements I'd found.

One doesn't know how much damage he has done to the enemy—just one man out front, camouflaged, knowing what to do and he could do something worth while. But it takes a lot of training. You have to be a good shot and you have to know how to sneak around. We learned a lot from cats, watching how they stalk their prey so silently, slowly one foot then the other.

A couple of snipers were often called to be 100 yards behind the initial force when the forward company was going into an attack. Then when the Germans started shooting, they were only concerned with the guys that were easiest to see. That let us move around and get into position, where we could get a bead on a machine gun or mortar crew. Believe me, when a bullet whizzes by your head, you don't know if it's two inches or two feet away; you duck and keep your head down. That's what allowed our forward troops to get up and go for the target. That was a pretty big role, and we did a lot of it.

When we took a town, there were always some underground people who appeared out of nowhere. As they helped us a lot, I was given the job of contacting them. The lady in charge of Lacappell wanted weapons and as we had a truck following us to pick up rifles and ammunition left behind by casualties, we unloaded it for her to issue to her "Freedom Fighters."

We had attacked Carpiquet air field, but we only owned half of it. Like all airports, it was pretty flat ground so we took an awful lot of artillery fire because they owned the high ground and could see every move we made. The day came when we went for the other half and we were so closely related to our mortars that we had good coverage. We could tell them to fire for a precise length of time (here again memory fails) then raise their fire 100 yards and we'd move up the 100. We did this several times, but during the night, the Germans moved out. Because there was no opposition, we went to our new positions too fast and got under our own mortar fire. One of my buddies from Brampton got hit with one of our own shells that cut through his wrist, leaving only a bit of skin with his hand hanging from it. We got a bandage around it, but he was only concerned about one thing. He said "Boots, get me out of here." We took him back to the Regimental Aid Station where the M.O. cut the rest of it away; I stuck a cigar in his mouth and gave him a half dozen more. He said, "So long buddy, I'll see you in Brampton." He wasn't even suffering; he just wanted to get out of there and keep on living. Boy! that's something real. When I have gone over and visited our cemeteries, I think of some of the campaigns I went through and realize when I look at those crosses that I have had another fifty five years more than those 18 - 19 - 20 year old kids. War is a terrible thing!

I found that on daylight patrols, just a couple of guys could almost get away with murder. In July, the wheat is way up and the Germans had been sitting there for years with big dugouts, even roofs over them and camouflaged so you couldn't see them, and they wouldn't give their positions away for a couple of snoops. They'd wait till they could get the whole gang. By not firing on us while we're patrolling around, we report everything is OK and then when the day comes for attack, they have guns all over the place and by not firing on a few guys poking around, they got a lot more.

I had a buddy who even under extreme danger, could always find something to laugh about. He was an Indian, a really good man, the guy I wanted with me when I went out on patrol. I had to blacken my face and he was already black, the blackest Indian I've ever seen. He had a great set of white teeth and he laughed at me every time I started putting on that damned charcoal. I told him, "One day you're going to laugh once too often and some German will put one right between those teeth of yours."

While we were at Carpiquet the forward company was in some chest high, old German trenches when they phoned for two snipers. As I said before, it was flat country and the ground gave no cover, so we snuck up through the grain to the position and reported to the company commander. "You called for a sniper, Sir?" "Yeah," he replied, "there's some shooting here for you." When we asked where it was, Jesus! It was like a little peanut on a pumpkin. I had to take my binoculars to make out that it was the top half of a guy on a machine gun and I could only see part of his chest and I said "Christ, Sir! You should be phoning for artillery. That's too far for a rifle." But he refused and ordered us to start shooting. The men were all enthusiastic about these two guys who were going to win the war for them and started razzing, "Ah, you snipers couldn't hit a barn anyway." So I said to my buddy, "We'd better shoot at him just to shut them up."

A sniper's sights only goes to 1000 yards, so I cranked it up to the 1000 mark and asked Frank to take a look, then fired a shot. The guy didn't even duck. Frank said I was about twenty yards short, so the only thing I could do was to lower the sight to the bottom and increase the range by aiming for the sky. An impossible shot, but I guess it went by close enough that the German ducked and the guys hollered "You got him. You got him." Remember, I'm in a chest high trench and he was so far away I could take a shot, put down my rifle, pick up my telescope and see him duck I took seven more shots before he quit ducking, and that smart officer who wouldn't listen to a man with experience and thought we were going to knock him off, got a lot of good men killed and wounded. While we were playing around there, the Germans were taping us and the next thing we knew, they had their big guns trained on our position. The officers that trained us in Canada and up till the time we lost them in Europe were really good leaders, but I'm telling you, in my experience, the new ones that came up right from training school had been taught so much discipline that we automatically did as they commanded. If I were ever to face the same problem again, I would listen to what he said, then go about it the way I thought was right.

Along with the regular ammunition, we had "tracers" that were just like a red guided light in the sky and "incendiary" ammunition that would flare up like a match when the bullet hit a hard object. It came in handy when there were three hay stacks in the field the day before and in the morning there were four. One shot and the bullet hit the tank, the hay stack caught fire and the tank would either get cooked or it would move out of there in a hurry. With tracer, if we spotted something and we had mortars handy, if they couldn't understand exactly where it was, we would tell them to watch for one tracer bullet that would put them on target. Then they knew what to do with their mortars.

As we moved in and took towns, we saw some terrible things. With their towns occupied by the Germans, people couldn't do anything without their approval. People had to do as the Germans said. Living conditions were horrible. As the battle got closer, homes were blown up and the food became more scarce.

During those peaceful times, before we went into France, Belgium, or Holland, there were some girls who, wanting the good things, would get a German boyfriend and would receive nice stuff like nylons, perfume, soap, etc. So they at least had a real good time. When we took over, the good girls who would have nothing to do with them would gang up on the few that had been consorting with the German soldiers. I've seen some of them beaten up, tied to street posts, or with their hair shaved off. It wasn't nice to see. In one of the towns we took, and I can't remember where it was now, there was a dead girl lying in the street. She had been bayoneted by her lover. When some guys returned, they were jealous and I guess they did that so we couldn't get their girlfriends. When we took a bunch of prisoners later, the locals pointed out her boyfriend among them. I don't remember exactly what happened to him, but it wasn't very pleasant—we fixed him up pretty good.

We were the first ground troops through to Nijmegan to support the Airborne when they got bottled up in the attack between Arnhem and Nijmegan (this scenario was made into the movie, *A Bridge Too Far*). My partner and I had a favourite pub in London, The Manor House, and one night we were sitting, watching those V2 rockets taking off and we thought "Boy oh boy! Wouldn't it be Hell if one of those things were to hit the Manor House. So we wrote a letter to the pub, gave them a load of baloney and enclosed a 100 Guilder note to cover drinks when we got back to England. We were lucky enough to get a 72 hour pass and being as we were the Colonel's body guard, we knew where he kept his liquor. So we liberated a couple of bottles and headed for the pub. It was flattering to see that they had put the letter in a nice wooden frame with the 100 Guilders attached, but the proprietor wasn't in, so we asked the bar lady for a piece of paper and a pencil and we signed our names on it. Of course, when she saw the signatures were the same, we had lots of friends. You couldn't buy liquor, but there was lots of it flowing that night.

In Nijmegan, my sniping buddy and I stayed for a week in a house with a family. One lady's leg was smashed from all the bombing and shelling, so I got her fixed up with our M.O. and of course, we became great friends. I digress to point out that we were short of food for the first three days in Normandy—we only had some big chocolate bars that were like chewing on a brick, but they kept us going. However, after that I can't remember ever being hungry. The food came up and our cooks kept us well fed. When meal time came, my buddy and I would load up our mess tins and bring food back to share with the family. They sat and slept on the floor because they had burnt up all their furniture to try to keep warm, but they kept everything clean and ate off their nice white plates on a beautiful lace tablecloth. There was no electricity, no water, no gas, no nothing, but before we left, we commandeered a Coleman stove for them so they would have something to cook on. They were terribly upset to see us go. But not us: we were going home.

After the war, I was in the heating business and got a job putting a furnace in an old farm house for a German immigrant owner who had been in the Wehrmacht. As he worked nights and it was a kind of a slow job in an old house that had never had a furnace in it, we got to know each other fairly well. He said to me one day, "Bill, do you ever stop to think we might have been shooting at each other?" and I said "You might have been shooting at me, but I wasn't shooting at you." "How can you be so sure?" he asked. I replied, "you're still here!" He didn't know I'd been a sniper.

Remembrance of Dieppe

Del McFadden, 3rd. Anti-Tank Regt.

On June 4th, 1944, we were in a compound that was more like a jail, near Southampton, guarded by English troops. No mail and no persons were allowed in or out of the area. In the afternoon, we were ordered to return to our equipment parked down the road and found everything had been waterproofed.

Soon we were on the move, follow the leader to somewhere. When we got to Southampton harbour that was full of ships of all sizes, we knew something big was about to happen.

There were all kinds of vehicles and equipment waiting at the dock and it was dark before we had our turn to board a Landing Ship Tank. First the trucks and jeeps were lifted onto the upper deck, then eight tanks onto the lower deck. Then the ramp was lifted, the doors closed and we pulled away from the dock to join the rest of the ships already loaded.

The next morning, we were still in the same place among the maze of ships and in the afternoon, we all started to move and gather in a group off the Isle of Wight, where they gave us a map that gave us no clue where we were, except that we had left Montreal and were going to land in New York. We began moving in what I figured to be a south-easterly direction. It was beginning to get dark, and before long, we couldn't see our destroyer escorts. In fact, we couldn't see anything. At first light, however, we received the correct map and were told our landing would be at Berniers Sur Mer, in support of the Queens Own Rifles.

While on the LST, the Major assembled the officers and NCOs and ordered all to remove everything from our uniforms and go ashore as privates, since snipers did not shoot privates. He also threatened to shoot the first man who saluted him when we got ashore.

The tide was out, so there was plenty of beach to ferry the tanks off. Then the Captain ran the LSI ashore and said, "Everyone out." We dropped off the ramp into three feet of water, and turned left down the beach. By this time, the battleship *Warspite,* sitting way out, was lobbing monster shells over our heads. I calculated it was about 8:30 when we landed and by 14:00 hrs., we were about a half mile from Berniers Sur Mer. We held this area for several days, during which time we helped the Padre bury fourteen of our comrades.

On the move again, we reached Colomby, although only temporarily and then on to Buissons, where two of our guns were overrun and two men were killed. The rest of them were captured and later murdered by German SS troops. Then we were sent east. I thought the English were to take Caen, but they couldn't do it, so we were given the job. It was at this time that the American bombers dropped a load on our troops, killing many, and wounding several, including our General; they missed us by about one hour.

Next stop Cormelles. Here we had long toms behind us and S.P twenty five pounders on the left, so we received all the short shot, and we were supposed to be resting. Next on to Bourgue and Roguancourt with not too much trouble. We were at a place called Cintheaux when our own Lancaster bombers caused many more casualties, some in our battery but mostly among the Polish Division. When the Lanc passed over me and dropped his load in the next field, that was enough for me. "Good-bye. Here comes another one," and I took off over the field. While I was out in the wheat field, a small plane flew over and shouted "what's wrong?" "They are bombing us" I shouted back, so he went up and started shooting yellow flares and the bombing stopped.

When the Falais Gap was closed, we were ordered northeast as fast as possible. We passed through Rouen near the end of August. From there, we went to Boulogne in support of the infantry, and managed to silence a few 88 mm guns. In a week all was over, so we moved on to Calais and went through the same process till the end of September.

After a short rest and getting re-supplied in October, we moved into the muddy area of the Leopold Canal. As we did not need the guns, we had the job of patrolling the south bank of part of the canal. Here we went fishing with hand grenades, but we didn't catch anything.

One night, the boys picked up a wet German walking down the road, so we dried him off and warmed him up with rum and coffee. The next day, we put him in black coveralls (just like we were all wearing instead of uniforms) and made him the cook's helper. As he hadn't seen food like that in months, he was very happy. However, it

186

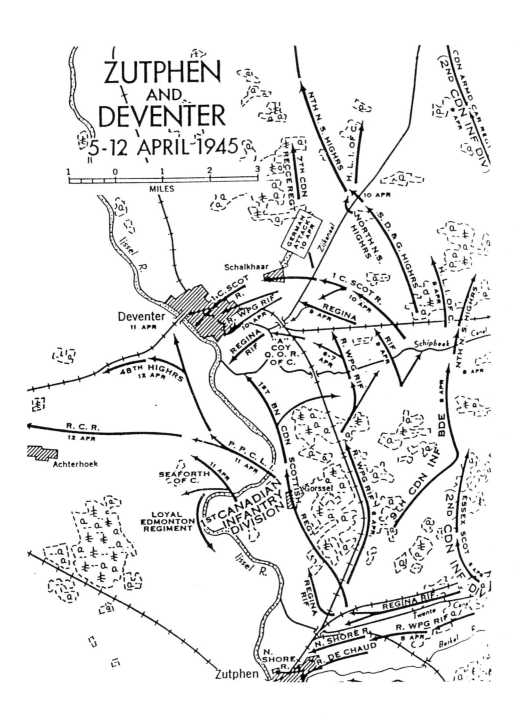

ZUTPHEN
AND
DEVENTER
5-12 APRIL 1945

MILES
1   0   1   2   3

(2ND CDN INF. DIV.)
CDN ARMD CAR REGT.

NTH N.S. HIGHRS
H.L. OF C.
10 APR

7TH CDN RECCE REGT
S.D. & G. HIGHRS
NORTH N.S. HIGHRS
H.L. OF C.
8 APR

GERMAN ATTACK 10 APR

Schalkhaar
1 C. SCOT R.
REGINA
1 C. SCOT R.
R.
10 APR
R. WPG RIF
REGINA RIF
8-7 APR
RIF
8 APR
R. WPG RIF
8 APR
Schipbeek
NTH N.S. HIGHRS
8 APR
Canal

Deventer
11 APR

REGINA RIF
"A" COY
Q.O.R. OF C.
1ST BN CDN

48TH HIGHRS
12 APR

R.C.R.
12 APR

Achterhoek

9TH CDN INF BDE 8 APR

R. WPG RIF 8 APR

(2ND CDN INF DIV.)
ESSEX SCOT 8 APR

SEAFORTH OF C.
11 APR
P.P.C.L.I.
11 APR

LOYAL EDMONTON REGIMENT

1ST CANADIAN INFANTRY DIVISION

Gorssel

SCOTTISH REGT.

Ijssel R.

REGINA RIF.

REGINA RIF.
Twente Canal
R. WPG RIF
8 APR
Berkel

N. SHORE R.
R. DE CHAUD

N. SHORE R.

Zutphen

Ijssel R.

didn't last long. The major spotted our new man and he sent him back to the POW compound.

From here the battery moved into the Scheldt with all its water and mud. Our battery was not too busy, even though the rest of the regiment did have quite a shoot at times.

In early November, the whole division moved into Ghent for a rest. Here we were spread out in individual homes with local people. Stan and I stayed with John Vits, on Rue de la Toil. They were using burnt barley as coffee, which was not good, so the cook truck supplied us with good stuff. At the end of the holiday, we moved through Antwerp to Nijmegan and from there into some abandoned houses in Groesbeek, where we sat for a long time as the whole area in front of us was flooded. Christmas day we were still there, and while waiting for the area to dry out, every unit was re-supplied. We traded in our six pounders for seventeen pounders, a much better gun, something like the German 88s. Our M10 Sherman tanks were traded for Valentines which had less armour and fixed 17 pounders (that meant you had to turn the tank to the direction in which you wanted to shoot). All units were re-supplied with everything—except men.

On February 8 at 0500 hrs., our 1600 guns began to fire into Reichwald Forest and Cleve. In we went through the forest to Cleve, then on to Voen. Mud conditions were bad and only tracked vehicles could get through. One of our batteries managed to get ahead of the rest of us and crossed the Rhine by ferry, but we had to wait for the bridge at Wesel.

Our last big contact with the enemy was in the area of Emmerich. From here everyone moved north into Holland. About this time (April), one of our officers was captured. The Germans let him sleep and when he woke up, they were gone. Our 17 pounders were tough on the German SPs. and we passed Deventer with very little resistance. Then some of the batteries headed for Groeningen. We and the 105 battery were told we were not needed, so we retired to a pasture field and played ball every day.

Although we knew it was coming, the first we heard that the Germans had quit, was in the broadcast by Winston on the morning of May 8th. I had to wake everyone up to tell them the news, which some did not believe at first.

In June, the battery moved to Barneveld for two or three weeks, then on to the barracks in Utrecht. Here I played baseball three days a week, and got leaves to look over the country. We all spent the time going on leave or whatever. In the fall, there were hockey games in Amsterdam twice a week. Finally in November, we were ordered back to Aldershot where we got more leave. On December 22nd, we left Aldershot for Southampton, boarded the *Queen Elizabeth*, celebrated Christmas in the middle of the ocean, and arrived in New York on December 27th.

And there it is: something I remember after all this time

I Remember the Joys of a Missed Youth

Ronald K. Haunts

In 1939, I was 16 and I joined the Army, and spent four years in Britain before Normandy.

As it became evident that the "beginning of the end" of the war was approaching, I found myself attached to 1 Echelon, 21 Army Group Headquarters, as an army engineer. My new assignment was one of locating areas for the acquisition of suitable sites for the construction of permanent burial places in the liberated countries.

This work came under the direction of Major-General E.L.M. Burns and his staff. I was assigned to Adegem, a small town in Belgium. This was unique, because there was to be only one Second World War Canadian cemetery in Belgium.

There were two reasons for choosing the Adegem site, which was located between Ghent and Brugge. The soil was most suitable for the re-burial of casualties and Maldegem, Leopold, and Schipdonk canals and the south Scheldt were central to the site.

To commence the task of laying out the cemetery, I supervised Canadian soldiers who took charge of work gangs, consisting of 60 Belgian civilians. One of my brothers, Gord, was assigned to this unit. I had authority to pay them and draw rations for noon lunch, which, on occasion, was eaten en route to and from the exhumation areas. A Jeep and trucks were at our disposal for transportation.

The 1,130 men buried in the cemetery included men of all services from Canada, the United Kingdom, Australia, France, Poland, and New Zealand. All religious denominations are noted on the permanent headstones. Padres were instrumental in supplying recorded map references of hastily dug graves during the conflict.

I remember returning to Adegem in September 1987. September was also the month in 1945 that Canadians liberated the area. I took greetings from city council and the citizens of Kingston, a parchment suitably framed and signed by then Mayor John Gerretson. This memento was presented to J. Rotsaart De Hertaing, the Mayor of Maldegem-Adegem, at a reception at the city hall.

In return, Mayor De Hertaing presented me with a large framed map of ancient Flanders to be presented to Kingston city council and the citizens of Kingston.

Dignitaries and Representatives from all over Belgium take part in ceremonies to remember the Canadians. Children parade and decorate the adopted graves and cenotaph, remembering the Canadian troops. During the ceremony, thousands of poppies are air-dropped. The people of Belgium do remember.

During the nine-day visit, I stayed with my host, Jozef Dekeyser who had been employed as an interpreter during the war. I occupied the same room of his home, in which I had stayed 42 years earlier. I enjoyed the daily tours of the battle sites and the ancient city of Brugge, as well as of Eeklo, Ghent, Ostend, Knocke-Heist, Brussels, and southern Holland.

I remember walking the rows of headstones, remembering how young those soldiers had been. Later, I recall signing the Golden Book of Remembrance, honouring those who lay buried in a distant land.

Whig Standard, Nov. 10, 1998.

Enemy Counter Attack?

Frank Sellers, 7th Field Regiment, R.A.

After all the heroics and horrors of War, perhaps this humorous, but absolutely true, interlude is called for.

We landed on Sword Beach in the early hours of D-Day and fought our way inland. D1 saw us established on the outskirts of the village of Beauville, and there our first (and most speedy job) was to dig in. My slit trench was quite a good one, about 6' x 2 1/2' and quite deep.

On D2, we 'stood to' at 4 a.m. in case of an enemy counter attack (this was to be our drill for some days). At 'stand down' I wearily made my way back to my slit trench, lay back and lit a cigarette. The sun was just coming through and, temporarily, all was at peace. Then suddenly there was a droning above my head and before my astonished gaze came a bee, and then another and another from the side of the trench. It seemed like hundreds of them, moving backwards and forwards, just carrying on with their daily routine. And then it sank in—I'd cut right through the entrance to a nest of wild bees! Whether they were grateful to me for providing them with a more convenient access, I don't know, but they never interfered with me and I certainly never interfered with them!

190

Liberation of Europe

Carpiquet

James Woodrow Blakely, Royal Winnipeg Rifles

I arrived in England on May 8, 1944 and on June 8 left for Normandy as a replacement for The Royal Winnipeg Rifles. The group I was with got to what was left of B Company on the evening of June 10. Despite having received replacements before we got to them, the losses suffered on the beach and as Pluto had wiped the company out; there were only seven men left. As we had not had the extensive training that the originals had, we were kept in reserve for quite a while. We experienced a few unpleasant times, but on July 4th we really got into the thick of things. This was the day that the Little Black Devils were to take Carpiquet Airfield that was defended by troops of the 12th SS Division and twenty of their Panther tanks.

At 0500 hrs., we were ordered out of the trenches in preparation for the advance onto the airfield. When we crawled out, our artillery began a thunderous barrage. The Germans must have been aware of our position for they soon responded with their artillery and mortars. The din from our guns together with the wails of descending mortar bombs, their explosions, and the explosions of shells was terrifying. Two of the fellows who were still in their trench were buried when a shell or bomb exploded near the edge. I heard afterward that they got out unscathed. A few yards from me, Norman Blue was hit. He apparently lived until the next day, for his gravestone in the Beny-sur-Mer Cemetery shows that he died on July 5th.

Woodrow Blakely, a stalwart member of Branch 78, R.C.L., Picton, Ontario.

He was only eighteen years old. It was heart wrenching that his brother was the corporal of the section in which he served and had to go forward with the rest of us, leaving his brother there.

We moved in single file past an isolated building that appeared to be a hangar. Then we spread out in line and advanced through a wheat field. I heard swishing sounds and realized that machine guns were firing at us. I do not think that anyone near me was hit as we made our way toward a copse of fairly short trees. We stopped when we got there and tried to dig trenches.

It was no use, for the soil was only a few inches deep and we hit rock. Mortar bombs were wailing toward us. Between attempts to dig I lay on the ground as flat as I could and tucked my hands under the rim of my helmet. I was afraid of getting my glasses broken. Without glasses I would have been in greater trouble. I must explain that I was short sighted and had got into the army by memorizing the first few lines of the eye chart. When a corporal tested my eyes, and subsequently prescribed glasses for me, I persuaded him to not tell the truth about my eyes. He didn't.

We suffered the barrage of mortars and Moaning Minnies for a long time. One fragment from a mortar bomb struck my helmet but fortunately at such an angle that it ricocheted off. Another hit me on the left shin but didn't cause real damage. The order finally came for us to advance. We went around the right side of the copse, and I could see a hangar ahead to my left. We came upon a huge crater, probably made by a large bomb dropped from an aircraft. All or most of 7 Platoon descended into it. It was about 0900 hrs. I was number two on the Bren Gun. Rifleman Engen was firing the Bren. After every 5 or 6 shots, the safety would snap on and stop the gun from firing. He finally took the gun apart and got it working properly.

A machine gun was firing at us from a position at or near the corner of the hangar. The lieutenant crawled over to us and told us and a lance corporal to crawl toward the hangar and try to take out this troublesome gun. So that I could crawl better, I removed my respirator and haversack and told a neighbouring comrade that I would be back for it. We started crawling toward the hangar. The grass was quite tall, and we couldn't help but make it move noticeably. We hadn't got very far before machine gun bullets were whizzing just inches above our heads. Mortar bombs began wailing down again. The lieutenant had said that if the mortar fire started again we needn't continue. I called to the lance corporal, "Remember what the lieutenant said?" "I sure do," he replied. We crawled back and dropped into a narrow shallow ditch. I heard someone in the direction from which we had crawled calling for help. I didn't have the courage to go back; I looked at the other two and neither of them made a move. The calls for help haunted me for days.

A few others crawled into the ditch. We lay there for quite a while. At 1330 hrs., word got to us that we were to go back a couple of hundred yards. Our artillery opened up again. The company re-assembled and moved forward in line, our artillery firing over our heads. A squadron of tanks of the Fort Garry Horse was assigned to support us this time. As we advanced, I became aware that the lad on my left was no longer there. He must have been hit, although I didn't see him fall. The sergeant was killed. We reached a position just past the hangar and dropped to the ground to await an expected counter attack. All the time there was the din of explosions and the rattle of small arms fire. It was a small crater made by a mortar bomb that I dropped into. I clawed and tried to kick at the shale, trying to get myself out of the hole.

Suddenly, Panther tanks loomed in front of us. They had been dug in and were not visible to us as we advanced. Some of our Sherman tanks were behind us, and the Germans naturally concentrated on them. Thus we had a chance to get out of the way. Instinctively, we ran to our right down a slight slope. I looked back and saw several of our tanks blazing. I could see many of our fellows running back - Engen with the Bren on his shoulder. I stopped running. It was now well into the afternoon. We had eaten breakfast at 0230hrs., been awake ever since, and had been going through hell for hours.

The unending stress, fear, hunger, and thirst must have affected me, for I just walked. Soon there was nobody within hundreds of yards of me. I didn't care. I heard the wail of an approaching mortar bomb and automatically dropped to the ground. It exploded a short distance away. I picked up my rifle and the case containing the spare Bren barrel and the extra ammunition and walked on. Another bomb wailed down. Again I dropped, and after the explosion, I picked up the equipment and walked on. Four more bombs were fired at me. Each time I reacted in the same way. I had no particular feelings. There was no fear. I just didn't care. I was like a robot, proceeding steadily, only stopping and going to ground whenever a bomb approached.

Finally, I found some comrades in a trench. One of them said, "Do you ever look white!" He shared some food with me. (I had never got back to the crater where I had left my respirator and haversack.) That food probably saved me from passing out.

At 2100 hrs. we were called back. The advance was called off. There had been 132 casualties. We spent the night in a ditch in the rain. Between the rain and the sounds of shell and mortar bomb explosions and eerie sounds that I did not recognize, I didn't get much, if any sleep, though I was dog tired.

I served in Normandy for a little over two months when on August 14th, I got hit. A large chunk from an 88mm shell struck me on the right ankle, removing two inches of the fibula, destroying flesh and most of the tendons. I refused amputation and have worn a special brace ever since. Complications had me in hospital for several operations over the next few years, but I have got along fairly well.

Since the fall of 1945, I have been a member of Branch 76 in Picton, and have been active in Legion affairs ever since. I have been in charge of Youth Education since 1975 and headed up Remembrance Day observances and all other parades and services since 1977. Remembrance is a priority for me.

Our Last Days

Howard Benn, 4th. Light Anti Aircraft Artillery

We landed in Normandy on D Day in an S.P (self-propelled). We were bombed by our own air force on the way to Caen. At Falais, the Luftwaffe came in strafing at rooftop level. We were under steady shelling from tanks, field guns, and aircraft.

The RAF came bombing at night, and they were all over the place, I hid under a truck and when the bombs hit, the ground heaved under me and I thought sure I was hit, but when it was all over I got up and found it was just the earth bouncing and I was only bruised from the earth's tossing me around. They killed a field full of cows, but the Germans were well dug in and didn't feel a thing.

We were involved in the Scheldt Estuary and spent the winter in Nijmegan. I watched our planes bombing Cleve. We crossed the Rhine at Emmerich and went up to Groningen.

The last few days we were in Germany taking in prisoners, herding them into their former Marine barracks and taking away everything they had stolen from the Dutch people; they were loaded with loot. There were lots of young fellows running around in civvies who we were sure had been wearing uniforms before we got there, and we put them in the bag too.

One of the saddest things I saw was in the Scheldt: three wounded kids coming to surrender, the two on the outside were in fairly good shape but the one in the middle who couldn't have been any more than 14 or 15 was bleeding badly. Still believing in the Master Race like many of the overzealous children we were facing by this time, he refused our offer of medical attention so we sent him back anyway. One of our guys who spoke a little German said "OK go ahead and bleed to death." The kid likely could have been saved.

We were billeted in a house with a mother, her daughter, and another old woman. Of course, they had been told we would go after the girl. She disappeared, till our German speaker told the mother to bring her back because nothing would happen to her as long as she stayed in her own room.

We weren't supposed to fraternize, but we couldn't help getting friendly with these frightened women. They started sharing letters with us from the father who had been captured in Normandy and who was a POW in Canada. He always wrote about how much he liked Canada and wanted to stay. So many prisoners started arranging for emigration as soon as they got home. Maybe they did come here to live.

After we left Germany and were waiting in Holland for our trip home, we had a hell of a good time.

Ada

Clifford Bolton, 6ᵗʰ Anti–tank Regt. R.C.A.

This is a story about our cat Ada, who was both our mascot and friend throughout many months of the war in Europe. Two weeks after landing on Juno Beach, we were driving our communications repair truck along a very dusty road on the way to Caen, before stopping to allow an armored convoy to pass. The vehicles raised great clouds of dust, and as it began to settle, we noticed a young kitten, with eyes as large as saucers. John jumped out of the truck and rescued the kitten. He handed her to me and I placed her in a bowler hat we'd found.

When we arrived at the 6ᵗʰ Anti-Tank Headquarters, we mixed some powdered milk with water and fed her. She must have been very hungry, as she made short work of it. We were going to call her Canada, but thought better of it, shortening it to the last three letters, "Ada." She became our mascot as we drove through France, Belgium, Holland and Germany. When the shelling began, she became scared, but someone always took care of her. Sleeping in a slit trench, it wasn't unusual for us to wake up and find Ada shivering and snuggled next to a shoulder for comfort.

Ada the sigs cat in the Reichwald

With four of us in the truck: Art Hamilton, Charlie Bird, John Leslie and myself, there was always someone to make sure Ada got her share of our rations. She never attempted to run away and always stayed close to the truck. On a stopover of about three weeks in the town of Battenburg, Ada made friends with the neighbourhood children, who played with her and pampered her to such an extent that we felt sure she'd want to stay with them. However, she was not ready to leave us yet, and as we were getting ready for departure, we found Ada sitting proudly in her corner of the truck, all set to go with us. She stayed with us through the Reichwald Forest, through the Hochwald and across the Rhine.

Ada died while we were in Germany, but as we were close to the border of Holland we drove across and buried her in Dutch soil. We all missed Ada; she left us with many happy memories of the very dark days of the war.

Feb. 6/45
Old Barns RR#1
Col. Co., N.S.

Dear Buck Brook:

Yesterday I received the letter you wrote my brother concerning my letter of Col. Oukafees. I want to thank you for your letter. I do not know if brother has written but I knew she, as well as the other members of the family, appreciated your letter very much.

His death has caused us so much sorrow but we are glad to know he played his part in this conflict. We are relieved to know he did not suffer.

I was afraid we would get no further word of him as we did not know any of the men he went with for the months and we knew of nobody to whom we could write to find out about his death.

It seems hard to realize that we will not see him again. He was a chum to me as well as a brother to me but I fear I did not do very much for him since he went over. How that it is too late to write him Brother I could have written him more often and in other ways shown my appreciation of what he was doing.

TO: Lieut. A.E. Brock
'C' Coy
48th Highlanders of Canada
C.A.O.

FROM:
(Sender's full name and address)
Miss M. Pulsifer
Old Barns, RR#1
Col. Co., N.S.
Canada

... us at home. Your description of the flight of his death helps me to understand how much he and the other men had to go through. Lloyd seldom mentioned it — the actual fighting and I never asked, as I hoped to hear what he wanted to tell me of the battle, etc. when he came home.

I also can appreciate your letter more when I know you wrote it after coming back from so long under brutal conditions as you described. It can't be pleasant — at the best of times — to write the details of the long ordeal as Lloyd has been killed.

This letter so poorly expressed but I wanted you to know how much it meant for my to hear something more of Lloyd.

Sincerely, Mildred Pulsifer

Fear In France

A. E. Brock, Captain

Old soldiers never die—they just tell war stories. While my memory of recent things is failing fast, some long ago happenings will stay with me so long as I live.

My infantry regiment went to France on 13 June, 1940. I was barely eighteen, a private with the Forty-eighth Highlanders, First Brigade, First Canadian Division. I had recently arrived at the Corunna Barracks, Aldershot, England.

The evacuation of those brave boys from the beaches at Dunkirk started on May 27. It was a sobering sight for us Friday-night soldiers to see truck loads of these exhausted and bedraggled men—some half naked and most half starved— straggling back to Aldershot, which was then the largest army base in Britain. These were the salvaged remnants of the proud British Expeditionary Force, which had been swept into the sea by the enemy's Blitzkrieg tactics, for which they were unprepared.

Even more sobering was the news that the First Canadian Division was being sent to France in a last-ditch effort to stop an enemy that neither the BEF nor the French Army could contain. An officer was heard to ask our Colonel, "This is a suicidal thing, isn't it? We will never come back, will we? You are going to take the Regiment to certain death."

The Colonel replied, "This is a time of great crisis; terrible decisions must be made, and desperate things may have to be attempted. If it leads to death—that's duty!" *

But morale was high as we boarded ship at Plymouth on 13 June, to the accompaniment of a British brass band. The Royal Canadian Regiment and Brigade HQ were also on our ship; the Hastings & Prince Edward Regiment were on another. The Shiny First Brigade was to be the spearhead of the First Canadian Division's heroic attempt to stop the unstoppable German Army.

The morning of the 14th saw us landed at Brest. The docks were crowded with civilians who all seemed determined to get aboard anything that would float—away from France! This was our first sight of genuine panic in the civilian population, and the seriousness of our situation started to sink in. Still, these were only civilians, and we were there to save them.

The Forty-eighth, along with Brigade HQ, was soon on a train to a proposed Divisional rendezvous in Paris. Our train was constantly side-tracked as the population of that city went by in the opposite direction. It was an amazing sight to see these terrified people, crammed into cattle cars, or travelling on foot, choking the parallel roads in desperate flight.

After two days of sporadic movement our train got to Sable, where we heard shouts of *"finis le guerre"* as the train crew deserted us at the double. We were now bad news, so far as the French were concerned, likely to draw fire from the Luftwaffe and from the advancing German Army, which was expected momentarily. Windows

200

were smashed out of the train to facilitate the coming battle and Bren gunners got ready to try for dive bombers.

The French had capitulated and left us in the lurch. The train's engineer had been held to his job at gun point. He turned the train around and we started our return journey—back to Brest, and then by ship to England.

Along the way, we got switched to a different track and arrived at St. Malo, many miles from our desired destination. By some miracle, there was one small ship still at this little sea port. It was badly overloaded with refugees, but was unable to sail until high tide, which would be early next morning. We packed ourselves on board and it was so crowded that at first we could only sit down on the deck by turns. The Channel was uncharacteristically calm that day and by afternoon we were safely docked at Southampton. Later that night we returned to Corunna barracks, which now looked like a palace to us.

---

* 3 Dileasý - *The 48th Highlanders of Canada* by Kim Beattie

219 Days in the Hands of the Germans: Hervé Couture
Translated by Jacques Aubin

It was January 1944. I was 19 years old. I left my home and my job at Paton to volunteer in the Royal Canadian Artillery. The war was on and I had always dreamed of driving a tank. It was my chance to see the world! Except that at 19, the Canadian Army had other plans for me and I found myself in Longueil, in the artillery.

After the initial training, towards the end of June 1944, I left Sherbrooke for Halifax by CPR train in the company of Marcel Bernier. We sailed from Halifax to Europe on a Dutch ship carrying 9,000 soldiers, seamen and medical personnel. I remember chewing gum to prevent getting sea sick. After landing in England, our platoon was assigned to guard a munitions depot in the Borden region, until the day when a Canadian Officer poked his nose in the camp to recruit 75 volunteers to join the allied troops at the front line in Douve, France.

I was among those who enlisted in the Fusiliers Mont-Royal and after having crossed La Manche and visited the cities of Caen, Lisieux, Rouen and Louch, our regiment went to Dunkirk, where the Germans were resolutely waiting for us."

At the Concentration Camp
17:00 hours, September 12, 1944

I remember it as if it was yesterday. Our platoon took position for the attack and suddenly our four machine gunners were shot, our platoon was surrounded. This was an experience I never imagined when I signed up in the Canadian Army. Out of the 25 soldiers in the platoon, 15 were killed and I found myself with a bullet hole in my arm and among the 7 survivors and prisoners of the Germans. Hospitalised for 11 days in Dunkirk, I was then taken to a kind of asylum where I recuperated a little before my transfer to a concentration camp.

If you Try to Escape, You're Dead.

Our camp housed 191 prisoners of all nationalities and upon our arrival, the commandant advised us in French that for any attempt to escape, we would be shot dead. This threat was validated when 2 German soldiers tried to flee their battalion. They were hanged and left there for 3 days in the yard of the camp. It could not have been clearer."

At Work Seven Days a Week, and a Reducing Diet

We worked seven days a week on a reducing diet. I was so hungry that I traded my boots for a piece of bread. Although not mistreated, we were bored to death, and all anxious to be liberated. Meanwhile, we had to follow the Nazi regime of the concentration camp and shield ourselves from the Allies' bombing of the region.

Christmas Festivities

There are times in life when the end justifies the means, especially when one is hungry. It was Christmas 1944. A cellmate came in to the barracks carrying a canvas bag containing . . . two cats! In spite of my love of animals and my disgust of this type of meat, I can assure you that these felines truly tasted like turkeys, especially when accompanied with carrots and Brussels sprouts. The truth is that we were forced to do things that would be considered today as being barbaric. Even upon my return, people had difficulties in believing my stories.

War is Over

In March 1945, the Red Cross arrived in our camp to announce that on the 18th of April, we would be escorted to the allied lines.

Allied and Nazis Exchange Prisoners and Evacuate 200 from Dunkirk

Lille, France, 18 (PA) - An exchange of prisoners and the evacuation of 200 civilians took place today in Dunkirk. This came in the wake of a 24-hour truce between the German garrison and the Allied forces that were besieging the port.

A Rock Forest Soldier Liberated from a Concentration Camp

Ottawa, 27. I was among the 191 officers and Canadian soldiers recently liberated from a German concentration camp. My parents learned about my injury and internment from successive telegrams.

Long Live Freedom

After a recuperating period in Glasgow in Scotland, we returned to Canada on June 7, 1945. I was proud of having served my country and enriched by an experience of which not many of the people of Sherbrooke could brag. I got married the following year on the 22nd of June 1946 and I returned to my job at Paton for the next 43 years until my retirement in 1983.

219 Jours Aux Mains des Allemands

Hervé Courture

Hervé Couture aura passé sa vie dans le quartier ouest et 43 années de vie active au service de Paton... Mais comme plusieurs de sa génération Hervé Couture aura eu une fin d'adolescence pas mal perturbée et fort différente de celle des jeunes d'aujourd'hui.

MATRICULE D-144104

"C'est le 15 janvier 1944, à 19 ans, que je quitte ma famille et mon emploi à la Paton pour me porter volontaire dans la Royal Canadian Artillery . . . C'était la guerre, j'avais toujours rêvé de "conduire" un char d'assaut . . . C'était ma chance de voir le monde!!"

"Sauf qu'à 19 ans l'armée canadienne avait d'autres visées pour moi et c'est à Longueil que je me retrouve . . . dans l'artillerie."

"Après l'entraînement d'usage, vers la fin du mois de juin 1944, je quittais Sherbrooke pour Halifax par le train de C.P.R. en compagnie de Marcel Bernier. A partir du port d'Halifax, c'est la traversée vers l'Europe sur un bateau Hollondais transportant 9 000 soldats, marins et personnel médical. Je me souviens avoir mâché de la gomme tout au long de la traversée afin de ne pas être malade en plus d'avoir servi comme garde de sécurité durant les 15 jours qu'a duré le voyage jusqu'à Liverpool."

"Dès notre débarquement en Angleterre, notre peloton fut assigné à la suveillance d'un dépot de munitions dans la région de Borden, jusqu'au jour où un officier canadien se pointa au campement afin de recruter 75 volontaires pour rejoindre les troupes alliées sur la ligne de feu à Douve en France. Je fus du nombre à être enrégimenté dans les FUSILIERS MONT-ROYAL et après avoir traversé la Manche et visité les villes de Caen, Lisieux, Rouen et Louch, notre régiment s'est rendu à DUNKERKE là où les Allemands nous attendaient de pied ferme."

AU CAMP DE CONCENTRATION

"Le 12 septembre 19944 à 5h00 p.m. (17 heures) . . . Je m'en souviens comme si c'était hier, notre peloton prend position pour l'attaque et, soudainement, nos 4 mitrailleurs se font tirer, notre peloton est encerclé et là commençait pour moi une autre expérience à laquelle je n'avais pas pensé au moment de mon engagement dans l'armée canadienne. Sur 25 soldats du peloton, 15 furent tués et à la fin des hostilités je me retrouvais au nombre des survivants avec un trou de balle à travers le bras . . . Et prisonnier des Allemands."

"Après une hospitalisation de 11 jours à Dunkerke, je fus transporté dans une espèce d'auspice où j'ai pu récupérer un peu avant mon transfert au camp de concentration"

SI TU T'ÉVADES, TU ES MORT...
"Notre camp abritait 191 prisonniers de toutes nationalités et lors de notre arrivée, le commandant allemand du camp, qui parlait français, nous avisa clairement qu'à la moindre tentative d'évasion, c'était la mort... Nous avons alors pu avoir confirmation de la véracité de cette menace lorsque deux soldats allemands ont tenté de fuir leur propre bataillon; ils sont demeurés pendus 3 jours dans la cour du camp. Comme message, ça ne pouvait être plus clair."

AU TRAVAIL 7 JOURS PAR SEMAINE... ET CURE D'AMAIGRISSEMENT
"Sand prétendre avoir été maltraités physiquement, nous n'étions pas au Hilton non plus.. Au début de notre internement, on nous fit déterrer des morts pour ensuite les transférer dans un cimetière militaire... pas particulièrement entiché de ce travail forcé, j'ai vite proposé au commandant d'utiliser mes talents de tailleur que j'avais développés à l'emploi de Lucien Trahan dont la boutique était située en haut de la Pharmacie Jean-Claude Savard; c'est ainsi que grâce à mon expérience de la machine à coudre, on m'affecta à la réparation des vêtements des prisonniers et à la confection de jaquettes pour les malades."

"Généralement les prisonniers étaient debout à 6h00 a.m., besognaient toute la journée et se couchaient sitôt le soleil disparu. Ajoutez à ça une cellule infectée de poux et de puces, un chauffage inadéquat, 6 soldats affamés qui, faute d'expérience, avaient troqué une bonne partie de leurs vêtements pour de la nourriture, un menu "gastronomique" composé le matin d'une unique tasse de chicoré, le midi d'une soupe à l'eau et le soir...Devinez?

Une autre soupe à l'eau. Grâce à ce régime amincissant, mon poids est passé de 125 à 104 livres en moins de 219 jours."

Il faut dire qu'écouter un tel récit plus de 50 ans après les faits nous a surtout fait apprécier l'excellente mémoire d'Hervé Couture et, surtout son sens de l'humour, qui lui a permis de passer à travers cette épreuve sans trop de séquelles: "C'est évident que je me suis ennuyé à mourir. On avait tous hâte d'être libérés. Mais en attendant, il fallait suivre le régime nazi des camps de concentration et se mettre à l'abri régulièrement contre les attaques aériennes des alliés qui pillonnaient la région."

FESTIN DE NOEL
Il y a des moments dans la vie où la fin justifie les moyens et quand tu as FAIM, tu prends les moyens.. Écoutons M. Couture: "C'était Noël 1944. Un compagnon de cellule s'amème dans le barraquement avec une poche de jute contenant... 2 chats!!

Malgré mon amour des animaux et mon dédain pour ce genre de viande, je peux vous assurer que ces félins avaient véritablement goût de dinde, surtout accompagnés de carottes et de choux de Bruxelles. C'est sûr qu'avec le recul, nous avons été contraints à poser des gestes qui seraient considérés comme barbares dans tout autre milieu. Même à mon retour, les gens avaient de la difficulté à croire ce que je leur racontais."

LA GUERRE EST FINIE

"En mars 1945, la Croix-Rouge s'est pointée au barraquement pour nous annoncer que le 18 avril nous serions escortés jusqu'aux lignes alliées . . . VIVE LA LIBERTÉ . . . Et après une période de récupération à Glasgow en Écosse, c'était le retour au Canada le 7 juin 1945 fier d'avoir servi mon pays et, malgré tout, plus riche d'une expérience que très peu de Sherbrookois peuvent se vanter d'avoir vécue. Je me suis marié l'anné d'ensuite le 22 juin 1946 et suis retourné à la Paton pour les 43 années suivantes jusqu'à ma retraite en 1983.

Letter, Written to a Daughter, to Educate School Children

Allison Chute, Submitted by Andrea Layton

October 29th, 1994

Dear Children,

At this time of the year, I usually sit down and reflect on that part of WWII in which I participated. However, at this time, I pen a note to you so you and your class will have an idea what I did during the war.

So, I have my "Log Book" which is a true record of every flight that I took, and I will highlight my participation with 403 Squadron in England and #5 Squadron in Burma.

I joined the RCAF in December 1940, first reporting to Manning Pool in Toronto, next down to Pictou for guard duty, and then to Victoriaville, PQ for initial ground school. First, flying was at Windsor Mills PQ, where we learned to fly 'Tiger Moths." Then to Summerside, P.E.I for service, flying on Harvard aircraft. I received my Pilot's Wings on August 30, 1941.

We departed from Halifax in September 14, 1941, and arrived in the U.K. September 20, 1941. I spent the next year flying different aircraft for an experimental and development unit for the RAF from Farnborough and Bude in Cornwall. My first wartime operationals started when I joined the 403 Squadron during August 1942.

#403 Squadron was a Canadian Squadron, with the majority of

the pilots from the Maritimes. From Kenley (south of London), we flew over France, Belgium, and Holland. Most of our sorties were to protect our bombers from German fighter aircraft. My task was to fly #2 to Wing Commander Johnnie Johnston, who was the top ace in the RAF. I covered his tail and made and kept the required Radio contact with RAF Fighter Command.

The majority of our flights were controlled by Radar until we made contact with the enemy. Our Squadron shot down approximately 20 enemy airplanes and we lost seven pilots who were also shot down. We were able to save two men whose aircraft were lost after they bailed out. I have flown 150 times in a Spitfire, and approximately 50 hours of this time was in direct war operations.

I was selected for further training to fly American airplanes and to also learn to fire rockets from these airplanes. On completion of this training, eight pilots were posted to India to teach the theory of rockets and low level flight. After training three Indian Air Force Squadrons, the RAF decided that we could do the same job while flying at the Squadron level. I was posted to #5 Squadron RAF at Lanka on the India, Burma border.

At this stage of the war, April 1944, the Japanese had been chased out of the sky over Burma, so all the Fighter Squadrons were utilized to support the British and Indian armies to chase the Japanese forces from Burma. We would take off in pairs and hunt for Japanese troops and their supply convoys. I recall one trip with Don Watts (a Canadian from the Winnipeg area). We were attacking trains at Wuntho. We made five attacks and blew up steam engines and started numerous fires on other trains. On the last attack, Don got shot at by ground fire and had a bullet pass through the upper part of his leg above the knee. On the way home, he passed out several times. I would scream over our radio and he would become alert. Finally we arrived at our base where he landed and then passed out. He was flown to a Military Hospital. I next saw Don at Trenton, Ontario when I re-enlisted in the RCAF. He made a complete recovery. I continued with #5 Squadron until October 1944, when my tour was finished, returning to the UK and Canada for leave.

Whilst in India, I visited Bombay, Calcutta, and Madras, also Columbo in Ceylon. I also visited with Bessie Lockhart at the Baptist Hospital at Vellone. This was where our Aunt Winnie served from 1946 until 1960.

I had leave at home in Nova Scotia during January and February 1945. This was the leave where I met your Mother and you have *heard about the romance. I was again posted overseas to UK when we were replacements for our Squadrons in Europe. However, we were not needed and returned to Canada in August 1945.*

You have heard all about the RCAF and our travels from 1951 to 1964. I have 7500 hours in the air. We aircrew members are the only service people who have a record in our logbooks of every flight. I hope this short epistle will relate to you some of the highlights of my military career.

Love, Dad, '94.

Children in Harm's Way

Art Enger, Calgary Highlanders

I had graduated from the signals school in Kingston, and was put to work operating the base switchboard . Running a switchboard was not what I signed up for. Three times I went before the C.O., pleading for a transfer to active duty, and was turned down every time. He kept telling me I was too important to let go.

It suddenly twigged in my mind to exploit the sensitive military brain where it was most vulnerable—its devotion to correct uniform. I went downtown and bought a pair of officer's brown shoes and brown gloves to match. I wore them on parade and, by God, one week later I was out of there.

We were in France when my platoon came across a large pig. To a soldier, a bunch of pork chops on the hoof looks like a great meal, and we all went after the pig. Although it got away safely, its squeals drew enemy fire and we took a lot of casualties. The pig was more lucky than we were that day.

One day about three months before VE Day, just outside of Wessel, Germany, we were moving in on an enemy machine gun, when a little boy about 10 years old with an even younger little sister, wandered into the line of fire. Bullets hit the dirt all around those two frightened kids, it seemed at the time a miracle that they were not hit, and I wondered what could prompt a German soldier to take pot shots at their own children. In retrospect though, I thought that possibly the gunner was ordered to shoot and was intentionally missing them, or

Art Enger

maybe he was just trying to scare them away from the field of fire. I would like to think one of those possibilities is close to the truth, but I still can't forget the scrambled emotions that ran through my brain over what I saw that day.

I had a great time in Holland after the war, while waiting to be shipped home. I presented three Dutch girls each with a jeep. They were the property of the British Army, who had got them from the Americans on Lend/Lease, and I got each of them for a carton of cigarettes. After all, the war was over, and what better way to dispose of war surplus?

Memories of D Day

Edwin Woollard

I was eighteen years old when I joined the Royal Navy in 1942. After the initial training I joined the HMS *Duke of York*, which was a 35,000 ton battleship and the flagship of the Home Fleet. It was commanded by Admiral Sir Bruce Fraser. Some months later I was sent for officer's training and served with a motor torpedo boat squadron operating from Poole, on the south coast of England. Next came a commando training course at Queensferry, Scotland, where we were taught to do many nasty things to inflict the greatest harm on the enemy. I was sent to join a landing ship which was part of an invasion force, and served in the Mediterranean during the North Africa, Sicily, Italy and South of France invasions. We were then ordered home to England to prepare for the invasion of Europe.

D-Day was planned for Monday, June 5, 1944. Bad weather and rough seas caused General Eisenhower to postpone the invasion.

Not all the assault forces were delayed. Combined-operation groups, special task forces, commandos, frogmen and others were already on their way to the French coast, and had to be ordered back until the next day.

The targets for these groups included underwater obstacles which had been built by the Germans. Some German and French workers had been used to build these, but mostly they were constructed by slave labour from concentration camps, and by Russian prisoners of war. The obstacles included large steel barriers known as "hedge-hogs," to which mines were attached. These were positioned to wreck landing craft on contact and to destroy the men before they reached shore. These obstacles had to be blown out of the way before the first assault craft and tanks headed into the beaches. The advance special tasks forces placed explosives on selected obstacles to provide areas of clear passage.

Our group, which included members of the United States assault forces, was assigned to the Aromanches coastal area, code-named "Gold." We were in position during the night of June 5 and 6, when we heard the sound of planes passing overhead. We learned later that these planes were bombers, and transport planes towing large gliders which carried three divisions of paratroopers assigned to attack special targets inland.

At dawn we could see the first ships of the invasion fleet and soon afterwards, shells from the war ships began to explode on the beach. The shells could be heard passing overhead and caused tremendous explosions as they landed amongst the German defensive positions higher up the beach.

As the cruisers and destroyers came closer, they too commenced firing until the air seemed to reverberate with the shells passing over. The air forces had now joined in and added their bombs to the devastation. The pillboxes and other concrete fortifications on and around the beach were treated to special attention and we could see chunks of concrete being blasted into the air. As the beach became saturated with the shelling, the warships gradually ranged their guns further inland, seeking out new targets.

By this time the sea appeared to be covered by ships as far as one could see. There were ships of all sizes, from great battleships to motor torpedoes. We could see the landing and troop ships beginning to off-load tanks, and the first assault troops getting down into the Landing Craft. We learned afterwards that the tanks had been especially modified so as to be water-tight and, by the attachment of a rubberized canvas skirt which trapped air and made them buoyant, were able to float. They were also equipped with rear-mounted propellers to enable propulsion. Included in this armada were landing craft fitted with pre-set rockets which were fired electronically and which seemed to wipe out whole areas of the beach.

It was difficult to imagine that many German soldiers would live through the massive fire storm which was directed at them from both air and sea. That some did survive, and were still ready to fight, soon became apparent.

As the first of the tanks and landing craft neared the beach, the Germans commenced firing with all types of armament, and large numbers of our men died before the craft touched land. As the men waded through the breakers on the beach, German guns zeroed in and hundreds of men were killed or wounded. Weighed down by their heavy equipment, some drowned. There was no shelter on that beach--only the obstacles with mines attached. There were mines on the beach as well. Some of our tanks were fitted with flails which exploded the mines as the tanks went forward.

It was a well prepared killing ground. The defences included coastal gun emplacements, machine gun pillboxes, anti-tank guns and heavy concrete bunkers. The noise, and the dead and wounded, are among my most vivid recollections of that terrible day. We subsequently heard that the Canadian-British landings at the beaches of Juno and Sword were making headway, as was the American landing at Utah, but that the American Rangers were having great difficulty in advancing from the beach known as Omaha as they had to contend with high cliffs from which the Germans poured down fire.

Eventually, even this impossible situation was overcome by sheer courage and desperation, but at very heavy cost in men's lives. Gradually, the force of men and equipment and the intense fire power forced the German survivors back inland.

The rest is also history: the marvel of Mulberry Harbour and the skill with which it was designed, built and put together, with its breakwater of old ships which protected it from the sea; the oil pipeline, code-named Pluto, which was laid from England to France. So much went into the planning and execution of the D-Day landings which, although successful, had a tremendous human cost. It is not a day that, fifty-five years later, calls for a celebration, but one that it is necessary to remember. Remember that so many of those who died that day and the following weeks and months were in their late teens or early twenties.

In 1989, I went with my wife, Muriel, who had been in the Women's Royal Naval Service, to visit the beaches of Normandy. There were still signs of the defence emplacements and of parts of Mulberry Harbour. It was a fine day in May and children were playing on the beach. Apart from the sounds they made, it was very quiet. The American, Anglo-Canadian and Polish military cemeteries were well kept but it was very sad to see that so many who had died were so young. Many were just schoolboys when the war started.

Billie Goat Goes to War

John Grainger, RCAF, Mechanic on Typhoons

It was late summer, 1944. We had moved to France and were on airfield B8, near the village of Bayeux, enjoying a day off duty by sitting outside the tent, sampling the local popular drink made from distilled apple cider, called Calvados.

This would not have caused any trouble had the farmer's goat not wandered by. It lapped up the first plateful so fast that we poured another and another. After three plates, that goat's eyes were glazed over and crossed, and its legs were like rubber. It probably would have gone to sleep right on the spot, but one of the lads whacked it on the backside and Billie took off in the general direction of the headquarters' tent. Billie zeroed in on the front door and galloped on through, dragging the tent with him.

The Squadron clerk was left sitting in the middle of a field beside the filing cabinet which was lying on the ground with its drawers emptied. The clerk's desk was upside down, the typewriter in his lap, and paper fluttering down around him. The tent/goat combination went on for another thirty yards before parting company. Then the drunken old goat staggered off into a nearby forest.

Fortunately, the C.O. was flying that day, so not only did he miss the party, but he never did find out what caused the goat to rampage through his headquarters and destroy so many of the squadron's records. We thoughtful "erks," being pure of heart, wanted to spare him the agonizing details. Besides, I had no desire to lose my hooks again.

1st Canadian Parachute Brigade

Jim Kingsley

I was a Bren gunner, attached to the 6th British Airborne and the only Canadian there. We landed in the Ardennes forest and dug in. They then moved us forward and again we had to dig in. But no sooner than we dug in the second time, we were ordered to move up. We spent the night moving and digging. It went like this for three nights, and by that time we were fed up with digging-in and then being moved.

The Paras' favourite sayings include "I never jumped once; I was pushed every time"; "It wasn't the jumping that gave you trouble; it was the sudden stop at the bottom"; and "Watch out for that first step, it's a dandy." One popular story concerned one of our new troopers. Making his first parachute jump, he stepped into the doorway of the plane and pulled the release on his reserve chute and was yanked outside. His main chute had inflated behind him automatically and he floated gently to earth with both chutes open. Our Sergeant gave him a typical military tongue-lashing, (readers can use their own imagination and memories as to the actual wording) "What exactly do you think you're doing soldier?" he thundered.

"Sarg," he replied, "I was told in jump school that if I'm ever in doubt, I'm to pull my reserve — and if I wasn't in doubt at the door of that plane, I wasn't ever going to be in doubt."

A Slit Trench Too Far

G.N. (Bud) Schaupmeyer

On the morning of August 14, 1944, the plan to close the gap at Falaise, France was under way. I was a corporal in the 10th Canadian Infantry Brigade, in the 4th Armoured Division.

It was hot that morning, and our position north of Falaise was flat, dusty, and incredibly hard. I tried digging a slit trench, but had opted for a dugout that had been used previously by a German Tiger Tank. They would drive into these with only the turret showing, offering little target for our tanks to fire at, and allowing maximum protection to their tank and crew. This was rather large for a slit trench, but with earth piled on three sides, it offered good protection. Many of the boys who tired of digging tried to sleep under vehicles.

We were told that morning a bombing attack would begin at noon, to soften enemy positions prior to the advance of our tanks and infantry. I was resting in my "slit trench" and beginning to feel the onslaught of dysentery, when a deafening explosion occurred a short distance away. Pieces of hot metal were landing like shrapnel all around my dugout. A half-track vehicle had driven over some tank mines that had been lifted, but not demobilized. So total was the destruction of the vehicle that the remains of the Corporal and trooper could not be found.

I was near a field hospital at noon when the first wave of our Lancasters and Halifax bombers arrived. They were flying very low, and as they approached our position, the bomb doors opened and bombs started falling on our lines! It was absolute pandemonium. There was very little cover, and you had to hope you were running away from the next bomb, not into the area it would fall.

Artillery Lysander and Auster spotter planes realized something was amiss, and some flew wing tip to wing tip with the bombers, trying to steer them from our positions. Some bombers did turn without releasing any bombs, but many, many casualties occurred. It was estimated ours were in the low hundreds, and the Polish Armoured Division to our left had many more.

By nightfall, I was back at my dug-out, bandaged from a bad head wound, suffering a big time headache and that fast approaching bout with dysentery. It was now dark, and I heard approaching aircraft returning to their bases in England from a raid over Germany. Or so I thought. Wrong! They were German planes and suddenly our whole marshalling area was lit up like a football stadium. The lights came from hundreds of phosphorus flares attached to parachutes. From the air, we were like sitting ducks, beautifully silhouetted against the dark night.

Bren guns and rifle fire were used to try and shoot the parachutes from the flares, allowing them to fall quickly to the ground where we could extinguish them with dirt. Every fourth shell was a tracer. As dangerous as the situation was, I could not help but note how beautiful a sight it was to see the coloured tracers arcing across the sky.

Suddenly a tracer went through the fuel tank of a truck loaded with 25 pound shells, a mere 40 yards from my slit trench. I was expecting one Hell of an explosion after the first shell went off. The heavy artillery behind us would start a new barrage, the ground would shake like jelly, and another shell from the burning truck would explode. It took all night for that damned truck to burn out, but I timed my mad dashes to the latrines with the lulls in the artillery barrages. I almost prayed for one of the oil bombs being dropped to end my misery.

Humour can be found in any situation. Two amusing incidents occurred during this hot night of August 14 that, to this day, make me laugh. The first one was of this young bronze Hercules of a man, Priest-Brown. Bare to the waist and down on one knee with his Bren gun cradled against his thigh, it's barrel red hot, he was shouting to his #2 on the gun, "Give me another mag. Give me another mag! (cartridge magazine)." At the time I thought he was up for an Oscar, it looked so much like a movie set! I doubt he hit one parachute!

The second incident was of this young soldier who had neglected to dig a slit trench. He was crawling across the bare rocky ground on hand and knees, his bare butt shining like a beacon.

Wartime Photographers

Lloyd H. Thompson

The role of wartime photographers in the R.C.A.F. and the part they played during WWII is known by few. I will not go into the realms of those photographers who saw duty with Bomber Command; Coastal Command; or public relations. Rather, I will concentrate on a unique role played by Mobile Field Photographic Sections.

The Units #5 and #6 MFPs performed a very important function as part of the 2nd Canadian Tactical Air Force and specifically part of 39 Recce Wing which was made up of a number of Squadrons: the 400 (The Bluebeard Squadron), 414 and 430. These three were fighter Recce Squadrons.

If you asked any infantryman who served in WWII his opinion of the Air Force, he will likely mention the Tactical Aircraft. This was the facet of the Air Force with which he was familiar. Bombers and Fighters saw their action at great heights, whilst the Tactical fighters were providing ground support, bombing and strafing. The three Squadrons mentioned were flying Spitfires and Mustangs. The 400 Squadron was the first R.C.A.F. Squadron to go overseas and 39 Recce wing the first airfield to cross the Rhine and also the Wing that pushed its way furthest into Germany.

Early in 1944, a number of R.C.A.F. photographers were chosen to go to #1 Photo Establishment at Rockcliffe in Ottawa to be prepared and trained to handle new complex rapid photographic processing machines. The monsters were large and, for their time, were far advanced over anything we had ever seen, and were still on the secret list.

The rest of our training came in England, following a rough ride over the North Atlantic and our arriving at Liverpool docks during an air raid. We were suddenly thrown into a real war. We were inexperienced Canadians who were ushered promptly onto a train and taken to Bournemouth " Sally Ann" on the south coast.

We met our Units — they were to be our home for the next year or so; they were located at Odiham in Hampshire. At this stage, our units became half R.A.F. and half Canadian, which occasioned some good-natured kidding. However, we found that we became very close in the following months.

The Units, when we first saw them, came as a surprise. We had been told very little whilst in Canada of the situation we would face. Our boys were split up, some going to #5 MFP and our group to #6. The first shock came when we saw everything was under canvas, along a hedgerow, under the trees and camouflaged!. Our monster machines were in long air-conditioned trailers and all these vehicles were destined to be hauled all across Europe.

There were generator trucks, water trucks, food and supply trucks, trucks to haul our tents. Both Units #5 and #6 had 2 negative processing, and 2 print processing vehicles.

Then came more training on our machines, plus military training like you wouldn't believe, ten-mile route marches, with full kit, gas training, and a short Commando course, for we had to protect our own Unit. Eighty men comprised #6 MFPS: forty were photographers, forty were mixed trades, drivers, plumbers, electricians, a medical orderly, dispatch rider (motorcycle). Each man carried arms, a Sten Gun, and because of my one good eye, I was in charge of 3 Bren Gun crews. We had to really work on those guns, disassemble and re-assemble in darkness or blindfolded.

Just before D-Day, we moved off to the marshalling yard on Salisbury Plain, later joining the invasion convoy in Portsmouth Harbour. Prior to sailing, we were taken off our Landing Barge a number of times because of motor problems. It broke down again in the middle of the English Channel. We were left adrift whilst the rest of the convoy proceeded on to Normandy. We were later to be towed onto the beach by a tug sent out from England — humiliating!

As we approached the beach at Gold Beach, our boys were sitting on top of the vehicles, taking pictures of the armada of ships spread along the coast as far as the eyes could see. Barrage Balloons were hanging over the ships and battleships were firing over our heads to the beach to the enemy lines.

As very inexperienced servicemen, the number of troops and supplies being unloaded on the beach awed us. The first night was extremely quiet. We slept beneath our vehicles and thought " Gee this is a piece of cake." That was the best night's sleep we were to have for the next six weeks. Every night, the ground shook with heavy gunfire and the beach was either bombed or strafed. We learned to dig slit trenches in a hurry and, as we moved our location frequently, we became gypsies or carnival hands setting up and tearing down tents.

For the most part, we were in the area of the town of Bayeaux. From this area we lost an airfield. 126 Squadron was completely disbanded. Personnel were dispersed to other airfields and some returned to England for re-grouping. Also from this location we watched the destruction of Caen during a 1,000-plane air raid a sight, which to say the least, was unforgettable.

The armies moved quickly after that and the breakthrough at the Falaise Gap. Our convoy rolled through town after town that had been destroyed by our firepower of artillery and bombers. It was difficult to get pictures back to the army there. We were moving quickly, although we were always located between the front lines and the first airfield.

In Holland, we spent the winter on the outskirts of Eindhoven. We were billeted in a schoolhouse formerly occupied by German troops and about a half mile from the airfield. We spent Christmas and New Year's there. On New Year's morning we had headaches on top of our hangovers after an evening of Calvados and French Cognac. At 9 am, we were surprised by an attack of 50 German Messerschmidt — one of the largest we had experienced. The German Luftwaffe was making its last strike on a number of Allied airfields all at the same time. After months of moderate enemy action, it came as a complete surprise. Our airfield lost personnel and many aircraft. Those that were destroyed were replaced the next day.

We moved from there early in March and were back under canvas. We were the first Allied airfield to cross the Rhine on March 30th; we hauled our convoy across a pontoon bridge erected by the Corps of Engineers at Xanten. This was six days after the "Operation Varsity" assault on March 24th. Prior to the Rhine crossing, Recce Pilots burned up the sky back and forth across the river. For this operation, more and more film poured into the 2 MFP's; the multi-printing machines were working around the clock, churning out prints at 1,000 per hour from each of four machines.

In the five days before the Rhine crossing, the 2 Units (#5 and #6) developed 32,091 negatives — 286,500 prints — used 2,000 gallons of chemicals, 3 tons of Hypo (or Fixer), four miles of film, 36 miles of roll photo paper, and 45,500 gallons of water, (all to be hauled by motor transport) and all of this for one phase of the war. We were processing for 3 armies. #39 Recce Wing made prints for the 1st Canadian, the 2nd British and the 9th American. The #39 Recce Wing (the Eyes of the Army) provided photos for practically every Paratrooper, and there were hundreds, that jumped behind enemy lines. They knew the location of every German trench, every Gun emplacement, even barbwire fences.

#39 Recce Wing penetrated further into Germany than any other airfield and ended its journey at the town of Lunenburgh in North Germany, not far from the Baltic Sea and almost up against the Russian front. It was here at Lunenburgh Heath that the German surrender was made to General Montgomery, VE-Day May 4th 1945.

Letter from the War to My Brother.

Raymond "Tony" Wallace

> *August 12, 1944*
> *I had a good newsy letter started for you, but I guess it's lost with the rest of my stuff. All the possessions I have are a clasp knife, comb and my pay book. I can't get in a comfortable position, so will not write all the stuff I had in my last letter. I will tell you all that when we are all home again. Or maybe I'll feel like writing it again some time.*

I was wounded on Aug. 12 at about 12 noon. We were on our way to Falaise, shutting the gap that you have no doubt read lots about. I didn't get very far unfortunately. Our Sergeant's tank in front of us was hit and brewed up. We couldn't see where the shot came from, but knew it was from an 88 mm. anti-tank gun. I knew that unless we got out fast, we would be the next to get it. Our officer hadn't any intentions of clearing out, so I was keeping my fingers crossed and yet knew that we would get it any minute.

The next ten minutes were hard on the nerves. We just sat there looking around trying to spot the anti-tank gun. All of a sudden, there was a Hell of a bang and the tank shook. Dirt and smoke flew every-where and I felt my both legs get a smack. I think I must have been stunned for a while, because when I realized what had happened, everything had quieted down again. I couldn't hear a word from the rest of the crew. The motor had stopped, and the turret was full of smoke. I knew that everything would burst into flames any minute so I wheeled around from my seat and pulled myself up through the escape hatch. I wasted no time dropping to the ground, as I knew snipers had been after us shortly before that.

When out on the ground, I was surprised not to see any of the crew, so I knew that they were still inside. I wanted to get back and try to get them out, but I couldn't even get up on my knees. I could see the co-driver's hatch was open, so I figured he, at least, got away. By this time, the flames were pouring out of the turret hatch. It was a terrible feeling to know that my officer and L.O. were still in there. I'll never forget that sight.

I had seen lots of tanks burn and knew that when the ammunition burns, it quite often blows the whole side out of the tank, and the shells blow for yards. So I had to get away as fast as I could.

It was very hard going, as I had to grab the grass and pull myself along. I could use my left leg a little, but my right was useless, and besides that, awfully sore. I was never so frightened in my life. There wasn't anyone around to help me and I didn't seem to be making much headway. The Germans were shelling and mortaring the sec-tion heavily. Dozens of times, the shells screamed so loud that I was sure they were going to drop right on me. I knew that the farther I crawled, the closer I would get to the spot they were mortaring. Still I had to get away from the tank and I had to get someone to help me.

After pulling myself along for about 150 yards, I stopped to fix my wounds. This was the first I had looked at them. I looked at my left leg first and got quite a shock. Around the knee were about four cuts which were bleeding freely, but weren't serious. The calf of the leg had a big piece out of it. I remember thinking that the quarter of a good size orange would just fit into it right. I took my shell dressing and put it into this cut. It nearly all sank away into the gash, but stopped the bleeding. Then I had a look at my right leg; it was easy to see that it was broken below the knee. There were some cuts on this leg too, so I used my field dressing on them.

I then started to crawl again and the shells and mortars kept howling overhead. At different times, I lay and hung onto the grass and prayed to God to spare me. My strength seemed to be going fast and I was really frightened when I heard someone talking, or shouting, rather. There was so much noise that I couldn't tell if it was English or German, and I was afraid to raise myself up so I could see better. I figured on crawling closer, so I could tell which language it was. Finally I had to rise up, as I was getting too tired to pull myself along. I was sure tickled to see a couple of stretcher-bearers running around helping infantry. I shouted to them but couldn't make them hear. I could see they were getting ready to leave with their jeep and a couple of wounded.

With my last strength, I crawled closer and shouted louder. Finally, an infantry-man saw me and came running over. He rolled me over on my back and the first words he said were, 'Give me your pistol will you, you won't need it now." Even though I was feeling about all in, it struck me as funny. I told him to get the stretcher-bearers, so he forgot about the pistol for a while, but managed to get it before I left.

Those stretcher-bearers do great work. They deserve a lot of thanks. They put a rifle on my leg for a splint. They just got me on the stretcher, when the mortars started coming again. Everyone flattened out on the ground and hung on. These ones were really close. The dirt dropped on top of us. I felt really helpless lying on the stretcher. They got up and asked if anyone was hit. Luckily no one was, so they placed me crossways over the back seat of the jeep and started off. Every bump in the field hurt my legs. We finally got on the road, but it wasn't much better. We came to a little grade where we stopped up on the top, as down in the bottom, the Bren-gun carriers were all jammed up in the road. The mortars had been falling here, and there were casualties lying all around. Everything was mixed up.

Just then, Jerry started to mortar us again. The driver and the fellow holding me jumped out and crouched at the side of the jeep. I just had to stay up on top. The jeep started to run down the grade and I thought, "Here's where I collide into all this junk at the bottom." I was sure hanging on for dear-life. The driver caught up, climbed in and got the brakes on.

We detoured around there and they got me to a dressing station. By this time, we had two more casualties, one a shell-shocked young fellow and the other a sergeant who had been shot in the arse.

The dressing station was a cave in the rocks. It was really quite a place. They didn't do anything to me here, just loaded me into an ambulance and took me to another dressing station. Here they took off the rifle, put my leg on a box splint, and dressed my wounds.

I was then put in another ambulance and taken to 74th Br.General Hospital. I was put to bed and went to the operating theatre, Sunday morning at 9:30 am. My leg was set by a Lt.-Col. Nothing but the best for me, eh? It was here I started taking penicillin. It's tough to take every three hours, but I guess it does a lot of good.

I was at the 74th for a few days, then came to England by boat. We went on a Red Cross train to a dispersal hospital where we stayed a half-day and then moved to this place.

This has turned out to be a novel, but I thought you might be interested. I hope I never have to go into action again. It seems to knock the nerve out of a fellow, and I can't forget the sight of the burning tank and two of my crew in it.

Unless a person is up there, he hasn't the least idea what it is like. The sights of death and suffering are terrible. The papers speak of "light casualties," but they don't show what those "light casualties" mean to some poor fellows and their families.

I realize that a lot of young fellows had it much worse than I.

War Starts and Ends a Friendship

Truman Wilcox, Argyll-Sutherland Highlanders, and Connie White

WWII was the start and end of a friendship that lasted four years and was cut short by a bullet. Two men, 23-year-old Truman Wilcox and 19-year-old Aubrey Cousens walked up the steps of a Toronto recruiting centre on Bay Street in November 1940. After talking to recruitment officers, the two decided to join the Argyll-Sutherland Highlanders. They did so together and became friends.

Aubrey hailed from Porquis Junction in northern Ontario, Truman from Monteagle Township near Bancroft, in eastern Ontario. The two were told to go home for the weekend and return for training Monday. The problem was that there was only one full kilt uniform.

Understanding Aubrey was going to northern Ontario for the weekend, Truman told Aubrey to take the kilt. Upon returning Monday, training began in earnest. En route to the Allenberg Barracks, south of St. Catherine, the two men sat together on the bus. For the next seven months, the two trained and took guard duty together. Like the other men in training with them, they would train one month, while for three other months, they rotated between Niagara-on-the-Lake, Chippewa Barracks and Allenberg, to guard canals and a power station.

In May 1941, the two were sent to Nanaimo, British Columbia for more training. "It was a real drag about, knock 'em out training," Truman recalls. In September, they were scheduled to go to Hong Kong, but that was cancelled. Instead, they were shipped to the West Indies. While there, they guarded a prison camp full of "naval type people" and the Governor of the Island. In May 1943, the two returned to Niagara Falls.

After a 10-day leave of absence, they were shipped to England and spent a year fighting together. Then, the two were separated: Truman went to France with the Highlanders, while Aubrey stayed behind in hospital, suffering from varicose veins, caused by a broken leg from years before. When he got out, he went to France as reinforcement and then joined the Queen's Own Rifle regiment.

While fighting in France, Truman and Aubrey remarkably met in an apple orchard, where they planned their future. Neither knew this would be the last conversation they would have. They both planned to return to northern Ontario to work on the railroad and they talked of a double wedding. Aubrey wanted to marry his high school sweetheart Julie, and Truman to marry Betty, a young woman he had been corresponding with.

Betty recalls how this idea for a double wedding came about. She and Julie had been friends since they were youngsters. Julie had encouraged Betty to write to Truman, and their letters were shipped back and forth over the next four years.

In June 1945, Truman was liberated after being a POW. In England, he met up with his Argyll friends. but during a big get-together, Truman was saddened to hear that Aubrey had died. Aubrey had been leading his men in an attack against Mooshof, when a sniper killed him. Aubrey was 24 years old and was awarded the Victoria Cross posthumously.

"I then went out and got drunk," said Truman. But that wasn't the only bad news. A few days later, he was informed that his mother, Annie, had been buried a month before. In 1996, the people of Latchford, where Aubrey was born, honoured his memory. A bridge over the Montreal River was dedicated to his memory and a plaque inside an adjacent small park explains his bravery. Truman attended the dedication ceremony and has also been to Grosbeak in Holland where Aubrey now lies.

Truman, 83, is a member of The Royal Canadian Legion and has been for more than 50 years. He is presently the Veterans Service Officer for The Royal Canadian Legion, Branch 181, in Bancroft, Ontario.

Attack on the Normandy Dry Dock, St. Nazaire, Mar. 1942

David Lloyd Davies, by Michael J. Wolstencroft

During the dark days of 1942, there was concern in the allied command that the great German battleship *Tirpitz* might emerge from the safety of Tromso fiord in Norway, and roam the Atlantic, sinking convoys of ships that were bringing vital food and armaments to England.

Though most of Europe was occupied by German forces, the only Atlantic port capable of repairing and refitting the *Tirpitz* was the huge dry dock at St Nazaire, six miles inland on the Loire River. The dockyard facility with its giant dry dock had been used by the French to construct the Liner *Normandie*, the dry dock taking its name from the liner.

Clearly, anything that could be done to damage the dockyard facility would impede the attacks by the German Navy on the Atlantic convoys of the allies and thus improve their chance of survival.

In a daring raid on the morning of March 28 1942, a small force of ships, army and navy commandoes and air force bombers attacked the docks at St Nazaire, achieving remarkable success. Such was the daring and valour of those involved, that a total of 85 decorations were awarded afterwards, including five Victoria Crosses. Fifty one people were mentioned in dispatches, twenty two of them posthumously.

One of the participants in the attack on St. Nazaire was my friend, David Lloyd Davies from Montreal. Lloyd joined the Canadian navy in 1939 at 23 years of age. After service in destroyers on the Arctic run, Lloyd was transferred to Coastal Forces and received special Commando training at Fort William and Oban in Scotland. When Britain asked Canada for one hundred naval officers, the exchange took place, and Lloyd became a Canadian member of the Royal Navy. His special duties, involved raids on German held French coastal installations along the English Channel.

In the Combined Operations Headquarters in England, chief naval planner Captain J Hughes-Hallett proposed the idea of ramming the gates of the St Nazaire dry dock with an expendable warship loaded with high explosive and fitted with a delayed action fuse to allow the crew to leave the ship before it exploded.

The eventual return of the crew to England was to be handled by a small fleet of sixteen motor launches, supplied by Costal Forces. The plan included elaborate precautions to confuse the German forces and allow the attacking fleet to enter the Loire River, and come within striking distance of the dock, before it became apparent to the Germans that the facility was under attack.

In addition to providing an escape route following the attack, the sixteen motor launches were to land a force of commandoes whose task was to set explosive charges and destroy other key dock facilities. These commandoes, under the command of Lieut Colonel A.C. Newman, were trained for their assault in the Scully Isles.

The commandos were divided into two groups. One group was responsible for demolition and the other for protection. Each demolition man carried 90 lbs of explosive and was armed only with a Colt 45 automatic pistol. The protection team members were armed with Bren guns, Thompson submachine guns, and mortars. It was their job to provide protective fire for the demolition teams.

A simultaneous torpedo attack on another set of dock gates providing access to submarine pens at St. Nazaire was also part of the plan. One of the motor torpedo boats was armed with delayed action torpedoes to be used against these gates. The delayed action fuses would allow the MTB to turn and escape before the explosives detonated.

The Admiralty was persuaded to release HMS *Campbeltown*, an old four funneled destroyer, formerly the USS Buchanan, which had been supplied under the Lease Lend agreement by the United States. This vessel was moved to Devonport, and was extensively modified so that she resembled a German torpedo boat, a force of which were at the time operating out of Atlantic ports on the Bay of Biscay.

Under the direction of naval and military explosive experts, the forward part of the destroyer was packed below decks with 24 depth charges, a total of four and a half tons of high explosive. The charges were stored in a steel tank placed 30 feet back from the bow to avoid detonation during the initial impact. The tank was also filled with concrete to lessen the possibility of accidental detonation of the explosive by defensive fire during assault on the gates of the dry dock. Long delay fuses were fitted to the charge which would be activated during the approach to the river mouth.

The Coastal Forces craft on which Lloyd Davies served were light fast attack vessels made of wood. They used speed, daring and the cover of darkness to make surprise attacks on German shipping. Some were armed with torpedoes, others with two pound Lewis guns. With the exception of light armament on the bridge, and at the gun positions, they carried no protection for the crew. Before the development of radar made sneak attacks under the cover of darkness more difficult, the crews of these dashing little vessels posed a constant threat to German coastal shipping movements.

The speedy motor torpedo boat, and motor gun boat of Costal Forces consumed fuel at a rapid rate, and had a short range. To overcome this handicap, the plan called for these two attack vessels to be towed to the Loire River by destroyers. To allow the 16 motor launches to reach St Nazaire and return under their own power, they were fitted with auxiliary flexible fuel cells, carried on deck. These were filled with aviation grade gasoline, a highly dangerous cargo to carry in view of the battle that was to ensue.

The small flotilla left Falmouth on March 26th and was made up of the disguised HMS *Campbeltown*, towing Motor Torpedo boat, No. 74, HMS *Atherstone* towing Motor Gun Boat No 314 and HMS *Tyndale* a second support destroyer, and 16 motor launches carrying the commandos . For the passage to the Loire River, the *Campbeltown*, under the command of Lieut. Commander S. H. Beattie, flew the German Insignia. This was replaced by the white ensign during the attack

The naval command was under Commander R.E.D. Ryder. Both Ryder and Newman set up temporary headquarters in HMS *Atherstone* for the crossing from Falmouth, transferring to MOB 314 as they entered the Loire River.

The passage from Falmouth was comparatively quiet. When the group met a group of French trawlers, Commander Ryder took off their crews, and had the craft scuttled, as he was determined to protect the secrecy of the mission.

Shortly after dawn on the 27th, a German U-Boat was sighted about seven miles away. The two supporting destroyers mounted an attack, but the U-Boat crash dived, and escaped.

The disguised destroyer, towing MTB 74 and flanked by two files of motor launches, deliberately steamed past St Nazaire, as if heading for Bordeaux. As darkness fell, the flotilla turned and headed back towards St Nazaire, where a partly submerged British submarine lay off the estuary of the Loire River, showing a light in their direction to guide them into the river

As the sea borne group began their stealthy entrance of the Loire River, 35 Whitley and 25 Wellington bombers of the RAF droned over St Nazaire with the intention of mounting a diversionary raid on the dock facilities. For security reasons, the pilots had not been advised of the attack from the sea. They had been instructed not to descend below the cloud cover, which that night was at 6000 feet. They were only to drop one bomb per run, and then, only if precision could be assured. As a result, only a few bombs fell, which unfortunately had the effect of alerting the defending garrison that something was underway. The commander of the German Naval Flack Brigade was alerted, and suspecting that something was about to happen, he put the entire port defence system on full alert.

Lloyd Davies recalls the feelings of mounting tension and excitement as the darkened fleet sailed quietly, deeper and deeper into enemy held territory. The sudden explosions of the RAF bombs made them realize that all the preparation and training for this attack was about to be tested.

At 1:22 on March 28th, searchlights stabbed the darkness, illuminating the group of ships, and simultaneously, signal lamps flashed from both shores . Preparations had been made for this challenge, and on HMS *Campbeltown* a leading seaman Pike, who was fluent in German, picked up his signal lamp and responded with a message to the effect that they were a German patrol entering the harbour according to orders, but did not say who's orders they were! Then with considerable flair which gained the group additional time, he stopped halfway through his message with a curt "Wait" and began to send the same signal to the other station.

For a few precious minutes, the bluff worked, and then for 10 minutes the air was filled with explosions and flying steel as every available weapon was directed at them. At the head of the column, Ryder and Newman crouched on the lightly armored bridge of the MOB as her captain Lieut D.M.C. Curtis steered her for one of the caissons of the Normandie Dock. As they passed an anchored flack ship, they came under heavy fire, but Able Seaman Savage, manning the forward Lewis Gun, attacked the vessel so effectively that she was temporarily put out of action.

As the great gates of the dock appeared, the MOB swung around in a tight turn to starboard, leaving the way clear for the *Campbeltown* to ram the gates. Then with engines racing emergency full ahead, the ancient destroyer smashed into the gates. With a tremendous crash of splintering wood and shrieking metal, the *Campbeltown* came to rest with her shattered bow projecting over the gates into the empty dry-dock. beyond. Lieutenant Commander Beattie immediately called for the ship to be scuttled to ensure that she remained firmly wedged in the entrance to the dry dock.

As the *Cambeltown* rammed the dock gates, Lieut Curtis steered the MOB along-side the mole, and Commander Newman and his second in command Major Copland scrambled ashore with the available uninjured commandos from *Cambeltown*. They immediately began to clear the way for the demolition parties, putting several gun positions out of action. The demolition teams managed to destroy the pump and winding house machinery for the gates which had so recently been rammed by the *Cambeltown*.

Another demolition team trying to repeat the process at the other end of the dry dock met strong resistance and suffered heavy casualties, but they managed to deto-nate charges suspended against the gates leading from the dock to the neighbouring basin, allowing water to drain from the submarine pens and escape through the now damaged dry dock.

The two columns of motor launches carrying additional commandos that had flanked the *Cambeltown* during her approach to the docks had sustained heavy dam-age from the withering fire by the defenders. On the port side, the first two launches were hit and put out of action with heavy losses. Only the third launch managed to reach the mole and put her commandos ashore, whilst the remaining three were forced to turn back after sustaining heavy casualties and severe damage.

The starboard column had similar experiences: two launches withdrew under heavy fire, four were sunk, set on fire or blown up, and only two launches from the star-board column managed to land commandos. Returning to motor launch 267, after providing covering fire onshore, Lloyd Davies was hit in the shoulder. He was blown into the water as the craft was struck repeatedly by heavy fire and sank. Lloyd and two of his crew members clung to wreckage in the water as the battle raged around them.

As daylight returned to the scene of devastation, Lloyd was one of only three survivors from his craft, still clinging to floating debris in the river. When seen by the German troops, they were arrested and taken for interrogation.

Also captured were Lieut Colonel Newman and Lieut Commander Beattie. While Beattie was under interrogation by the Germans, he was informed that the British obviously had no idea of the strength of the dock gates if they thought they could destroy them with an ancient destroyer. At that very moment, the windows were blown in as the explosive charge in the *Campbeltown* detonated, killing many Germans who were close to the vessel, and causing a small tidal wave which washed the sunken destroyer into the dock.

The facility was put out of commission for the rest of the war, and the *Tirpitz* never did escape into the Atlantic to prey on the convoys there. Lloyd Davies and the surviving captured members of the raid were quickly transported to a prison camp in Hamburg where they remained until the end of the war.

The bullet that found its mark in Lloyd's shoulder in 1942 is still there and gives him frequent reminders of that night in St Nazaire. "There aren't many of us left now," he remarked, "but I can still remember the names and faces of my friends and colleagues who died to make this world a better place. It was a privilege to serve with them. I feel proud to have been part of that action, to have fought among so many brave men."

As a result of the daring raid on the dockyards at St Nazaire, the dry-dock was put out of commission for the rest of the war. The U-boat pens behind the dry-dock became a tidal basin when the lock gates that separated them from the Loire River were destroyed. This severely hampered maintenance operations on the German fleet of U boats then operating in the Atlantic.

Lloyd Davies recalls his impressions of the attack. He prefers not to elaborate on the specifics of his duties as one of the attacking Naval commandoes providing cover for those men carrying explosives. As one of the 700 men who took part in the attack, he has vivid recollections of what happened to him, and how the action developed. It is easy to understand why Lloyd remains silent regarding details of the death and destruction for which he was responsible.

Lloyd believes that each of the survivors of the raid would give a different account of what happened that night. Seen from their perspective, colored by the closeness of violence and death around them, and inspired by the heroism and valour or their comrades, each would have his own vivid memories of the action. Every man taking part in the raid on *St Nazaire* risked his life. For those captured, it was their last active duty of the war. Sadly, for many it was the last thing they ever did. There is no doubt that the raid played an important part in the eventual defeat of the German armies in Europe.

Fogbound

Ted Hutton, RCAF Bomb Aimer

Of the 36 operations I flew, this one stands out in my mind. The date was Tuesday, December 26, 1944 and the target was St.Vith, Belgium

For several days, Yorkshire had been blanketed under a thick mantle of fog. Although we had been called to briefing several times, the ops had been scrubbed before we got to our aircraft. We passed the time playing cards and snooker. The daily newspapers were full of the new German offensive and breakthrough in the Ardennes forest area.

A few days before, the enemy had launched a sudden and heavy attack against the American 1st Army, pushing them back more than twenty miles. Because of the fog, allied aircraft were grounded and unable to help our ground forces. The German objective was to recapture the city of Antwerp. Historians later referred to this as the Battle of the Bulge.

On the day before Christmas, we'd been briefed to fly a cross-country training flight. Because the weather had not improved, the exercise was cancelled at the last moment. It was Christmas Eve, so we didn't mind. The mess was crowded with many of the lads celebrating early and we were quick to join them at the bar. Christmas Day, no duty, no parades, and we were permitted to sleep in uncommon luxury for aircrew; I slept until noon.

Christmas dinner was served in the late afternoon. The meal consisted of celery hearts, mixed pickles, roast turkey, hot mince pie, plum pudding with rum sauce, beer and cigarettes. The bar was open until midnight. I was relaxing in the lounge with the boys, when our Skipper, Sqdn. Leader Pierce, came in announcing that he had "a bottle of Scotch that wasn't doing anything." We then rounded up the rest of the crew. In addition to the Skipper's bottle, other liquor appeared, along with a fruitcake that had traveled from Canada in a food parcel. Canada. By midnight, we'd finished the lot.

Returning to our quarters, the fog was still dense. "No flying tomorrow, Guys," someone shouted light-heartedly. "Sleep in as long as you like. You have my permission." Distant village church bells added a final touch of peace and tranquility to the end of a good day.

The next day: Boxing Day—I awoke to the airfield Tannoy blaring repeatedly: "All Aircrews to the briefing room immediately." At 0830 hrs, I dressed and hurried down to the Flight room where we were told to get ready for ops immediately, as the skies over Europe were clearing. Our target was to be the small town of St.Vith in Belgium.

"I can't over-emphasize the importance of this mission," the Commanding Officer explained. "As you know, this area has been fogged in for the past two weeks, so the Germans have been able to attack anywhere, without worry of interference from the air. By the time you reach the target, there will be very little fog." Pointing to the map, he said, "St. Vith is being used by Von Runstedt's troops as an army base and supply centre. Your job is to knock it out . . . You're to be airborne in one hour. . . Good luck, lads. And give 'em Hell!"

An hour later, we climbed aboard our aircraft *Y-Yokum*. The engines idling, we prepared for takeoff and watched closely as the first bomber sped down the runway, disappearing into the fog.

I was going to say I couldn't see the end of the runway, but thought I'd better not to worry the others. With throttles wide open, we roared down the runway into the misty white veil. At 120 mph, the skipper pulled back on the stick and we were airborne, clearing the fence by several feet. He kept close watch on the instrument panel, while I peered intently ahead, until suddenly, at 1000 feet, we emerged into a clear bright sunny day. "OK, Chaps" the Skipper called to the crew, "come out and enjoy the sunshine."

As we headed down over England, we joined the main force: a total of 270 Halifax's and Lancasters. Then, over the Channel we climbed to our bombing height of 18,000 ft. and altered course in the direction of Belgium. The bad weather conditions plaguing Britain had now disappeared. We now had excellent visibility for bombing.

"Ten minutes to target," advised Frankie, the Navigator. I moved into the nose of the aircraft and got ready for the bombing run. I switched on the bombsight, selected all the bomb switches, and checked the camera. Everything was ready.

The first wave of bombers dropped their bombs, causing a large column of black smoke to rise in the still air. "Bomb the centre of the smoke," The master bomber called repeatedly. Ignore the t.i.s." Nearing the aiming point, I saw a large cluster of t.i.'s sparkling in the snow, some distance to starboard, obviously dropped in error.

"Bomb doors open" I shouted. "Bomb doors open" acknowledged the Skipper. "We're coming up nicely Skipper . . . hold it there . . . " At that moment, a Halifax on our starboard side started streaming black smoke, and quickly losing height. Before diving straight to the ground, it pulled up and made a complete loop before heading for the ground.

"Jeez, did you see that?" exclaimed one of the gunners excitedly "...that Hally did a complete loop and three guys bailed out...." Suddenly, three bursts of flak rocked our aircraft, peppering the fuselage with shrapnel¾a frightening sound, but it caused no damage.

At the aiming point, I pressed the bomb release, sending a two thousand pound high explosive bomb and ten cans of incendiaries into the target. Then we saw another Halifax hit, trailing black smoke and with flames spreading along the fuselage. Someone counted the 'chutes' as they blossomed out in the flak-filled sky.

With a fleeting moment of sadness, we watched them drift slowly out of sight. For them it had been a one-way flight, while for us, we managed to return home. Once again we were thankful we'd beaten the odds and escaped ending up being a statistic. This had been our 25th op and we would go on to complete 34 before VE Day.

Nearing the coast of England, we received a diversion call, ordering us to land at Leuchars, a coastal command airfield in Scotland, as Skipton was still fog-bound!

We Done Good

Charles Clark, RCAF

On my 18th birthday, September 8, 1942, I asked for the day off from my work at a Montreal armament factory and headed for the RCAF recruiting office on St Catherine Street. After a short physical I was told that I couldn't fly because I wore eyeglasses. But no problem, they needed ground crew.

I soon found myself on draft to RCAF Manning Pool, Toronto. We did our basic training at the Royal Winter Fair animal buildings, which had been turned into temporary barracks. Our building had been used to house sheep and its unpleasant smell still lingers in my memory.

Our basic training lasted from before early morning to late evening. We marched and carried out intricate drills along the lakeshore, until we could do the manoeuvres in our sleep. After a battery of tests, I was selected to train as an electrician at the technical school in St. Thomas, Ontario.

During the training our class got a 48-hour pass. A group of us headed to Detroit as the USO was open to us for free accommodation. Free dances and food made a leave in Detroit a real good deal. On the first night, we all went to a dance, but I developed real rosy countenance and what turned out to be a bad case of measles. Consequently, my friend and I spent 2 weeks in quarantine at the Windsor hospital.

In 1943, I was posted to Dorval Airport, a staging airfield where I was to service aircraft before flights to the UK. The work was mostly routine; I made sure that the electrical components were in good shape for the trip over the Atlantic. We were issued bicycles for getting around the airfield to service the planes. Sometimes when the engine mechanics were warming up the planes, we found that by coming into the slipstream at just the right place on the tarmac, we could pick up the propeller blast and coast for hundreds of feet down the concrete lanes.

In October 1943, I was posted overseas, ending up in Kenley, near London, England. This was one of the airfields used by our Spitfires and Hurricanes that fought against German bombers in the Battle of Britain. I remember one Canadian ace who had the habit of tossing his hat in the air after a successful sortie, then shooting it down with his pistol.

My job during the winter of 1943-44 was to do electrical work on the Spitfires. Around January '44, as 127 Wing, 2nd Tactical Air Force, we moved to the southern part of England, went under canvas, locating our workshops on trucks so that we could pick up and move at a few hours notice. I was now running the mobile generators and laying electrical cables to the various trucks and tents that required electricity. We practised moving our mobile airfield to various sites, setting up, and going operational in the shortest time possible. Rumours circulated that as soon as a landing field across the channel had been prepared, we were slated to invade. We were issued khaki uniforms for the invasion, for Air Force blue was too close to the colour of the German uniforms. Towards the end of May and as ready as we could be, we broke camp and joined the convoys travelling to the embarkation ports.

The weather turned bad around June 4th, but the invasion went as scheduled on June 6th. We spent more than 6 days, however, waiting for the airfield to be prepared before finally leaving for Normandy. Our airfield was located near Bayeux, and the squadrons operated out of that airfield from about June 14 or 15, until the allies broke out of Normandy. Then a call came from Britain for technicians to help modify the Typhoon fighter-bomber, and because there was a relative stalemate at the time, a group of us were flown back to do the modifications. Afterwards, I was posted to 126 Wing, still with 2nd TAF, which was now located in Holland, then to Germany proper, quite close to the border of France and Belgium.

The Germans didn't appreciate us being on their territory, so they blew out the dikes that held back the local river, and flooded the airfield. Then to reinforce their territory, they bombed us with anti-personnel bombs, tough on us and hell on the aircraft. Just as we were packing up to get out of there, a German fighter dropped more anti-personnel bombs. I heard them coming and jumped into a slit trench headfirst. Because it was full of water, I got soaked, but also I got a piece of the bomb in my backside.

Before I knew what had happened, our medical people pulled me out of the trench, cut my uniform pants off me, stuck a bandage on the wound, and sent me off to hospital at Eindhoven. All I can remember is that I was given a local anaesthetic, laid belly down on the operating table. The surgeon looked at the wound, and found that the bit of metal had fallen out on the table. With that, he poured a glass of iodine on me and sent me on my way. I was happy to get out of there.

I knew I had to get back to the airfield. I had lost my pants and there were no clothing stores either in the hospital or in the local area. What to do? I would be in deep trouble if I appeared outside, out of uniform as it were. Finally, while walking around the hospital I found a pair of army pants being aired out on a clothesline. Faster than I can type this, I grabbed the pants and was soon hitching a ride back to squadron.

When I rejoined the airfield, we were based at Brussels main airport. Because there was no living accommodation there, we were billeted with friendly families that lived close by. Belgium is a bi-lingual country, with French and Flemish speaking people, but mostly Flemish speaking people lived around the airport. Picking up the new language was difficult. However, most people understood English and we got along fine. In fact, some soon found Flemish girl friends who they later married.

Work at the airfield continued. Our squadrons kept busy harassing the enemy, softening up the ground defences with bombs and canon fire. There wasn't much of the Luftwaffe left to get involved in aerial fighting. The Germans introduced the Buzz bombs, or V1's, most of which flew over our heads in a westerly direction. Our pilots would try and deflect them by flying up to them and trying to tip their wings, and cause the rockets to lose control and crash in open ground where they did little damage. The V2's were a lot worse, and were in effect until our army overran the launching sites.

Close to the end of 1944, we were in for a huge surprise. The Germans had assembled a potent army and air force for a final push to drive us out of Northern France, Belgium and Holland—the Battle of the Bulge. Our airfields were the targets of their air attacks. One morning after celebrating the festive season too well, I awoke to the sound of aircraft flying very low. They looked the same colour as our planes, but all sported German black crosses. In the distance we could see black smoke billowing up, so we dressed as fast as possible and headed back to the airport. To our horror, our neatly parked aircraft were all on fire. Very few had managed to take off to tackle the Germans. Later we heard that every one of our fields had received simultaneous attacks, and many of our planes sustained substantial damage. However, we were soon supplied with new planes.

VE day found us at Eindhoven, Holland, but not for long. We moved into Germany as officially designated occupation troops, ending up at Hamburg, which was in terrible shape! We had to use a bulldozer to clear the road to enable our trucks to get into the airport. This was also a mess, with so many damaged planes of all types. Still, it was interesting to see the famous German aircraft up close.

I arrived back in Canada at the end of January 1946, not yet twenty-one years of age. I was discharged from the RCAF in Ottawa, May 1946.

Dutch Resistance Fighters
Karel Berkman, Vancouver Consul General, The Netherlands

The first clandestine newspaper hit the streets of Amsterdam two days after the Nazis marched into Holland. Unlike the larger countries, there were no natural hiding places such as mountains, caves, or large forests. The Dutch "Underground" operated out of cellars and attics.

The biggest challenge was funding. In 1940 Mrs. Kuipers, a mother of five, headed up the task. Father Stomp aided her, with the co-operation of the Catholic Church. By 1944, there were 300,000 members of the "Loyal Order of Divers" in the Underground. They were producing 220, 000 phoney ration cards, travel documents and ID's each month. Each Diver unit had a small executive committee which spawned other specialized units for sabotage, fighting and rescue of allied airmen. Sabotage was deemed to be their most important business.

German vehicle convoys were obstructed, communications were destroyed and Dutch traitors, Jew hunters and ranking Nazis were executed. In one raid just prior to Montgomery's failed "Operation Market Garden," 1500 Freedom Fighters rescued fifty political prisoners who were being held in Arnhem.

By the end of the war, 350,000 Dutch nationals were in hiding and being provided for by the Underground. While in the field, the total confrontation was made up of 45,000 fighters, plus a 60,000-strong illegal army.

Mrs. Kuipers died in a prison camp in 1942. She was one of 15,000 who had been arrested; 10,000 of them were killed. Overall losses from the German invasion were 230,000; 110, 000 of them were Jews.

Special Operations Executive Len Mulholland
Gordon Bell

Len left his home in the Dutch East Indies in 1939 to study at the Merchant Navy College in Amsterdam. Eight months later, the Germans marched in and he was forced to complete his training under the occupation. He graduated in 1941 and after a year's apprenticeship, received his second mate's ticket. During his apprenticeship, he was asked to deliver important papers to the underground in neutral Sweden. In 1943, the Germans had banned Dutch ships from going to Sweden, because of an increase in Dutch sailors jumping ship; this meant the end of the pipeline between Holland and the Allies. So Len decided to escape via Sweden to England to join the Allied forces, jumping ship in Swedish waters. "I had the coldest swim of my life," he recounts, "the water was between 5 and 10 C degrees and it felt like being stung by thousands of needles."

In Stockholm, Len worked for the British Embassy, where he interrogated escapees and identified suspected German agents. Four months later, he was sent to Scotland, and volunteered for the Special Operations Executive (SOE) in Holland. His extensive training involved everything from silent killing to railroad engineering, coding, decoding, wireless, commando, and demolition for infrastructure. Anything the Germans used to fight the war was a target for sabotage. Coping with fatigue was also an important element. "By the time I graduated I felt I could handle anything. I was alert even when extremely tired," he recalls.

As a final test, he was sent in civilian clothes to Liverpool. With false papers and a fabricated story to tell if caught, he was to act as a German spy, trying to find out in which part of the city a bombing raid would do the most damage. With most young men in uniform in Britain, it was extremely difficult for a young male civilian to avoid attracting attention. To make it more difficult, British Intelligence advised police of a spy in the area whom they wanted captured for interrogation and even provided Len's description. Lasting a week before being picked up, Len underwent intensive interrogation, sticking to his story for two days until British Intelligence finally alerted the police of his true identity. Len passed the test that failed 90% of candidates.

On the night of July 7 1944, accompanied by another agent and a wireless operator, Len parachuted out of a Hudson bomber over Holland. But because the Gestapo had infiltrated the Dutch Freedom Fighters, their arrival was unannounced. Len's task was to contact groups that had not been penetrated, and reorganize them into an active force. Most clandestine activity had halted, due to heavy losses and low morale. Len's leadership soon renewed their efforts of receiving airdrops of arms and explosives, etc. He also transmitted valuable information on enemy movements and rocket launching sites. He arranged the sinking of three ships at their moorings, severed the main railway routes used by the Germans, and in conjunction with the Allied Airborne troops in the field, delivered valuable intelligence through the German lines.

After a month, he was picked up by the Germans in a *rassia,* (general round-up) and transported with hundreds of others in cattle cars to southern Germany. His papers showed that he was on a two-week leave as second officer on a German ship. Because they were due to expire, he went to the man in charge of the Deutsche Reichsbahn in Bamberg, and explained that he would be regarded as a deserter if he were found with expired papers. Len told him he would have to either go back to his ship in Hamburg, or stay in Bamberg to work for the railroad, in which case he would need different papers. Knowing there was a critical shortage of manpower, his gamble paid off: he was given a compete set of legitimate papers bearing his false name. "I never could figure out why they let me work as a baggage handler, but with my new papers I had authority to go anywhere in Germany the trains went," said Mulholland.

Len witnessed how forced labour under German supervision could work miracles when, in February 1945, their train was stopped outside Nuremberg during a major air raid. After only three days, they passed through the devastated city. "It was unbelievable that track could be laid that quickly with rubble and bomb craters all around," Len says.

He then proceeded to find a new way to wreak havoc.He knew the routine of trains inside cities during air raids. Everyone left the train to find an air raid shelter, remaining there until the raid ended. Because of the total blackout, Len found it quite easy to stay behind and board the locomotive, open the throttle, then jump off and hide somewhere until the "all clear" siren sounded. By then, the train would be several miles away, probably already piled up against whatever was in its way. He says it was hard for him to keep a straight face when the crew came back and found their train had disappeared.

When the Americans came through, Len was captured again and sent to an intelligence unit for intense interrogation. Things were in such turmoil toward the end that contact with SOE had become impossible. It took a long while for him to convince his captors of his real identity. Len recalls, "The Americans were full of apologies then; they made me a special guest and treated me like a hero."

"It is not fair to blame all Germans for the Nazi atrocities," said Len, "only about ten per cent knew what was happening in the concentration camps. There were guerrillas fighting in Germany just as hard as anywhere else. I worked with three of them, one of whom had been sent to a concentration camp in 1932, and he was the most dedicated of the lot. I only used silent killing once, when I took out two soldiers. But they must have recovered because their deaths were never reported."

Len's exploits in Holland are recounted in *Night drop at Ede* by John Windsor.

My Time in Europe During the War Years.

D.F. (Doug) Beasley, Pte., Army Service Corps

I enlisted in the army at age 18. By the time I reached Europe, most of the serious battles were over and I was never personally involved in any fighting. The sound of distant explosions was all I heard of the battles.

I was a truck driver in the Army Service Corps and I drove hundreds of miles through Belgium, Holland, and later, Germany. I spent many a boring day driving at a snail's pace in long convoys.

Later, while stationed in Hilversum, Holland I got a better assignment. My major contribution to the war effort was to drive my Mack truck to Brussels every few days to haul kegs of beer for the canteens from Wieleman's brewery—a good job for a teetotaler like myself. I often made the trip as a single truck with a Sergeant riding with me, but once in a while there would be two trucks.

My driving job gave me the opportunity to see much of the countryside and the devastation caused by the war and the occupation. Many of the major highways had been badly damaged. Much of my driving was over narrow, tree-lined cobblestone country roads. There were no bridges that escaped damage. Rivers were crossed on a makeshift ferry, or on a rickety Bailey bridge.

The high point of my stay in Europe was the day I drove my truck into Brussels and found the streets crowded with happy people. It was VE-Day.

The Sound of Bagpipes in Holland

Sietske Van Houten

I was a twenty-year-old schoolteacher in Holland at the time of the German occupation. I remember the hunger, the lack of clothes, especially in the winter, and how all the men from 16 to 60 had been taken away to work in German war plants. I remember the allies bringing us food during a ceasefire and the beautiful sunny morning, April 16/45 when I awoke to the sound of bagpipes, looked out the window and saw the Canadian Scottish.

My Momentary Claim to Fame

Bernard Quigley, Irish Regt. of Can. and Lanark & Renfrew Scottish

In June 1940, Canada had been at war for eight months, but for us the world had not changed much. Business was pretty much as usual; money and jobs were still scarce.

Some Militia units had mobilized—a sprinkling of uniforms filled the streets and newspapers were full of patriotic advertisements and notices. I was 19 years old, had just graduated from Parkdale Collegiate in Toronto, and was lucky enough to have a job delivering handbills when I read in the paper that the Irish Regiment of Canada was 'going active.' Inspired by my Celtic heritage, the thought that the kilt and bonnet looked attractive, and some vague idea about keeping the world safe for democracy, I knew the time had come. I jumped on my bike the next morning, peddled down to Fort York Armouries, and enlisted.

After several years training and guard duty in Nova Scotia and the U.K., we found ourselves in Italy as part of the Fifth Canadian Armoured Division in Montgomery's Eighth Army, also known from Lady Astor's remark to the British House of Commons as the D-Day Dodgers. Since the fighting through the river valleys and mountains of Italy was more suited to infantry, an additional infantry brigade was added to the Fifth Division, and I was transferred to the signal platoon of the newly formed, Lanark and Renfrew Scottish.

On May 4, 1945, we were bivouacked in isolation and put under wireless silence, somewhere near Apeldoorn. Called to attention sometime after dark, we were told that we were to take up a position the next day at a map reference that was well behind the German lines. There was no explanation. I was designated signaller to the advance party and assigned to a jeep along with a young officer and a driver.

The next morning before dawn, the advance party, armed as for a fighting patrol was lined up ready to move out. Our young Lieutenant, who, incidentally, had just arrived from England a day or so before, was not on hand. The time came for departure, but there was still no Lieutenant, so the advance party moved off without us. Moments later, he arrived, puffing and panting, still doing up his equipment. "They've gone, Sir," we said, trying not to show our relief. "What'll I do?" he panted. "Better report to the Colonel," we suggested.

He gathered himself together, marched over to the Orderly Room tent to talk to the Colonel. After giving a smart parade ground salute, he apologized, telling him we'd missed the advance party. The Colonel barely raised his eyes from the paper he was studying, and snarled, "Well, get the hell out of here and catch up to them." As the Lieutenant returned to us, our driver, Roly, Rory or some such name, said "Never mind, Sir, I know a short-cut."

So, off we went, the driver and the Lieutenant in the front seats, and me with my Sten gun at the ready in the back. To get ahead of the story, in that short cut we unknowingly passed the advance party, and driving as fast as we could through the countryside, we got farther and farther ahead of them. As we got closer to the more populated areas near Haarlem, we began to see more and more people standing by the roadside waving. Then there were crowds, cheering and throwing tulips. By this time my Sten was on the floor and I was sitting up on the back of the jeep, waving as if I were in the Santa Claus Parade.

My first indication that something weird was going on was when we approached a bridge over a canal guarded by German sentries. They presented arms, and with my heart beating at the double, I returned the salute as casually as any General. Our next hazard was trying to pass a hospital where we were mobbed by a horde of hugging and kissing nurses. Keep in mind that we were under the impression that there was an advance party ahead of us and that we had to catch up, so it was: "Nurses, stand back, we have no time for fun and games!"

We arrived at our destination, Bergen, just outside Alkmaar, sometime around noon. The Burgemeister was in jail and the *Orangerie* (the underground) were in control of the town. First they fed us potato soup. We were hungry and although we knew that the civilian population had little food, we had no idea the sacrifice they were making in sharing with us the little that they had. They invited the young Lieutenant to the *Stadhuis*, to discuss a matter of authority, I presumed.

Roly and I were left at the roadside with the jeep where a happy crowd gathered. We communicated without much difficulty, mainly by disjointed words and sign language. A meije with a two-seated bicycle indicated to me that perhaps I would like to go for a ride. Of course I accepted. Without a care in the world, I / we rode along a quiet country road, when suddenly, marching along towards me, three abreast and with light machine guns in front, was what looked like the whole German Army. I still didn't really know what was going on, but by this time I had some pretty strong assumptions. With my heart in my mouth and looking straight ahead, we peddled past. To my great relief, there was no reaction then, or when we passed them again on the way back.

The rest of the advance party arrived about four o'clock, and the remainder of the battalion the next day. And I returned to the obscurity of a simple private. Later, I was told by some of the Dutch people who had witnessed our premature arrival that they thought the person sitting on the back of our jeep was General Montgomery.

Reflections

Ernie Ratelle

Where was I on VE Day? I was with D Company, in Holland near Leewarden. I wrote on the inside cover of my pay book that we had received word to cease fire. It was 20 minutes past 5:00 PM on May 4th, 1945. Yet the enemy did not cease fire until 9:00 PM that night.

The next day, we were moved to Emden, Germany to take over a barracks. On arrival, armed guards saluted us, before they handed over their weapons. We also took over the officers' mess, which had loads of champagne and peach brandy.

A Humorous event? We were in Viex Cason, France a couple of weeks after landing on June 6, 1944, waiting to enter Caen. Since there were cows in the vicinity, some of our company being farmers decided to get some milk. After milking the cows, they offered some to the Company Commander, who commented, "I wonder if this milk is pasteurized?" I piped up and said "It should be, it went 'past your eyes' a few minutes ago." "Get out of here, Ratelle," he said; "That was puny."

A Memorable event? Probably landing in France on June 6, 1944. The fear, anticipation of what might lie ahead was something to remember for a lifetime.

VE Day

John A. Spence, Gunner, 1st Division, Antitank Red Patch.

It was May 7, 1945, my birthday. What great day! We had just received orders of "Cease Fire." The end of a long war: VE DAY. First the guns were quiet around us; then sounds of cheers of happy soldiers and civilians, followed by a long evening of celebrations.

My next duty was as an Honour Guard for the "Signing of the Peace Treaty" by British, USA, Russian, and German officials. I then I remained in Holland for the next six months of the Rehabilitation period.

I returned safely to Canada aboard the *A La France* on October 2, 1945. When I had originally sailed overseas on the *Queen Elizabeth*, I believed I would never see Canada again. But I was one of the fortunate veterans.

John A. Spence, died Dec. 3, 1994

Denmark Occupation

Ely Bull

For five long years, I saw the face of the enemy very close up. From April 9, 1940 to May 8, 1945 the Germans occupied my country of Denmark. I was 12 years old in 1940.

The first few years were quiet and uneventful, but in 1943, the Danes started a Resistance movement, blowing up railways, German troop convoys and things started to get very nasty. Eight men from our neighbourhood were executed for taking part.

From 1943 to 1944, we noticed the German troops were looking younger and younger; we called them "the boy troops." Some were as young as 14-15. We saw them marching to the railway station and some were crying. I asked my mum why they were crying and she said they were going to fight in Russia and would probably never come out alive. How sad war is for everybody. Do we ever learn?

On V-E day I was celebrating with my school friends in the town square in Randen. I was 17 then. Five years later in 1950, I married my English "Fly Boy" F/Sgt. R.A. Bull in my homeland. He was by then finished with the RAF and flying in the Berlin airlift.

My Brother's Last Letter Home

Jon Robert McQuay, 7th Battalion, Royal Welsh Fusiliers by Brian McQuay

My Brother John Robert McQuay was with the 7th Battalion Royal Welsh Fusiliers and was killed crossing a bridge over the Rhine.

An officer, wanting to be one of the first men to enter Germany, asked if anyone could drive a Bren gun carrier that was sitting there. John, being a truck driver volunteered. They were half way across, when a German cannon shell blew them up.

The following two pages are excerpted from his last letter home. In his letter, he forecasts the German General would be coming to surrender. He also mentions Stalin.

236

are expecting him, here in Holland in a few
days, ofcouse the high ups say he will have
to stop soon and that the British army
has a hard fight a head, ofcouse thats
just to keep up our spairet, off, but I think
the war wont last long with Germaney
if joe keeps on going. I am longing for the
end if the keep me on over leae till I get my
ticket, but if they are going to send me
to the far East I sooner the war last with
jerry a nother 2 years. Jerry never worrys
me I think I am las good has any jerry
but the jap whil thats a difent story.
I want to post this letter to night so Pat
will have to waite a few days for her letter
but tell her I was very please to hear from
her and allgoning well she could
get a letter a few days from this one I shell
also put the date on letter letter and
next time you write will you tell me
how long it takes to get to you, a letter
reseved from Pat arrived on the 24d I could
not see when she posted it, but the avge
time is about 7 days for the letters to get
to us, they have taken longe to get to me
because I have move about.
                              Well thats
about all for now so all my love and I
hope I shell hear from you soon.
            your loving son.
            John,

P.S enclosing a few stamps for Briet
and by the way the price for Postige
After you to me is 1½d

Germany

Life in Nazi Germany

Peter Buttuls

Compassion for the Enemy

As a 7-year old, living in Nazi Germany in 1944, I, together with some other school-boys, heard about an American plane that had crashed in the woods above the village of Weiler bei Bingerbrueck. On approaching the plane, we were told by other spectators that the American pilot was taken to the Rhine River and drowned. Even though we were taught in school that the Americans were our enemies, I was shaken by the information. Something inside me said, "This action is wrong" and has shaped some of my thinking ever since.

Fear of the Barber

On visiting the barber, my fear of being poked in the eye by his long pair of scissors was less frightening than his constant and inevitable talking about my joining the Hitler Youth. I was so scared about being forced to do so, that I let my hair grow as long as my mother would put up with it.

Our Fearless Father

After a night of heavy artillery fire, all our family remained in the basement. The following morning, we heard that the Americans had captured the town. To my surprise, my father dragged me outside. Upon seeing an approaching tank, he jumped right on it and practised his English—to the astonishment and uneasiness of the tank commander.

Navigating Wellington Bombers

Howard Dale, Navigator

We were ready to go to Bremen, when the mission was scrubbed due to bad weather. Following our usual procedure, we repaired to the Mess and proceeded to tip a few. After a couple of hours of joyful imbibing, we were told to get over to the flight line, the weather had cleared and we were going.

None of our crew was in fit condition to fly by this time, but we went anyway. I was trying to plot a course with map references doubling up and moving about, on top of which, I was feeling sick. I made several trips back to the elsan to barf it up, but finally settled down in time to go to my other job as bomb-aimer. I had never seen the flack any heavier than it was that night; it seemed every anti-aircraft battery in Germany was having a go at us. But we finally got on target and I let the bombs go. I then hollered to the skipper "Get us the hell out of here."

Next day I was called in to the Navigations Officer and asked some very pertinent questions like, "Where did you go last night?" "Bremen" I answered. "You got good pictures?" "Yes Sir," I replied. "Well why the hell then are the pictures from Emden?"

No wonder we had got so much flack, we were the only aircraft in the area.

Riddled Bomber

James A. Duff

Flight engineer Sergt. J.A. Duff was one of the crew of a Halifax bomber that a wounded pilot, sitting in a flak-ridden cockpit, brought safely home from a raid on Germany after the crew had put out a fire on board.

"S for Sugar" was approaching the target on a raid when heavy flak burst just below the plane, throwing the Halifax over on its back, and pitching the crew violently in all directions. Flight-Sergt R.E. Crockett of London wrestled with his controls, but the bomber went into a spin and plunged earthwards. It fell over a mile before the pilot could right it. Then Flight-Sergt. Crockett found that shell fragments had wounded him and Sergeant J.A. Duff. The cockpit in which he sat was "holed like a pepper-pot" and smoke began to appear in front of the instruments.

Bomb Bay Hit. With all the bombs still on board, a shell had caused a blaze just forward of the main spar and all the crew, which could be spared, tackled it with fire extinguishers. Meanwhile, Flight- Sergt. Crockett had found a suitable target on which to release his bombs. It was only then that he realized the extent of the damage. There had been hits in the bomb bay, and one of the doors had been wrenched off, and the bomb aimer was able to drop only a small portion of his load. Flight Sergt. Crockett turned for home with the fire still burning and the smoke swirling into his cockpit. It became so thick that he could not see his instrument panel; yet, despite his wounds he stuck at his controls encouraging the others that were still fighting the blaze. After about ten minutes, when all the extinguishers had been used, the fire was put out.

The pilot brought the charred and battered bomber back to base and "S for Sugar" settled down on the runway as smoothly as though her crew had been on a test flight.

James A. Duff came to live in Canada in 1956, and joined the R.C.A.F.

Joining the Luftwaffe

Walter Gulick, German Paratrooper

I had just turned 16 when I got a summons to an office of the Waffen S.S. in my hometown of Bremen. Knowing full well what could happen by not showing up, I was on time. A Friendly SS man in immaculate uniform greeted me at the door. The gist of this meeting was that he told me that if I would like to drive a panzer in Russia, all I would have to do is have my father sign the papers in triplicate. I would then belong to the SS.

At home my father refused to sign any such thing. "What happened to the Luftwaffe?" he asked. I had flown gliders earlier and still belonged to that group. So I went to see the highest-ranking officer in our town, a General der Luftwaffe in charge of anti-aircraft and night fighter installations. After a very long wait, I finally stood in front of his huge desk and was asked what I wanted. "I would like to join the Luftwaffe, " I said. "Wha-a-at!" he replied. "Why do you think I have a bunch of officers in my outer office. Do not bother me. Get out!" I retreated, saying to myself, "Now the SS will get me." The general hollered at me "What was that? Close the door and repeat what you said." I then told him about my meeting with the SS. He asked "Why didn't you say that in the beginning?" (As if I had a chance to.) His tone revealed there was no love lost between the Luftwaffe and the SS. Reaching into his desk, he gave me some papers (in triplicate) "Have your dad sign these papers and the SS can not touch you anymore," he said more agreeably. "Leave your name and address in my office and bring one signed copy back. Now get out."

A few days later I had to show up at the SS office, but my visit there was short. When asked if my father signed the paper, I said yes and gave him one form from the Luftwaffe. Now it was his turn to get red in the face. He threw the paper at me with a string of dirty words, opened the door and pushed me out. For good measure he kicked me there where I normally sit. And that is the way I volunteered.

I have vivid memories of the American Flying Fortresses, not that I got to see much of them—I was too busy running for cover. It was the Focke Wulf factory they were after, but it always seemed to me that I was the real target. I was a student, apprenticed to the railway roundhouse. We never got hit, but we did have some close calls.

One time when the air raid siren sounded I was running for the shelter when I saw that old Fort with the bomb doors open coming right up the track at me. I knew I wouldn't make it to the shelter and leaped into a ditch just as it dropped its load. The rail yard control tower on the other side of the tracks took a direct hit and disappeared. The planes kept on going, so I turned around and went back to work. Another time a friend and I were going home from work on a streetcar when the air raid warning sounded. The motorman stopped and most passengers got off to run for the bunker, but we were only four blocks from home and decided to stay on. But once the bombs started falling, the driver ran for the bunker and we did too. I looked back and saw the streetcar blown to pieces, but we made it to our cellar.

The FW plant was never badly damaged until the Forts started coming over in the daylight. Father who was a guard at the plant told me how the guards would stand on the roof of the factory feeling quite safe as they watched the night bombers work over the farm field where the company built and kept on building a false plywood "factory" and airport for the night bombers to blow up. The farmer didn't like what the bombs were doing to his potato patch, but the guards were happy.

Because my father had refused to join the Nazi party, he was sent to the Russian front. He was home, recovering from wounds, when I was called up in February 1945. I expected to be trained as a pilot because of my experience with gliders, but was put in a paratrooper unit. In April I was wounded and with a 45% disability was sent home—a wounded veteran at age 16.

Note—Walter became a Canadian in 1951. He retired from the Pacific Biological Station, is an avid modeller, and a popular volunteer with Air Cadets.

Life as a Tail Gunner
Gordon Hunt

I guess it's time to hear from the rear. I know there is not too many of us tail gunners left and although some will say what it was like in the rear turret, all will agree it was the loneliest place in the aircraft.

Our crew was on our third trip going to bomb Dusseldorf and we were to bomb from an altitude of 22,000 ft. because of the cloud base. After "Bombs Away" at 02:30 hrs., we turned to starboard and headed for home. But twenty minutes after leaving the target, we came under attack by a Focke Wulf night fighter, clearly visible in the light from the target area.

He came up from underneath on the port side and we all heard the loud bang as our inner starboard engine was hit and caught fire. At the same time, another cannon shell hit the tail plane. We fired at the fighter and knew we hit him numerous times, as we could see the flashes on the aircraft body near the engine. We then corkscrewed to starboard to get out of his line of sight. When we levelled off, the fighter never returned.

By this time, our starboard wing was well ablaze and the flames were nearly reaching the tail plane. I saw a black cloud on the starboard side and told Mac, my pilot, to fly into it, to try to put out the fire. Mac then ordered the crew to prepare to bail out, as he was afraid that the wing might burn off. I told him that I could not get out, as the turret doors had jammed. Mac then said "no one leaves the aircraft until we get Gordy out of the turret." Dick, our wireless operator, was coming down the fuselage with a big flashlight and I was silhouetted against the black sky.

I could not communicate with Dick because he did not have his intercom plugged in. By then, however, the fire had died down. On the way to base Mac said he would

244

have to use the emergency air because the hydraulics had been damaged. "There will be a little oil coming your way Gordy, as the air will displace the oil" he said. That was a great understatement, as I was covered in oil from head to foot.

The next day, we went to see the damage, because it could not be seen at night. The hole in the starboard wing was big enough to climb through and the reason we could not extinguish the fire was that the fire extinguisher had been hit and was gone. The hole in the tail plane was about three feet from the turret, so there was no doubt what the fighter had been aiming for. The plane must have veered slightly to port and that's what saved me from being the target.

Another time I flew as a spare with another crew and Mailey Le Camp was our target, it being the base set up to repel the Allied forces and very heavily defended. Shrapnel was hitting the aircraft like stones on a tin roof. We bombed our target from about 10,000 feet, before leaving for safer areas. My mid-upper gunner from my regular crew was also flying as a spare, but he never returned. We also lost 42 aircraft. We know the Germans were expecting us, as there were so many fighters.

I lost a lot of my buddies on those two raids and many more on the two raids on Revigny, another hot target. It was not pleasant to see all the empty bunks and service people gathering all the crew's effects—not pleasant at all. But because of the times and our youth, we never thought that we might be next. I will say, however, that I would do it all over again, serving with the finest bunch of men anywhere in the world. Unfortunately, the youth of today will never experience the companionship we had, even under the conditions in which we served.

A Canadian Family Trapped in Germany

Rosaline Mandalik

My father, Helmut Jaenisgh Walter, was born in 1894, in Breslau, Germany and was a pilot in the Luftwaffe in WW1. He moved to Canada in the early twenties and homesteaded in Deer Creek, Saskatchewan, which is no longer on the map. He also ran a ferry across the river. In 1933, Mother came from Germany and married him; they settled in St. Walburt, Sask. and had three sons.

In 1939 Father received word that he had inherited an estate and as he had to return to Germany to claim it, decided to take the family and make it a holiday in which his family could see their homeland. Three days after they had completed their business and were returning to Canada, the war started. Their ship turned back to its home port. A fourth son was then born in Leipzig, where Father was working till 1944.

As the Russians were closing in, all men of any age and all teen age boys were called up to become soldiers in the Volksturm. Even though he was a Canadian citizen, Father was sent to the frontline. Meanwhile, allied bombers were adding to the turmoil in Leipzig. It was during an air raid that Mother sent the whole family down to the cellar for safety. At the last minute, remembering she had forgotten something, turned around and went back upstairs. It was while she was there that a bomb came through the roof, went right through the house and exploded in the cellar, killing the four boys.

I was born in January 1945, and my dear mother told me long ago that Father did get to see me, but because the Russians were on the outskirts, he returned to the fighting and was killed. There were Russians everywhere and she was mighty scared of them, so she put me in the baby carriage and started pushing me west so she could get to the Americans. She could see the Russian soldiers stopping people everywhere, but she just kept her head down and without making eye contact, kept pushing past them and was never stopped.

In 1951 she had saved enough money to come back home, but when we got to Halifax we needed $5.00 to get on the train or we would be sent back to Germany, and she only had $3.00 left. I slipped under the rope that was keeping us out of Canada and started begging till we had $2.00 more.

A Soldier's Diary: Brief Notes to Give my Mom

Tom Mansfield, British Black Watch

Feb. 21, 1945 We have got to the front line, about 10 miles from the River Rhine.

Feb. 22   We are going into a bit of a fight tonight at 10:45, at a place called Ghoh.

Feb. 22   Ghoh is taken.

Feb. 24   Another small town to take - the name is Clave. Night has come. We are still fighting for the town.

Feb. 25   Morning. Very hard fighting. Not much more of the town left. Night time 11:45 The town is taken.

Feb. 26   A bit of a rest.

Feb. 27   We have just had orders that the Hochwald Forest has to be taken before we can cross the Rhine. We go in tonight - we have to cross a field about 200 yards wide. We can't take the forest. The 43rd. Division came up to help next morning. The place is taken we lost over 40 men.

Feb. 28   We are on the banks of the Rhine. Only ones to go across tonight. We are the first across. I can't tell you what it's like - just plain murder.

Feb. 29   We have been cut off by the Jerries. They are throwing everything at us. The cannons are here. We have got out at last. Six men left of the platoon. I was very lucky tonight.

Feb. 30	A short rest.
Mar. 1	We have to take the town of Dichenlow. We go in at 7:00 hrs. Only a few Jerries left behind. And #1 rec. goes in — recce brings back 9 more.
Mar. 2	Orders came that we are having 3 days rest. About time too??
Mar. 6	We go into Holland again. The name of the town is Esgeade. It's big and I think it will be hard to take.
Mar. 7	We are now fighting for the town.
Mar. 8	Still fighting. We have lost another 8 men out of platoon.
Mar. 9	Town is taken
Mar. 11	We are moving out again. Don't know where yet. We arrive at a small village tonight. We start a 48hr. push to clear a pocket of Jerries.
Mar 12	No Jerries yet
Mar 13	We have entered the village, and in it are about 30 kids — 14 to 16 and they are holding the place.
Mar 14	The village is taken and 11 of the kids are left alive.
Mar 15	Resting
Mar 18	There is a small town to take. Disley, is the name.
Mar 19	We don't have to take the place now. The mayor came out to us and said there were no German troops left.
Mar 21	The river Ems to cross tonight.
Mar 22	We are across the river — fighting hard.
Mar 23	We got a small village anyway.
Mar 24	The 43rd. div. is taking over and we are having a week's rest.
April 1.	We have got to get to Bremen somehow. I hear it is about 26 miles to cover.
April 2	We're off on the road to Bremen.
April 3	Small village taken
April 4	10 miles to Bremen.
April 5	We are outside of city. We are getting shelled like hell.
April 7	Still holding the outskirts
April 8	Moving out. 43rd. coming in.
April 9	We are around the other side of Bremen.
April 10	We are all going in to take the city.
April 11	Bremen is ours.
April 12	Rest at last.
April 18	We have got to fight our way into Denmark.
April 19	The push has started.
April 20	Small town to take
April 21	It was easy.
April 22	Still flushing them out.
April 23	A few small woods to clear.

April 24	4 out of the 5 woods taken.
April 25	Very hard fighting for the last wood.
April 26	The wood is taken.
April 27	A couple of farm houses to clear. That is one thing I don't like—clearing farm houses.
April 28	The farm houses are cleared. Rest again.
May 1	We are moving to a big town called Bremerhaven tonight.
May 2	We are dug-in outside of town
May 3	The artillery is shelling the place to hell.
May 4	We are expecting them to give in. I don't think they will?
May 5	Still on the outskirts. Nighttime: the Jerries have given in.

I got blind drunk that night. We were behind the lines on our side of Cologne, Germany, resting, when I found a chicken coop full of chickens and lots of eggs. I was just as well received by the farmer as we had been as we came through France, Belgium, and Holland. The farmer certainly was not a Nazi. He let me have a bunch of eggs. His wife even fried them for me and gave me a bowl to carry them back to my buddies. I fancied I would be a real hero in their eyes when they feasted on real food for the first time since the war started.

While walking back, a squadron of tanks went by; I was so savouring the treat we were about to enjoy that I wasn't even thinking about the dust a dozen tanks can kick up, till we sat down to eat. We found the eggs all crusted over. I'll swear the dust was about an inch thick. It wasn't funny then, but I've had many a laugh with my buddies, at reunions.

Tom Mansfield

My Brother with the Royal Engineers was killed. He was about fifty miles away, so I asked the Colonel for a short leave so I could go and pay my respects. He was a heartless old sod and my request was denied, so I did the next best thing.

I checked the motor pool and found the vehicle with the most gas in it and drove over to my brother's outfit in a 15 CWT. There I was treated properly by the C.O. Of course, he assumed I had done it legally and showed me every courtesy. He gave me all my brother's belongings, including a carton of cigarettes that Mom had just sent him, (and I didn't even smoke).

When I got back to my outfit, the Military Police were waiting for me, but it never went to court martial. They decided on the merit of the circumstances and I only got a minor detention.

My Father's War

Goody Niosi

My father never talked much about the war, not to us children — not even to my mother. Photographs show him in a smart sergeant's uniform, dark hair slicked back, looking, for all the world, like a handsome Hollywood movie star. There are photos of him on the steps of the Berlin City Hall, his arm linked through that of my mother, a brand new bride. Willie and Heidi met during the war.

My mother worked in an office and was given a suggested list of names of young soldiers to write to. It was the patriotic thing to do, so my mother dashed off five or six letters. My father's reply came first. The minute my mother opened the letter, she knew this was the man she was going to marry.

Willi was stationed in Norway at the time. A photograph shows him on board a troop carrier with his platoon: all of them shaved bald as bowling balls. It seems they'd got into the rum ration the night before and thought it might be fun to shave each other's heads.

The photograph unmistakably picks up the hangovers in the men's faces. Willi spent most of the war behind a desk in Bergen, in the far north of Norway. As the war dragged on and the tide began to turn, he applied for a transfer to the air force, hoping to see some action.

Willi was made a Master Sergeant in the Air Force and shipped to the Italian Front. By then, the entire war was mass chaos. Willi ended up on the ground, in some of the fiercest battles of the latter stages of the war. He never talked about it — never went into details. As officers were killed, my father was promoted eventually to the rank of Captain. He led his men through the final stages of the war and was finally shot in the leg. He was taken to an American Army hospital. Germans weren't treated very well there, he said, but, at least they operated and got most of the shrapnel out of his leg.

When the war ended, he returned back home to his wife and baby son. My mother had been caught behind the Russian lines at the end of the war — but that's another story altogether. The German soldiers and women who ended up in the hands of the Americans knew, without a doubt, how lucky they were.

My Father carried bits of shrapnel in his leg for the rest of his life. When the war began, Willi was one of 13 children. When the war ended he had one brother and one sister left.

Behind Enemy Lines

Goody Niosi

Berlin was a bad place to be at the end of World War 2. The early part of the war had been exciting. Berlin was one of the most glamorous capitals in Europe. My mother was young, single and pretty. She worked in an office in the heart of downtown. The way my mother tells it, the entire staff was under-worked and overpaid and spent far more time having fun than doing actual work.

Then Heidi met Willi, my father, and they fell in love. They got married on one of his leaves. On Willi's last leave, before being posted to Italy, my mother became pregnant. Her son was born on March 9, 1945. Willi had also left his six-year-old son by his first marriage in her care. By then Berlin was being bombed to shreds. The air raid signals sounded day and night. There was little or no food for the baby and no sleep for Heidi. Every night the sirens sounded and every night she ran to the underground air raid shelter with her baby and young Freddie.

Miraculously, as her friends and co-workers died around her, Heidi survived. But days before the war ended, the Russians began moving into Berlin. The horror stories of Russian atrocities swept through the city. Heidi's own brother had been gunned down, execution-style, by the Russians.

The women who had huddled together every night in the bomb shelter and helped each other find food for their children devised a plan to escape. They would have to leave Berlin by night through the forest of the Tierwald. From there, it wasn't far to the American lines. In the dead of night, Heidi tucked her baby into his carriage, loading whatever household clothing and supplies she could around him. Holding Freddie by the hand and pushing the carriage, she fled with the other women.

The women crept soundlessly through the woods. At the border between east and west, double rows of barbed wire had been strung. Russian soldiers patrolled the line. The women timed the patrol. When they saw their opportunity, one ran forward and cut the wire. Freddie was frozen in fear by now and couldn't move so Heidi left him in the bushes and pushed her baby carriage through the cut wires to the other side.

Then she went back for Freddie. Too late, the patrol, sensing something suspicious, had turned back. The other women made it, but my mother was caught. She pleaded with the soldier but he spoke no German and she spoke no Russian. He took her to the bunker where his commander sat behind a desk. The man glared at her. Heidi's only thought was for the baby and the young child hidden in the woods. "Please let me go to my babies," she pleaded.

The commander spoke German. He listened to her and while she begged him, his eyes strayed to the framed photograph on his desk. Smiling out from the picture was a pretty woman holding a young child. He finally held up his hand and turned it palm up. "Give me your watch," he said, Heidi took off her watch and handed it to him.

"Go," he said. "You have 20 minutes to disappear." Dizzy with relief, Heidi rushed back along the line and collected Freddie. She rushed across the border and there was little Rick, soundly asleep in his pram. Fifteen minutes later, she walked into the American camp. "It was," Heidi recalls, "the most beautiful sight of my life."

Moment of Compassion

Franz Stigler, Luftwaffe

On December 20, 1943, U.S B17 #42-3167 flown by Lt. Charles Brown, took part in an attack on Bremen and was severely damaged by flak during the bomb run. Fifteen Luftwaffe fighters then attacked the battered Flying Fortress, which was returning to base before it ran out of fuel and/or ammunition.

Franz Stigler, former Messerschmidt ME 109 pilot, had already shot down three aircraft that day and was on the ground with his aircraft, which had just refuelled. When he saw the straggler, he took off after it.

Left: *Franz Stigler, Luftwaffe, May 1944;* right, *Charles Brown, USAF, 1943*

Stigler says "I closed on the bomber from the rear and was ready to fire when I noticed the tail gunner was dead and slumped over his weapon. As there was no danger there, I moved up to within a few meters to get a look at the rest of the aircraft. The rudder was riddled to pieces, the left elevator was gone, I could see through the whole left side of the fuselage, the wing had a big hole in it, the nose was shattered with some pieces of Perspex still attached to the aircraft, and there was one dead engine. I pulled up alongside the cockpit where the pilot was struggling for control; it looked like he was the only member of the crew still in business and he was wounded. Our eyes met, and seeing the look of disbelief on his face, I couldn't shoot; it would have been like shooting a man in his parachute. I didn't believe he could make it back to Britain, so I pointed in the direc-

Franz Stigler and Charles Brown, September 1990

tion of Sweden, where he would be able to land in a neutral country. He chose to stay on course, so I peeled off and went home."

After a full post war career, retired USAF Colonel Brown who lives in Florida had never forgotten the strange encounter and, aided by a German veterans organization, found the pilot (Stigler) who indeed remembered the facts relating to the engagement. He then contacted Stigler at his home in Surrey B. C. The two old combatants visited back and forth and were popular guests at service clubs, till the aging process made travel too difficult.

Lucky Wrong Turn

Tom Crawshaw, O.C. #4 Company Canadian Provost Corps 3rd Canadian Infantry Division

We were near the Rhine River and I was driving forward to check with certain regiments regarding the immediate action and handling of prisoners, etc. Watching for regimental signs, I inexcusably missed our own last sign!

Shortly after, I turned downhill into a wooded section and immediately took a machine-gun burst on the side of the Jeep. I stopped instantly and took cover under the jeep, behind a wheel. The firing continued onto a steep meadow where a group of British troops from a forward reconnaissance squad were running after a pig! Having caught it, they were laughing and yelling, while they dragged it to some cover in the trees.

I could see the puffs of dust of the bullets very close to them. I jumped into the Jeep, and quickly wheeled it behind a nearby barn. "Didn't you know you were under fire?" I shouted to the N.C.O. in charge. He then replied with a real Cockney accent, "Aw Guv'nor, them bastards been shootin' at us since D-day, and we ain't had a feed of pork since we left 'ome!"

I drove out of there real fast, taking with me a big chunk of that pig's rear end for the Company. And I was a hero! But I never did mention I'd missed the last sign.

A German Perspective

Alex Maldacker, Wireless Operator, German Navy

This is an account of my experiences being in Germany during the war. It starts with my being on my last ship, the four previous ones had been sunk. 1945 was a bad year for us. To understand German losses is not easy for people here. Out of 37 minelayers (average 3000, tons), we had 3 left afloat, and these were out of commission. We had been in the Baltic Sea, in Swinemuende, a small town on the Baltic, with a load of 500 mines on board. Apparently nobody knew what to do with them, as it was too late in the war to use them properly.

At the time, Swinemuende was filled with refugees from the east; people who were trying to get away from the Russian front. A lot of them had gone through tremendous hardships. Whole families traveled on horse-driven farm wagons in the cold winter. Some freezing to death. Some wagons broke through the ice on the rivers they had to cross. Some were being shot at from the air. Swinemuende was only a small town, but counting the refugees, it might have contained up to 70,000 people. It had no military importance, with mostly old people, women and children.

Next day, at 10:00 a.m., the Captain decided to move the ship out and we dropped anchor outside the harbour that held 31 ships. We knew the war was lost; the Russians were coming in from the east, the Americans from the west, but the war went on. We had *very* little left to defend ourselves with and our losses were tremendous. In the early afternoon, I got the report of 500 bombers and 250 fighter planes coming our way (I was the wireless operator). Soon we could hear them. It was unlikely that they would attack an unimportant town like Swinemuende, but that was what they did.

Seven anti-aircraft guns blasted away at the enemy, which was flying above the clouds; we could not see them, but their noise was enough. We thought they were after us, but the bombs fell on the town. The first ones came down on the trains: the empty tank cars exploded one by one, the flames shooting out, I thought of the refugees on the train next to it, How much can human beings suffer?

The guns on the beach fell silent and we were entirely defenseless. As the bombs fell, we watched the destruction of the town, knowing that thousands of people were dying there. Soon there was only smoke and rubble and fire.

We were still alive. We would have understood the destruction of our ships, but this? There was no use for our mines any more. So we got orders to go to Kiel to unload them at the end of a pier. Just as they were lined up, right from our ship to the underground ammunition depot, we had another air raid. There was a clear sky, so we could see the planes bombing the town, covered mostly with artificial fog. Some 34 bombers came our way as they could see the mines and us. Soon we watched the bombs coming down, wiggling in the sunshine, right on target. The planes had no opposition, no guns shooting.

We were sure to be dead this time, but the bombs had merely fallen around us. The ship had suffered a few splinters. Just unreal! There were lots of dead fish in the water, which we ate that evening—an inexpensive meal provided by those bombers.

Having been ordered to Kiel harbour, our ship did get hit on her stern by a bomb. But luckily, we got the ship moored and everybody got off. I was last, as I had the foresight to get food. The ship being on her side, I had to hang on the doorframe to get to the food! We were hungry all the time, as had been the whole of Germany for four long years.

With no hope left, the military was still fighting. We were sent to fight for Berlin. Standing in the mud with an Italian rifle, being bombed and shot at from the air, and with Russian tanks closing in on us, war was no fun. We were driven back to a swamp were the tanks stopped, so as not to get bogged down. As it was getting dark, I took a fellow soldier with me to get out, as I was sure the tanks would wipe us out. The remarkable fact is that I had prepared for the end — one year before already. I had a compass and some civilian clothing with me, even fishing hooks!

So with the help of the compass, we crept along the edge of the swamp. It was easy enough to avoid the tanks as they were shooting. We got through by going north, then changing to a westerly direction. Then we were utterly alone in an empty deserted village, with no sound at all.

I changed into civilian clothes: a fur-trimmed jacket, silk shawl, and white shirt. I had an old jacket for my partner to wear. I told him to say nothing if we got stopped by the SS, as I would have had to kill them, or they would do us in! I had a pistol with me, but we met no opposition. We made it to the river Elbe by joining some French POWs, also on their way home. Fortunately, my partner spoke French. We traveled with them on a farm tractor, which was better than walking. At the river, we ran into heavy traffic: thousands of trucks and cars were stalled. Everybody wanted to go to the other side of the river, away from the Russians! That day was the day of the capitulation!

At the river, we climbed on a truck loaded with food. I then found a bicycle and a bag, which I filled with 7 bottles of drinks—Schnapps etc. I met my first American who said, "How are you?" I told him I was from Switzerland and happy to see him. I also traded him my pistol for his chocolate.

The Americans had closed the only bridge in the area, as they did not know what to do with all the people. I had learned English out of books. As a wireless operator in the Navy, I could listen to the English Radio stations, so I could speak good enough. Even as a child I had in mind to come over here.

I slept in a car that night. I did hear a woman scream, so thought "the Russians are close." On the river next day, I told some soldiers that I was in the Navy, and sent them out to look for rubber rafts. They found two good-sized rafts, which we inflated. I put my bicycle and possessions into the raft. Having 6 men for each raft, I told the second crew to go down river 400 yards ahead. It was good thinking because, when we got halfway over, an American in a rowboat met us, telling us to go back. "OK Johnny, I said and told my crew to stop paddling. The American boat then proceeded down river to stop the other raft. "Row like hell" I commanded, and we took off, making it to the other side, only to be rounded up in a group by American soldiers.

An American officer asked if anybody spoke English. I told him I did and that I was from Switzerland. He got me to line up the group consisting of civilians and soldiers who were then marched off to some prison compound. I went along with the soldiers to the next village where I found my sleeping quarters. By then I had established the fact that I was from Switzerland; I told them stories about my poor mother in Zurich, that she didn't know where I was, since I had worked for the Standard Royal Oil Company in Denmark. I gave them lots of details about Switzerland, that even the Germans believed me!

After a week I left and rode south toward home. Stopping to eat, I met a group of young people also traveling and ended up with three of the girls for 6 weeks. Walking through Germany, we had a lot of fun and laughs; there was always some danger, too, as there was no law in place. We usually found food and sleeping quarters, as the people were generous towards us. We had some bad times though, like the time we ran into a Russian patrol. I started to speak some Russian and grabbed one girl and pretended to be drunk. We got through.

One day, we encountered three Poles on the road ahead who had just robbed 3 soldiers. They were armed with pistols. I gave my bike to the girl I was with, telling her to take off downhill if they started shooting! I put my hand in my pocket to make it look like I had a pistol too and walked up to them, close enough to hit them before they would think of shooting me. If they attacked me, I hoped I might have been able to hit the middle one with a right on the chin, the second with my left in the stomach, and kick the other one with my right foot in the belly. It might have worked too as I was in top shape, but luckily it was not necessary! Although they wanted the girl and the bike, I flatly refused. They seemed shaken by my apparent wild and aggressive appearance. On top of that, I asked them for a smoke and got tobacco and a paper from them. I rolled a cigarette, then got a light too! The girl had walked past us by then and I so went to join her. Fortunately they were gone when we passed that spot later. I managed to deliver the three girls safely to Sonneberg, Thueringen, then went on my way home.

I arrived at Bamberg, Bayreuth, where there were posters that said, "Soldiers will be shot if they don't give themselves up to the US Army." I went into the town and ended up in a large POW camp in Bayreuth. We had nothing to eat for two days, before we got some soup. First thing I did was walk along the fence to find a weak spot, in case I wanted to get out. I found a place where the wire was rusted and screened by bush.

Soon I went to work, with a guard, of course, as I could speak English. I sometimes got extra food to bring back to the camp for my starving friends. Since I had no identification on me, I could not get a discharge from the camp. I stayed for about 3 months, dressed in my civilian clothes quite nicely, and even had a necktie.

The Camp Commander didn't like me (he was Austrian), because I talked and ate sometimes with the US soldiers and I was dressed much better than the 3000 men in uniform. So, one day, he abused 2 of my sick friends who were Flemish and Dutch. I retaliated by calling him names like traitor. I didn't know that the soldier in US uniform standing beside us was Polish who also understood German. They took me to the building where they had the SS man under special guard, and after some slightly rough treatment, they put me into a room with 65 S.S. men. There was hardly enough room to lay down, so it was not comfortable. We were all given short haircuts, including me, to distinguish us from the rest of the prisoners. We worked inside the prison camp, under extra guards, fixing the roads. My friends could come close enough to hear me, so I gave them instruction to get my clothes ready, a bit of bread, socks and soap in my raincoat, as I was going to break out.

I cut one arm off my sweater; tied one end and rolled up the other which made up a nice cap to hide my baldhead! I found out that the guard on the main door was absent for 5 minutes every evening when he brought back another group of prisoners to their room. We had to clean the building every evening, one guard per room observing and accounting for his men. The third day I was in there, we had to clean the downstairs hall. Afterwards, the guard took us back to our room, counting the men in. I told the guard that I had left my pail downstairs and was going to get it. As he was counting the men he had no time to pay attention, so I went down, put on my rolled cap, and walked out while the guard on the main door was absent. Shortly before 9:00 o'clock in the evening, I was in the general area of the prison camp, where my two friends were waiting. I slipped into my coat, said 'goodbye' to my friends and slowly walked to the area where I knew the fence to be weak. I made sure nobody was looking my way, then dropped into a little cornfield and slid along the ground to my escape hole in the fence.

I didn't have much time before the alarm would be raised, and I had to get outside before that! When I got to the fence and was working a hole in the wire I heard some girls laughing, and I thought that the outside guards were certainly with them; yet when I poked my head through the hole, I saw 2 pairs of boots marching right for my head. Luckily I was shielded by the bush and was not seen. As I slid through the hole I rolled over the path and downhill, sticking to the ground as it was still light enough to be seen. Not too far away, I rose up, only to see another guard patrolling, so I dropped down again.

It got dark quickly and I made my way to the river. I went into the water and walked downstream 500 yards, then walked out on the other side. It was dark, really dark! I went across a street, which was used by US cars and trucks, hoping it would help to hide my scent, as I knew they would send the dogs after me. Four escapees were caught before and got 4 years hard labour for trying to flee! I went for the woods and nearly ran into more danger. An outside guard of a US hospital was sitting behind a bush, smoking a cigarette; I had seen the light of his cigarette, mistaking it for maybe that of a farmhouse, but when I heard the click of the rifle I knew better.

The guard probably could hear me and got his rifle ready. I got away carefully in stocking-feet and went into the dark woods. By then the prison camp had sent up rocket flares to signal my escape. I selected some dense brush and slid under it to spend the night, cold and wet, but free! Searchlights were on at the camp!

The next day, I went south through the woods to the other side. By the way, I had a compass around my neck all the time. I wore it on a thin string, towards my back so that it was hard to see. When I came to the end of the woodland I spread my clothes on bushes in the sun to let them dry, then climbed a tree and watched the open land! I noticed a man walking in the fields, about a mile away. Soon I heard and saw a small spotter-plane, and not long after, a Jeep came along to pick the man up. I knew they were looking for me most likely. A matter of pride, they couldn't let a prisoner escape; especially as I was in with the SS. Doppelguard!

After my clothes dried, I planned my route home through open land which had some trees under which I could find cover and shelter. Aided by my compass, I started southwest on my way home. When I arrived I found our house was still there. But the city was in rubble.

Life in the R.A.F.

Ron Bull, R.A.F.

I joined the R.A.F. as aircrew cadet 6.12.1943, aged 17 years and 9 months. Our first trip was to Munich, with eight hours flying time. Take off was OK, but on our climb, we lost our port outer engine. We might have been a green crew, but we knew we would not be able to go to Munich on three engines. So we were to dump our bomb load of 12000 lbs at a safe area in the North Sea.

We were an unhappy crew when we landed at base. After a full investigation was carried out, along with the system, we were cleared of any wrongdoing.

With our first trip behind us it was training and ops over Germany. By the time the war ended, we had 17 ops to our credit.

May 8th 1945 was spent in Newark-on-Trent. The best trip was to Berchtesgarden, our last one. After May 8th, we went back to work flying our ground crew over bombed-out Germany, and also flying down to Bari, Italy to bring the British 8th army home. Not too much comfort with 24 soldiers per Lancaster, but in 6 hours flying time, they were home and on their way.

My last flight in a Lancaster was 7.9.45. Leaving the RAF, I went to Civil Airlines. I finished my flying days on the Berlin Airlift 1948. In 1955, I came to Canada, joined the RCAF, and after 24 years retired from 435 Squadron, at CFB Edmonton.

Ron Bull

To all Prisoners of War!

The escape from prison camps is no longer a sport!

GERMANY HAS ALWAYS KEPT TO THE HAGUE CONVENTION AND ONLY PUNISHED RECAPTURED PRISONERS OF WAR WITH MINOR DISCIPLINARY PUNISHMENT.

GERMANY WILL STILL MAINTAIN THESE PRINCIPLES OF INTERNATIONAL LAW.

BUT ENGLAND HAS, BESIDES FIGHTING AT THE FRONT IN AN HONEST MANNER, INSTITUTED AN ILLEGAL WARFARE IN NON-COMBAT ZONES IN THE FORM OF GANGSTER COMMANDOS, TERROR BANDITS AND SABOTAGE TROOPS EVEN UP TO THE FRONTIERS OF GERMANY.

THEY SAY IN A CAPTURED SECRET AND CONFIDENTIAL ENGLISH MILITARY PAMPHLET,

THE HANDBOOK OF MODERN IRREGULAR WARFARE:

".... THE DAYS WHEN WE COULD PRACTICE THE RULES OF SPORTS-MANSHIP ARE OVER. FOR THE TIME BEING EVERY SOLDIER MUST BE A POTENTIAL GANGSTER AND MUST BE PREPARED TO ADOPT THEIR METHODS WHENEVER NECESSARY"

"THE SPHERE OF OPERATIONS SHOULD ALWAYS INCLUDE THE ENEMY'S OWN COUNTRY, ANY OCCUPIED TERRITORY AND, IN CERTAIN CIRCUM-STANCES, SUCH NEUTRAL COUNTRIES AS HE IS USING AS A SOURCE OF SUPPLY"

ENGLAND HAS WITH THESE INSTRUCTIONS OPENED UP A NON-MILITARY FORM OF GANGSTER WAR!

GERMANY IS DETERMINED TO SAFEGUARD HER HOMELAND AND ESPECIALLY HER WAR INDUSTRY AND PROVISIONAL CENTRES FOR THE FIGHTING FRONTS. THEREFORE IT HAS BECOME NECESSARY TO CREATE STRICTLY FORBIDDEN ZONES CALLED DEATH ZONES IN WHICH ALL UNAUTHORIZED TRESPASSERS WILL BE IMMEDIATELY SHOT ON SIGHT.

ESCAPING PRISONERS OF WAR, ENTERING SUCH DEATH ZONES WILL CERTAINLY LOSE THEIR LIVES. THEY ARE THEREFORE IN CONSTANT DANGER OF BEING MISTAKEN FOR ENEMY AGENTS OR SABOTAGE GROUPS.

URGENT WARNING IS GIVEN AGAINST MAKING FUTURE ESCAPES!

IN PLAIN ENGLISH: STAY IN THE CAMP WHERE YOU WILL BE SAFE!

BREAKING OUT OF IT NOW IS A DAMNED DANGEROUS ACT.

THE CHANCES OF PRESERVING YOUR LIFE ARE ALMOST NIL!

ALL POLICE AND MILITARY GUARDS HAVE BEEN GIVEN THE MOST STRICT ORDERS TO SHOOT ON SIGHT ALL SUSPECTED PERSONS.

Escaping from prison camps has ceased to be a sport!

Image courtesy of Vancouver Island Military Museum & Ron Buxton

Prisoners of War

WHEN YOU PAUSE TO SEE THE TIME OF THE DAY, REMEMBER THE CANADIANS WHO FLEW FROM THIS AIRFIELD BRAVE AND COURAGEOUS, SOME NEVER RETURNED, OTHERS RETURNED WITH LIFETIME MEMORIES.

DEDICATED BY THE MEMBERS OF 437 (T) HUSKY SQUADRON WITH THE GRACIOUS HELP OF THE PEOPLE OF CRICKLADE ON 25TH SEPTEMBER 1994 NO. 437 SQUADRON ROYAL CANADIAN AIRFORCE R.A.F. BLAKEHILL FARM 14TH SEPT 1944 - 7TH MAY 1945

Organ Music

Lorne Shetler, 429 Squadron Bomb-Aimer

It was on a trip to Neurenberg that we first met fighters with what the Germans called "Pipe Organ." (Upward firing guns mounted in their night fighters.) We lost 96 aircraft that night, 6 of them were from our squadron, and when asked at debriefing what had happened, all I could say was "I don't know, I didn't see anybody get shot down. There were just a lot of balls of fire in the air." That was a sobering experience and then a few nights later we were told that our target was Aachen, and that we would overfly a Luftwaffe Fighter Base where, according to intelligence reports, there were 45 aircraft stationed.

It was May 24th, and back home people would be celebrating the holiday with parades, picnics, and band concerts when we took off on our 26th trip in the Halifax Bomber. Our plane had nose art depicting Hitler being flushed down a toilet and with the name "Reich Express" that our skipper had chosen to have painted on it. Our flight in was not too bad, with only the usual flack, and it didn't come close. It was on the way out, over Holland and while we were thinking about the good breakfast and our warm beds that the fighter got under us and fired into our midsection. The explosion ripped us apart, and we were now one of those balls of fire I had seen on the trip to Nuremberg.

Only our Navigator, Wireless Operator, and I got out of it alive. I landed in a tree, then bounced off a stump before hitting the ground. It was still dark and, in spite of terrible pain in my backside, I managed to hobble away. Some hours later I got to a farm where I was taken in and cared for by a friendly Dutch family. I spent the next four days in bed, being treated by a Dutch doctor until I was able to get around. Finally a Freedom fighter came to guide me and we worked our way to a safe house in Tillburg, where I met up with three other airmen that the family had taken in. We stayed in a row house in which a German Officer was billeted next door, on the other side of the wall of our room. We sure kept quiet the few nights we were there, until our next guide came along and led us to another farm house where we were given civilian clothes and Dutch documents.

This, too, became a close call. The invasion had begun and more troops were coming in from the Russian front. Six soldiers came on a truck looking for billets and were dropped off at the front door. So we pedaled away on bicycles that the family insisted we take. They explained that it was "better to have our bicycles stolen than be shot for harbouring allied airmen."

We reached Antwerp and were put up by a young girl who kept us hidden till the next guide took over. And this was where our tour of the lowlands ended. He was one of the Belgians who found it profitable to sell escapees to the Gestapo and that's how come we ended up in Herman Goering's Stalag Luft 7 in Poland. The girl's father who didn't even know about her activities was taken away and executed. Her involvement was undiscovered until she was caught in a later operation and subsequently sentenced to death. Luckily, however, when our army reached Antwerp, she was set free before the sentence could be carried out.

I was in several Prisoner of War camps, because as the Russians got closer they took us further into Germany and made us walk or sometimes put us in boxcars. Red Cross parcels helped us to survive the camps, as the meals were usually terrible. They got worse toward the end of the war, and all that walking on an empty stomach was more than many men could handle; even our guards were going hungry.

We were in Stalag 3A when we woke up to find the guards had gone during the night. We mostly stayed near the camp, scavenging locally for food. I was walking around with another guy, somewhat lost in this strange country, when an American jeep came along. The officer had his driver stop, gave us chocolate bars and cigarettes and asked, "Where are you guys from." The other airman said "Prince Albert Saskatchewan" and I told him "Napanee, Ontario." He then started telling me about all my friends he knew at the Paisley House Hotel. Before the war, he had called on the bar while selling Pepsi Cola.

Two days after, we took possession of camp 3A and the Americans came and flew us to Brussels, where they fed us and cleaned us up. They threw away all our old stuff and gave us new clothes, regardless of who had worn them before. I ended up in a British Army Captain's uniform, complete with all the insignia, which did seem fitting since I had received my commission while in prison camp. The camp commandant at the time had offered to have me moved to an officer's camp, but I figured it wouldn't be that much better and by this time I had made several friends and didn't want to start all over again. We were only in Brussels a short time before the RCAF flew us back to Britain and I went on leave in Edinborough in my British Army uniform.

Since the war, I have learned that one of their most successful night fighters, Oberst Lieutenant Heinz Schnaufer, was the pilot that got us. He ended up a Major and Kommodore of NJG 4. Interviewed by a couple of RAF gunners in 1946, he told them "pilots had the greatest respect for the mid-upper turret, because at the beginning of a corkscrew with a dive in their direction, the gunner could get a clear shot." He was convinced that the bomber gunners didn't fire enough or soon enough and had they fired more and used brighter tracers, many of the Luftwaffe pilots, especially the newer ones would not have attacked. He recalled one occasion when he was shot at 800 meters and the fire was so accurate he could not approach the bomber.

In 1947 the Belgian Judas was found working for the Americans in Brussels and met a firing squad. The girl from Antwerp is married to an American Air Force Colonel and lives in Los Angeles. We still correspond.

The Escape Committee

Max Sikal, RCAF

It was late 1942 in the Prisoner of War compound at Barth, near Lubeck and we were busy digging an escape tunnel. We had trouble disposing of the sand, so came up with the plan of carrying the sand out of the tunnel in long tubes inside our pant leg, as later shown in *The Great Escape*. When eventually we had no place left to put the sand, we started dumping it down the holes in our 80-holer.

Everything was going fine until one of the guards happened to look down into the latrine and spotted all the sand. That put us out of business. Next night, after we got the signal that the guard was coming, we left the door ajar and stood a can of water on top. The Gestapo pushed the door open, walked in, and the full load of water dumped on him.

The Commandant called us all on parade and chewed us out for spilling urine all over his officer. He gave us one week of no basketball, or baseball. All sports were cancelled. It didn't cause us too much trouble, but we were all sorry we hadn't thought of using urine instead of plain water.

Our "ex" committee bribed guards with coffee, cigarettes, sugar, etc. from our Red Cross parcels. The Red Cross was wonderful to us. It was verboten for anyone, except our committee, to work with the goons. Any POW caught trading was severely reprimanded by our own men. We had an understanding with one of the goons who was a decent sort, although I can't remember his name now. Shortly after I got to know him fairly well, he told me, "Now it's your job to try to escape, and it's my job to stop you." And that's what it boiled down to. There was no malice intended by either of us.

Shot Down over Russia

Tony Ruppert, Luftwaffe / by Lynn Welburn

"I tried out as a pilot on a Messershmidt 109 fighter, but I was too young and careless and tried to buzz a girlfriend's house. After the crash, I was court-martialled and sent back to flight school to learn to be a flight engineer," says Tony Ruppert.

"I really didn't want to be in the service, because I was a skilled gymnast, having thoughts of being in the Olympics one day. I was offered a job in a circus that was going to South America—a perfect chance to escape the war that I knew was surely coming." He'd already been drafted to the submarine service, but he was under-aged and his father wouldn't let him go. "You stay here with the fatherland," he said. So that was when Tony decided to try for the air force.

"It wasn't what I wanted to do, but I didn't have many choices. I was not a Nazi supporter, although I was glad they kept the communists out. We didn't really know much about it when I was growing up; we were poor and didn't have much food till after Hitler took power." Tony says that in the beginning, they saw only good things, but then his father spent time in prison for refusing to put a 'No Jews Allowed' notice in his barbershop. He says his mother never got used to saying "Heil Hitler" as a greeting, always preferring a traditional religious greeting.

Tony Ruppert, Luftwaffe, 1942

So at age 20, he was in Russia, flying a 1937 Heinkel 111. By 1942, it was to be too slow for their anti-aircraft artillery and was replaced with the faster, but more cramped JV88. This one didn't land as well and tended to crash more easily. Tony says that they had new guns, but they weren't much use against ground fire. Stationed at an air base in Pskov near the front lines, they flew a lot of bombing missions over the ever-approaching Russian soldiers. Planes were being lost fast and furiously. "We knew we were being B.S'd. by our superiors who told us about the Russian losses only," says Tony. "Starting with 81 planes, we had only 4 left by the time I was shot down."

On Christmas Eve 1942, his Commanding Officer asked for volunteers for a mercy flight to help some 6000 German soldiers trapped behind the lines. "Those were our boys, half of them wounded. They'd had no supplies for 50 days, they were almost starving." So four of them volunteered to drop a shipment of food and Christmas goodies to them, with a message from the C.O., asking them to lay a German flag out on the ground. When they got there, however, they saw about 25 flags, because the Russians had broken their code and were trying to trick them.

They flew to about the middle at about only 300 meters above ground to parachute drop the supplies. As soon as the food dropped, the ground fire started. They had about 60 holes in their belly and the pilot's left leg was shot off at the knee and was bleeding profusely. Tony then swung the yoke over to his side, attempting to fly them out, but with oil lines broken and being so close to the ground it was difficult to get the nose up. He says he knew they'd had it. He then decided to crash land. As he aimed for a clearing in the forest, he saw his right wing break off, then the left one, and then they hit the snow. In the last couple of seconds, Tony says he saw his life, his childhood pass like a very fast dream. Then they were sitting quietly in the snow.

They had been told never to be taken prisoner and to save their last bullet for themselves. But he was only twenty, "too young, too yellow, maybe?" he asks. He decided to take a chance. Only one of the other crew members took the same route. But before the others killed themselves, they used their machine guns to kill two Russians from the village nearby. Later, village women began beating him and the other remaining officer, until the sergeant stopped the women. Tony says they were very polite and he knew then that those people were not cruel brutes as their leaders had told them.

He was a prisoner of war in Russia for six years, until 1948. At one time, he was down to 81 pounds in weight. He describes other men around him who were dying like rats. He still doesn't know where he got the will power or strength to live through the ordeal.

When he was finally repatriated, he found many things had changed, including his view of the war. This was especially true when he found out about the death camp atrocities, which he had originally thought to be propaganda. He says he was shocked when he learned the truth and ashamed of what had been done in his country.

"As a soldier, you just do your own thing. It was a stupid, horrible war that should never have been fought. It killed and maimed so many children and old people, along with young men and women who served. I should never have been in it. I just wanted to make my living with my gymnastics, but that just didn't happen."

Wartime Wings

Ted Barsby, RAF Pathfinder Squadron

I got my wings, my commission, and was married to Babe all on the same day. But one of my funniest experiences came when I first joined up. Standing over the urinal to fill the bottle, an old veteran from the first war asked, "Will you do me a favour?" "Yeah! I said, "What do you want?" "I've drunk a lot of beer in the past 20 years" he said, "and I don't know what kind of shape my kidneys are in. Will you please pee in my bottle?" So I did him the favour. Since I only saw him that once, I don't know if he got in—but if he did, it could be my fault.

I did one tour of ops with the RCAF 405 Halifax Squadron, 6 group, Bomber Command, then was posted to the RAF Pathfinder Squadron and flew Lancasters for the rest of the war. My crew, except for our Flight Engineer, went on leave to Birmingham for Christmas 1944. We were due

Ted Barsby

back by 23:59 hrs, but the train was full. We had to wait for the next one, and didn't get back to base till morning. Having had no sleep, we arrived just in time for the only daylight trip we ever made. The weather had finally broken. Up until then, it had been favouring the Germans for their big attack in the 'Battle of the Bulge.' We were among the first bombers sent in to help turn the tide.

On VE Day, I flew to Lubeck, Germany to bring home prisoners of war, and spent the day in the air, returning with about 25 very happy servicemen. Since the Lancasters were not built for carrying people, my passengers could not have been very comfortable, but they sure weren't complaining. Experiencing their joy made shuttling men back to freedom one of my most pleasant memories.

WARNING ORDER. No. 4382.
"Forbidden on pain of imprisonment or death to have intercourse with the daughters of the Reich."

Image courtesy of Vancouver Island Military Museum & Ron Buxton

Pacific

High Jinks in Northern India

Maurice Lonsdale, Captain, Royal Engineers, by Nick Lonsdale

Before being demobbed, my dad, Maurice Lonsdale, spent the last two years in northern India, near the Khyber Pass, although I think that he was in other areas for brief spells of duty. He was, at this time, a Captain in the Royal Engineers and had the responsibility for the maintenance of the Air Force Base(s) in his area. He was generally the only Army type amongst a bunch of RAF personnel. The following are some of the tales he recounted, usually when we went to cricket matches with his long time friend and our family doctor Tony Gill, who served as a medic in the same area and so could verify, or dispute the stories. A few brandies also helped.

Maurice Lonsdale was a mason during his time in India, although I never recall his being involved afterwards. He was also a member of the Lodge established by Rudyard Kipling.

My father had his own Jeep and driver, whereas the RAF guys did not. One night some of them stole his Jeep and were racing it up and down the drive and around the Lodge pool, until they drove it into the pool. He made them pull it out, take it to the workshop, strip it and rebuild it. Since he was Army and they were RAF, I suppose they had no option.

One night, returning from the mess to his bungalow, at his front steps he encountered a cobra in striking position. As an understatement, like me he didn't particularly like snakes, so you can imagine his reaction, until he heard some laughing from behind the bushes. Some of these characters had purloined a preserved cobra from a specimen jar (one of several kept for identification reasons) in the doctor's office (the same doctor mentioned earlier), and had mounted the snake on a stick.

The Officers' Mess in India was situated in a large imposing building, commandeered for the Mess. It had an enormous, long, highly polished dining table and a wide shelf all the way round the room, at about 8 feet off the ground. On Mess nights, after dinner and no doubt after more than a few drinks, the RAF officers would try and walk all the way round the room on the shelf without falling off. The table also provided entertainment. After it was cleared, they would get the smallest and drunkest of the party, and then slide him down the table to see how far he would go before falling off. The ones sliding him farthest would win. What? I don't know.

My father talked of an Australian pilot named Wright, whom they called Wilbur. He was always depressed through lack of action in that area and regularly asked the CO for a Spitfire to fly home to Australia for a few days to see his family. Of course, he was always refused. To vent his displeasure, he would go up in a Spitfire and fly at about 400 mph at a very low level and 'beat up' the airfield. Of course, he knew that his chances of any serious punishment for these antics were slim, for apparently he was the best pilot the squadron had at the time.

Finally, Wilbur Wright, my father and others went off into the Mountains in Jeeps—sight-seeing I think! They met a caravan of locals on donkeys or camels, traveling in the opposite direction. The merchants were all asleep, but because their animals had done the trip so many times, they knew their own way to market. Wilbur got out of the jeep at the head of the caravan and, without any of the travelers knowing, he turned the leading animal round 180 degrees, sending the caravan back to where they'd come from.

The last time I heard these tales was about 30 years ago, when I was driving the two fairly well oiled veterans from an England v Australia cricket match, in Nottingham. Unfortunately my father died in 1982 and Dr. Tony Gill died just last year, so I can't ask them for more details. I always knew, however, that they'd had a good time over there. But much of what they got up to was probably out of boredom, bearing in mind that at the time, they were all only in their early to mid-twenties.

The Forgotten War

George Maycock, Bolingbroke Squadron #115, by Vivian Maycock

My husband, George, had many good stories, but he died 12 years ago and I wanted to share with future generations this brief account about the "forgotten war."

George's Bolingbroke Squadron #115 was formed in Ottawa as a fighter squadron and posted to Patricia Bay B.C. Then in June '42, six months after Pearl Harbour, they were converted to a bomber squadron and rushed to Annette Island, Alaska to help the Americans stop the Japanese advance up the Aleutian chain.

The Squadron was active throughout the campaign and took part in the final blow that drove the Japs off their stronghold "Kiska." This assured our Pacific allies that these island stepping-stones were not going to be the route the Japanese Empire would take to bring troops to North America.

George spent 18 months in that isolated outpost; I had to send his mail by way of Seattle, Wash. He was never issued Canada badges, and how our Canadian 115 Bomber Squadron saved North America after the US Navy was destroyed at Pearl Harbour is a story that has never been told. Their part in the History of WWII has been neglected.

The news clips we saw at shows were about all we knew of where our men were. And the only clips I can recall were about mounties rounding up the Japanese people. Up until then, we were wondering what had happened to a Japanese boy from our school; his parents' restaurant had closed so suddenly.

George's own account of the year and a half he spent on that remote Island would have been filled with humour, as that was what kept them going.

Life in the Forgotten Air Force in South East Asia

Gil Green, 159 RAF Squadron

We celebrated VE Day with a real great party in the Officers' Mess, drinking to our hopes of more and better equipped B.24 Liberators, (Loran and Radar) because we had just received word that we would continue operations through the wet monsoon season. We really thought we were the forgotten Air Force because it was not until July 11th that we had the pleasure of air testing a shiny new 'Q' Liberator. With no camouflage paint, no more girlie art, this was going to increase our cruising air-speed, and it did by seven mph.

The Loran was a great navigational aid; we could pinpoint our position at any time to within a quarter of a mile. Unfortunately, we only had three more trips to complete our 400 hr. tour. Then we were off to Nani-Tal (A military garrisoned hill-station in north central India with a lake 8500 feet above sea-level). We sure had a great holiday: horse-back riding, roller- skating, and dancing at the Yacht Club, with mostly waiting in line for the few available ladies. We arrived back at our base, Digri, at the end of July to find the war over and another new 'Q" K.N. 812, #4. "Q" K.L.671, #3 had crashed into a mountain in Burma, on its sixth trip, losing all crew.

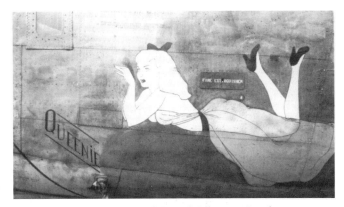

"Nose" art on Gil Green's Liberator Bomber

There was an interesting seventh operation on February 15, 1945. We were in "Q" K.N. 215, #1, along with two other aircraft. We had just finished destroying a road and railway bridge at mile 41, on the Burma Siam railroad, and as normal practice, we continued flying along the tracks, hunting for locomotives. We found two on a siding, blew the boiler on one, and made a second pass for the other when all hell broke loose; I guess they had found some guns. I knew we were hit somewhere in the starboard tail section; I could feel it on the controls. I was busy adding power and weaving as best I could to get out of range of the guns and gain some height. After getting settled down and on course for home, I went back to the waist hatch to assess the damaged tail. Most of the top of the starboard fin and rudder were missing, but thanks be to God, a Liberator has two. Now we were faced with a six and a half hour flight home, mostly over water, hundreds of miles from land. With the extra drag of the damaged tail and full rudder trim, we wondered if we would make it on the fuel we had left.

As we sighted the land of the Ganges Delta, the Flight Engineer reported the gas

Gil Green, in the peaked hat, with crew members

level going out of sight and we still had ninety miles to go! After getting permission for an emergency night landing, I was sure thankful to touch down. When the ground crew dip-sticked the main tanks, 2 and 3 showed ¼"; 1 just wet the dipstick bottom, and 4 had no markings! The Engineering Officer also found the main spar in the stabilizer broken and cracked in several places. This was the end of "Q" K.N.215's flying; it would be useful only for spare parts.

Its replacement, E.W.246 "Q"#2, an older model Liberator, arrived on the base two days later and we certainly did a fuel consumption test for the next operational trip. We did three more operational trips with "Q"E.W.246, but no night landings. I pointed out to the ground crew that there were a lot of heat marks on the stabilizer of the tail section, immediately behind the motors.

Our fourth trip was to Bangkok to bomb the Railway Locomotive works. Our first run in was to drop four flares at one-minute intervals at two thousand feet, then to climb to five thousand feet for the bombing run. Bangkok was equipped with Radar searchlights and their beams had already found the aircraft ahead of us. With only 20 seconds to 'bombs away,' I immediately closed the throttles and lost height to lose the searchlights. The Navigator called me to say that the two starboard engines were on fire. While everyone watched those two motors, I increased the two port motors to maximum power and trimmed accordingly, feathering 3 and 4 motors. We were heading south away from Bangkok at two thousand feet with the fire in 3 and 4 motors out. Next came the big decision to try and start these motors. If we were to get back home, we had a 10,000-foot mountain range to get over. I told the second pilot to select the fire extinguisher to #4 but to pull the ring only if it went on fire again. It fired up safely, so we repeated the procedure with #3 motor.

We joined our circuit and approached to land. I closed the throttles and lo' and behold! We had four of the longest flames from the exhausts sweeping back over the tail-section and blinding our night vision! After we had slowed down on the runway and I needed more power to taxi, the flames disappeared. This, then, was the cause of the burn marks we'd reported previously.

At de-briefing we were told that one of our planes had reportedly been shot down in flames, and they'd thought it was the "Q" E.W.246. We told them about our problems that had occurred after the bombing-run, and how we had all concentrated on looking at the #3 and #4 motors, until we landed and found we had FOUR! flaming motors. The ground crew did everything they could to correct the carburetors but were not too successful. I just had to live with landing with the throttle on.

Commonwealth Air Training Plan

John Mills, R.A.F., by Eileen M. Mills

Even at the age of fourteen, John Mills had always been fascinated with aircraft, so when war broke out in 1939, he was one of the first to apply to join the Air Training Corps. in England. Anxious "to do his bit" for King and country, John worked hard at learning the Morse code and completing other preliminary requirements before Dec.7th 1942 when, at age seventeen, he reported to the London recruiting office and was accepted into the Royal Air Force.

In the next several weeks, he was checked out, and to his delight, he was elected to become a pilot. He started his flying training on the Tiger Moth in Scoone, Scotland. In October 1943 John sailed aboard the troopship *Queen Mary* for Canada, via New York and New Brunswick. He continued on the now retired railroad system to Moose Jaw, Saskatchewan to be a part of the Commonwealth Air Training Plan. After a while, he continued on to a station in Alberta.

At long last, his dream come true and he received his Wings, his favourite plane being the Oxford. He believed his mission was to help eliminate Hitler's regime. During the Christmas short leave of 1943, John and a couple of his buddies hitched a ride on a USA aircraft to Seattle. On arrival, the three gladly accepted an invitation to spend a few days on someone's ranch in the Cascade Mountains. At the ranch, they were shown around and given clothing so that their uniforms would be protected. They were also encouraged to help themselves to as much food or meat as they wanted.

A very amusing thing happened the next morning. The ranch foreman invited them on a trail ride to check the cattle, but John had never ridden a horse before. After a short while, he pointed out that his horse was making some very strange noises from the rear. His foreman then told him he was "very lucky to be on that particular horse, as a farting horse never tires." But at the end of the two-hour horse ride, it was John who was tired, having a very sore rear end. Nevertheless, all three of the friends enjoyed the experience.

In March of 1944, John and all the graduates were sent back to England as Air Crew, ready to do their bit. They found that D-Day had passed and there had been many casualties as a result of the war. John was then sent to a glider station in Chester, from which aircraft transported men and equipment to wherever they were needed. During this time, John met many other Commonwealth servicemen, enjoying their friendship and camaraderie, especially that of the Aussies!

John was listed to participate in the Arnhem raid, but unfortunately, he was put on the sick list because of a viral infection—verucca warts had been found on his foot. His buddy Harry went in his place and to John's dismay, Harry was shot down and never came back. Fate is very strange.

Soon after, in September 1945, the war in Europe ended. John was then sent to India for 18 months to close down RAF stations, as the Indian Empire was going to do its own governing. In May of 1948, John and family returned to Canada, where they have enjoyed a good lifestyle.

VE Day and Other Reminiscences

W. E. (Bill) Howell,

At 2345 hours on May 7, 1945 we were steaming through the Philippine Sea toward the Ryuku Islands with other units of the British Pacific Fleet; we were moving into position to bombard and bomb airfields on Miyako Jimo Island, to the north east of Formosa (now Taiwan). I was sailing in the 6-inch cruiser HMCS *Uganda,* along with nine hundred other Canadian matelots. I was just going off watch when news came over the intercom that Germany had agreed to unconditional surrender. My gun crew toasted the victory with hot chocolate and graham wafers—some celebration!

The funniest thing I saw during the war was when we were at anchor in Alexandria Harbour in Egypt in January 1945. It was about 2100 hours and shore leave was drawing to a close when a commotion started off the port quarter. Looking over the side, I saw an Arab in a rowboat pulling away from the ship, and an inebriated sailor pushing and lifting a donkey up the gangway and on to the quarterdeck. The officer of the watch had a great laugh, but had to order the boson to slip the guardrail and shove the donkey over the side, whereupon the drunken matelot jumped in right behind the donkey. When last seen, the two were swimming side by side for shore.

My most frightening experience was during a 24-hour naval engagement carried out in total darkness inside the Arctic Circle on December 26, 1943. Three ships of the 10th Cruiser Squadron out of Scapa Flow were shadowing a convoy from North America, on the Murmansk run. Early that day, we had intercepted the German battleship *Scharnhorst*, which had left its base at Altenfjord, Norway to raid the convoy. Our group consisted of two 6-inch cruisers, HMS *Sheffield* and *Belfast*, and an 8-inch cruiser, HMS *Norfolk*. The *Scharnhor*st carried 11-inch guns.

Survival time in the waters of the Arctic was two minutes maximum. Only 26 of the nearly 2,000 of *Scharnhorst*'s men survived, following shelling from our ships, HMS *Duke of York*, her escort cruisers, and torpedoes from accompanying destroyers.

It was our lucky Boxing Day to have survived.

274

A Funny Experience

Peter J. Eastick, Merchant Navy

One day in July 1943, we arrived at the River Mersey, tying up at Liverpool Docks. There were 12 gunners on our ship: 9 Navy (a Petty Officer and 8 ratings) and 3 Maritime Royal Artillery. As soon as we docked, a DEMS officer had come aboard, informing us that half of us could go on a 72 hour leave in the morning, and the other half could go when the first ones returned. He then gave us some guff, including the fact that Base Gunnery Maintenance ratings would come aboard in the morning.

The Petty Officer and the three MRA gunners were quartered in cabins amidships, whilst we eight ratings, with a Leading Seaman (killick) in charge, ate, slept and performed our duties in an area under the poop deck. Early next morning, four of us were in the washhouse. The killick and another guy were shaving, while another and myself were showering. We were in a good frame of mind, discussing our leave plans.

Without any warning, the washhouse door was suddenly pushed open and a feminine voice said, "Where's the Petty Officer?" You could have cut the air with a knife! In shock, none of us spoke for a full two or three seconds, as we saw two Wrens dressed in coveralls standing there.

"Sorry" said the older Wren (she was at least 25 or 26!), as she looked us all over. "We thought this was the mess deck." With water still pouring out of the shower, the other chap and myself each grabbed a towel, but in our haste, reached for the same one and stood there, with just the one towel doing its best to hide our modesties!

The killick was the first to gain his voice. With lather over half his face, and wearing only his jocks, he yelled at the Wren, "Read the bloody sign on the door, it says 'Wash house' don't it?" Then in a more apologetic tone he said, "You'll find the P.O. in his cabin amidships."

The two Wrens turned to leave, but with a quick glance at the two of us doing our best to hide behind the towel, they looked at each other and with huge grins on their faces muttered, "OO-LA-LA." Embarrassed? Who me? Only 17 years old, and 8 months in the Navy? I won't bore you with the remarks we made after the Wrens had gone!

The 'Forgotten' War

Peter J. Eastick

VE-Day was just another very hot and humid day as we swung our anchor out in midstream of the lrrawaddy River. Oil tanks and other fires were still burning in and around the city of Rangoon. The SS *Khalistan*, a 5,862-ton freighter of the British India Steamship Navigation Company on which I was serving as a Royal Navy DEMS gunner had followed (General) Bill Slim's boys as they advanced down the Burma coast from Akyab. We had been supplying the 14th Army with food, oil, truck parts and medical supplies as we sailed to obscure ports like Kyeintala and Gwa.

We had traveled in small convoys, escorted by ships of the British, Australian and Indian Navies, been bombed and subjected to Japanese 'Kamikaze' (suicide) air attacks. In one single day, four freighters and an escort vessel had been sunk. We and two other merchant ships were the sole survivors of the original eleven that had set out two months previous. We finally arrived at Rangoon on 5th May, two days after the Japanese garrison had supposedly surrendered or fled south.

We were both happy and relieved for the troops in Europe; their war was now over and they fully deserved their celebrations. We, however, still had a job to do. All we wanted on that Tuesday, 8th May, was to have the remainder of our cargo unloaded and then get the hell out into the open sea. We wanted to leave the stench, the torrid heat and the random bullets that would ricochet off the ship's superstructure and keep our heads ducked whenever we were on the open deck or at our gun positions.

More important to us than VE-Day, was the knowledge that we knew were heading back to our base at Colombo (Ceylon). This meant our eagerly anticipated mail delivery from home, fresh victuals, lazing on the beach at nearby Mount Lavinia, or, if we were particularly lucky, a few days of "R and R" at an upcountry tea plantation.

In a week or ten days, we would once again join a convoy and sail eastwards across the Indian Ocean to take our place in the final push to Singapore. We had no idea how much longer it would take our army to rid the Malayan peninsula of Japanese forces. But we lived in hope that we, too, could soon celebrate: the end of the 'forgotten' war.

> *When you go home*
> *Tell them of us and say*
> *For your tomorrow*
> *We gave our today*
>
> *– The Kohirna (Burma) Epitaph*

HMCS *UGANDA*

Fred H. Broadbent

On VE Day I was aboard the HMCS *Uganda*, the first Canadian cruiser, and we were swinging at anchor in Leyte Gulf in the Philippine Islands. It was July 1945 and our ship was part of the British Pacific Fleet. The fleet was made up of two or three large aircraft carriers, several small carriers, three or four battleships, six or eight cruisers, and twenty destroyers. Japan at this time was reduced to suicide bombers (Kamikazes). The Fleet stood off Japan at about one hundred miles. At night, we would then move in to about eighty miles offshore; in the forenoon, the carriers would launch their planes to bomb Japan. I never saw land for months. Supply ships brought in our mail, food, oil, etc.

It was just after we had taken on fuel oil from a tanker that a very disturbing thing happened. The oil hose that was about eight inches in diameter had been unhooked at our end and thrown over the side for the tanker to reel in—Murphy hadn't been mentioned until then. The hose became entangled around our propellers. The ship stopped, and a diver was sent down to untangle the hose. We were left bobbing about in a large swell as the fleet sailed away from us towards Japan We were left with only one destroyer, which circled us about a half mile way. One Seafire aircraft also remained, and it also circled us, but its pilot would periodically fly between our masts and generally raise hell about our ship in order to stop himself going bananas from boredom! Meanwhile we were a sitting duck, waiting for the torpedoes to hit us. Luckily we got underway after what seemed to us as an eternity, but what was only about four hours.

One of the funnier moments involved a lad who had been caught misbehaving. For punishment, he was ordered to scour the Captain's motorboat that sat amidships. Things seemed to be going well, so the lad decided to have a smoke—bad idea! He had just lit up, when the commander came by and asked him if he was smoking. The boy had just inhaled deeply, so when he replied "No Sir," he blew smoke in the Commander's face. I had a hard time staying on my feet, laughing so hard! And I think our lad might still be in "Chokee" (that's jail).

I had originally left Edmonton going east in July 1943 and was still going east when I got home in August 1945. We crossed the International Date Line on July 32, 1945, a day in which very few have lived. On my next birthday, I will be 75 years plus one day old, unless I go back around the world from west to east.

Nagasaki

Koos Van Houten, Dutch East Indian Army

I was born in Bandung, Java and was a soldier in the Dutch East Indian Army. We were taken prisoner by the Japanese, herded through several Prisoner of War camps and ended up in Nagasaki, where they used us as forced labour in the Mitsubishi factory.

We were kept in a compound 10 Km from the shipyard and had to run to work, do a ten-hour shift, and then run back to camp. I was 1600 meters from ground zero on August 9/45 when the second atomic bomb destroyed the city. It immediately killed 60,000 people, with thousands more victims dying every year since.

It was like the whole world changed in a white flame. I had no clothes—they were all burnt off and a Japanese soldier gave me his coat. We tried throwing buckets of water at the fires but it was a futile attempt; there was nothing we could do. I saw one of my friends with a huge steel beam across his back. There were about twenty of us still living and we used shaving cream to treat burns. A group of us ran back into the factory to get some food, because there were Red Cross parcels that the Japanese had kept from us. Then we ran into the hills and stayed for two days.

When we returned, we were put to work burying the dead. There were not many to bury, as most had been cremated. Then we were taken to another camp 60 miles away.

On August 15th, when the Japs surrendered, we were still in the camp. Planes came over and dropped food, and on the 29th, the Americans arrived. We were first taken to Okinawa, then flown to Manila, Hong Kong, and finally Singapore, where we boarded a ship to Holland. My father advised me to go to Friesien, where he had a brother, and my whole family moved back. I met Sietske in 1946, and we were married in 1949.

In a 1995 interview, when asked "how come you survived the bomb and are still healthy?" Koos, then in his eighties, replied, "The only thing I can think of is that when I first saw the explosion, I laid down flat on the ground and didn't even look up till I heard other people moving about. The blast and fallout must have gone right over me, because the ones that had stayed standing to watch the show were all gone.

After

PASSENGER LIST

A/C —JT-975   SERVICE — PW-41
DATE — 8-30-45
FROM — HAMILTON FLD. TO — SYDNEY, AUS.

1. "VIP" RT.HON. PETER FRASER   TO AUCK
2. MR. A. D. MCINTOSH   "
3. MR. J. V. WILSON   "
4. MISS K. G. JORDAN   "
5. MISS M. H. BROWNE   "

CREW
1. F*L H. J. BARRON
2. F*L T. L. DONALDSON
3. F*O C. A. CROSS
4. F*O J. G. MCARTHUR
5. F*S H. YOUNG
6. F*C LAC J. HAWKINS
7.

Just A Penny Note

H.J.'Pat' Barron, R.A.F..

At the dinner table that evening, there were admirals, generals, colonels, commanders, etc. from the U.S.A. Pacific Forces. In addition, there was a New Zealand captain and two RAF pilots: Tom Donaldson and myself.

After the toasts, one USA Admiral had asked Prime Minister Peter Fraser of New Zealand what was the future thrust for the newly formed United Nations Organization. His answer was: "I pray the U.N. will be the Ombudsman of the World!" Complete silence followed.

Then I asked, "Sir; what is an Ombudsman?" The Prime Minister thought for a minute or so, and with his eyes twinkling, it was clear that he was of the opinion that the high-ranking officers around the dinner table didn't have a clue as to the function of an Ombudsman. Sitting well 'below the salt,' with my Reserve Captain, Tom Donaldson, we didn't know either. But long before joining the Royal Air Force, my favourite Classics professor had hammered into me: "Barron, if you don't know, then ask."

That afternoon, July 2, 1945, we had landed our 'Liberator' Aircraft on the one long coral runway at Canton Island after 9 hours flying time from Honolulu. Canton is 20 degrees below the Equator and warm. We were en-route from the first United Nations Conference in San Francisco in June 1945 to Auckland, New Zealand, flying their Prime Minister and party home.

For the next 10 minutes, the New Zealand leader told us in clear terms what the Ombudsman function was, and in particular how the Ombudsman sought to maintain a 'level playing field' for all citizens of the country. He dwelt on the background and history of the office and how well it currently helped protect grass-roots democracy, particularly in Scandinavia. The Prime Minister's audience was spell bound by his clarity and grasp of detail, and after the address, gave a strong round of applause. It was an evening long to be remembered.

The following day, we flew to Nandi, Fiji for another night stopover. That evening, Prime Minister Fraser presented me with a small reminder of the previous evening at Canton. "Skipper," he said, "Here is a 'Penny Note' from Fiji. That's used because copper is very scarce. I've signed it so you can add it to your collection of 'short snorter' notes.

Flying the oceans of the world in those days was quite a feat and conclusions of flights called for a 'short snort' in the bar. In addition, someone who had previously completed that flight usually presented us with a signed currency bill—maybe a dollar bill or a ten-shilling note. Heaven help you if you were later challenged by aircrew to produce your "Short Snorter Bill" and couldn't do so. If you couldn't, the next round of refreshment in the bar was totally paid for by you. Expensive? Yes.

The Prime Minister then invited me with my fellow crewmembers to have a drink on him before dinner to christen my new 'Short Snorter Penny Note." To this day, I keep it in my Log Book together with the Passenger List dated 30 June 1945. The following day, we safely delivered the Prime Minister to a waiting crowd of New Zealanders at Whenuapai Airport at Auckland. Courteous and gracious as always, he personally shook hands with each crewmember, thanking everyone for a safe and pleasant flight.

Peter Fraser had begun his career as an apprentice carpenter in Scotland and had emigrated to New Zealand in 1910 to work as a dock labourer. He became a Member of Parliament in 1918, subsequently holding several cabinet posts and becoming Prime Minister in 1940—the same year as Winston Churchill in the UK. After traveling to many countries during WW II, visiting N.Z. troops, and conferring with many allied leaders, he received many honours from different universities for his WW II leadership and involvement. He died in 1949.

In 1960, I was flying for the United Nations in the former Belgian Congo. Many flights took me to Scandinavia to bring back sorely needed medical and food supplies. As my "Penny Note" reminded me, such Scandinavian countries had Ombudsmen. Having made many visits to these Ombudsman offices, I gradually learned more and more about them.

For eight years thereafter, my wife Barbara, our seven children and I lived in the little country of Luxembourg. We loved it, even though I was away a lot flying internationally. Finally we moved to North America, settling in Nanaimo, located on Vancouver Island. It was a happy choice.

Shortly after settling in, I visited the late Mayor Frank Ney and found that both of us had flown as pilots with the Royal Air Force during WW II. I told him the "Penny Note" story from twenty-three years before, and asked him for the name of our British Columbia Ombudsman.

"We don't have one," replied Frank. "And furthermore, we don't want any vigilantes in our town, Pat." In parting Frank warned, "You'll do well in this town Pat, if you don't rock the boat." Standing at the Cenotaph a couple of minutes later, I pondered Frank's advice, and my thoughts returned to Peter Fraser's gift of the "Penny Note" and the word Ombudsman.

1976 saw the first International Ombudsman Conference, held in Edmonton, Alberta. Attending, were Ombudsmen from all over the world, together with many government officials. I was privileged to represent the Justice Councils of British Columbia and to address the Conference as a "Voice of the Voiceless" — the everyday citizen. Meeting Sir Guy Powles, the New Zealand Ombudsman, I related the story of the "Penny Note." He was intrigued with the story as he had been a longtime friend of the late Peter Fraser.

Baroness Bea Serota, Ombudsman for London, England, identified the problem, claiming "The greatest opposition to having an Ombudsman came from elected politicians." Following my brief address to the Conference, I had a 'lively' discussion over a drink with B.C. Attorney General Garde Gardom about the thrust for an Ombudsman in B.C. As coordinator, working through the forty-two Justice Councils, I had noticed the politicians in our province were finally taking heed. We parted as friends, and I felt that I had provided some new aspects for the Attorney General's consideration.

Finally 1978 saw results, brought about by pressure from many political parties and their leaders, together with ongoing requests from many organizations in BC. Attorney General Gardom tabled Legislation Bill #63 for action by the Legislative Assembly, with these words:

> The Ombudsman will be a person who can question and deal specifically with misadministration and injustice, with power to investigate, criticize, and make public his findings. This legislation is a great democratic step forward in our province.

> This Office will be another safeguard to the individual against excesses and abuses, and a hallmark in this province for an additional guarantee for the legal rights of an individual.

The Ombudsman Bill #63 passed unanimously.

Yes! Just a "Penny Note." But I could have sworn that when I opened my logbook, the note smiled at me after 33 years of waiting. Certainly there was a smile in my heart.

—Excerpt from *At the Going Down of the Sun* by H.J.'Pat' Barron

Military Units Mentioned

Canadian General Hospitals # 3, 4, 5, 6, 8, 14, 15, 19
#3 Canadian Military Prison
#5 & #6 Mobile Field Photograph Units
10th Canadian Infantry Brigade
4th Armoured Division
10th Field Battery RCA 17th Field Regiment
10th SM - Flotilla
1st Canadian Army
1st Canadian Parachute Brigade
6th British Airborne
1st Hussars
22nd Field Ambulance
2nd British Army
2nd Canadian Infantry Brigade
2nd Canadian Tactical Air Force, 39 Recce Wing
400-414-430 Fighter Recce Squadron
48th Highlanders
4th Anti Tank Regiment 5th Armoured Division
4th Field Ambulance
57th Timber wolf Division
74 British General Hospital
7th Canadian Light field Ambulance
7th Field Regiment Royal Artillery
82nd Anti Tank Battery
90th Anti Tank Battery
9th American Army
Argyll & Sutherland Highlanders

Armed Merchantman 'Prince David'
ATS British Auxiliary Territorial Service
Black Watch
British 8th Army
Calgary Highlanders
Cameronian Scottish Rifles
Canadian Provost Corps #4 Company 3rd Canadian Division
Canadian Scottish
Canadian Women's Army Corps
Cape Breton Highlanders
Carleton & York Regiment
Depot Ships Montclair
Wolfe
Dundurn Detention Centre
RMS Queen Elizabeth, Queen Mary, Andes,
Empress of Canada

Empress of Scotland, Duchess of York,
S.S. Khalistan, Lancastria , Oronsay, Aquitania,
Monterey, Santa Elena, Troop Ship Moritania,
Dorsetshire, Louis Pasteur,
Essex Scottish
Fairmiles   QO 80-72-74-79-80-82-83
Fleet Air Arm
Fort Garry Horse
Fusiliers Mount Royal
German Ship Scharnhorst
Geschwader Horst Wessel
Hastings & Prince Edward Regiment
Canadian ships HMCS - Naden, St. Croix, Ottawa,
Shediac, Assinaboine, Coppercliffe, Fraser, Iroquois,
Magog, Shawnigan, Waskesiu, Montreal, Skeena,
Uganda, Campbelltown, Nonsuch, Cornwallis, Niobi,
St. Laurent

Royal Navy Ships HMLST (Landing Ship Tank) #1021,
HMS Primrose, Glasgow, Belfast, Trumper, Alaric,
Alaric, Ambush, Aphis, Atherton, Belfast, Courageous,
Cyclops, Diomede, Dolphin, Tuna, United, Dutcher,
Duke of York, Hood, Malpan, Hermes, Terror, Motway, Nabob,
Norfolk, Prince of Wales, Repulse, Sesame, Sheffield,
Norfolk, St.Vincent, Suffolk, Sunfish, Thane,
Trident, Tudor, Tyndale, Victory, Warspite, Wessex,
Hospital Ship Letitia, Atherstone, Tyndale,
Motor Torpedo Boat #74 Gunboat 314

Irish Regiment of Canada,
Lanark & Renfrew Scottish,
Lord Strathcona Horse,
Loyal Edmonton Regiment,
Maritime Royal Artillery,
Merchant Navy,
Mobile Field Photographic Sections,
Naval Commandos,
New Brunswick Rangers,
North Shore New Brunswick Regiment,
Polish Armoured Division
Polish Army,
French Foreign Legion,
Princess Patricias Canadian Light Infantry,
Queen's Own Rifles
Queen's Own Cameron Highlanders

RAF Squadrons 103, 148 Special Duties Squadron, 159,
RCAF Squadrons115, 405,419, 426, 429,

RCAF Women's Division (WD)
Regina Rifles

Royal 22nd Regiment "Van Doos"
Royal Air Force 2nd Tactical Air Force 126 Wing 210 Kittyhawk
Royal Canadian Air Force
Royal Canadian Army Medical Corps
#24 Canadian Army Hospital
Royal Canadian Army Service Corps
Royal Canadian Artillery
Royal Canadian Corps of Signals
Royal Canadian Electrical & Mechanical Engineers 2nd Field Workshop
Royal Canadian Engineers
Royal Canadian Ordinance Corps
Royal Canadian Regiment

Desert Rats 8th Army
Royal Engineers
Royal Marines
Royal Netherlands Armed Forces
Royal Winnipeg Rifles
Saskatoon Light Infantry
Seaforth Highlanders
Sherbrooke Fusiliers
South Alberta Regiment
South Saskatchewan Regiment
Stormont Dundas & Glengarry Highlanders
Perth Regiment
7Th Field Regiment Royal Artillery
Three Rivers Regiment
USS Panay
Welsh Fusiliers
West Nova Scotia Regiment
Women's Auxiliary Air Force (British)
Women's Royal Navy Service

Military Terms & Abreviations

AAA   Anti Aircraft Artillery
AG   Air Gunner
ARP   Air Raid Patrol
ASDIC   Anti Submarine Detection
ATS   Women's Army Service (British)
Coxn   Coxswain

CRÈME	Canadian Regiment Electrical & Mechanical Engineers
CWAC	Canadian Women's Army Corps
D.Day	Allied landings in Normandy June 6
DEMS	Defensively Equipped Merchant Ship
ERA	Engine Room Articifer
FE	Flight Engineer
FGH	Fort Garry Horse Tanks
FL	Flight Lieutenant
Hasty Ps	Hastings Prince Edward Regiment
HD	High Definition Warning Surface
HE	High Explosive
HMCS	His Majesty's Canadian Ship
HMCS	Shediac " " " " Shediac
HMCS	Naden " " " " Naden
HMCS St. Croix	" " " " St. Croix
HMLST	His Majesty's Landing Ship Tank
HMS	His Majesty's Ship
HMS	Belfast " " " Belfast
HMS	Etchen " " " Etchen
HMS	Glasgow " " " Glasgow
HMT	His Majesty's Transport
HQ	Headquarters R prefix Regiment C prefix Company
ITS	Initial Training School
LACW	Leading Aircraft Woman
MID	Mention in Dispatches
MM	Military Medal
MRA	Maritime Royal Artillery
N	Navigator
NCO	Non Commissioned Officer
O	Observer
Ops	Operations
OTU	Operational Training Unit
PLUTO	Pipe line under the Ocean
POW	Prisoner of War
PPCLI	Princess Patricia's Canadian Light Infantry
QOR	Queens Own Rifles
RAP	Regimental Aid Post
RCA	Royal Canadian Artillery
RCAF	Royal Canadian Air Force
RCAMC	Royal Canadian Army Medical Corps
RCASC	Royal Canadian Army Service Corps

RCE   Royal Canadian Engineers
RCN   Royal Canadian Navy
RMS   Reserve Majesty's Ship
RN   Royal Navy
SAR   Search and Rescue
SEAC   South East Asia Command
SP   Self propelled Gun
SQDN   Squadron
SS   German Storm Troopers
TAF   Tactical Air Force
TI   Target Identification
TU   Training Unit
WAAF   Women's Auxiliary Air Force (British)
WAG   Wireless Air Gunner
WLA   Women's Land Army
WOP   Wireless operator
WR   West Riding Division (British)

Acknowledgments

I would like to thank all my comrades at Legion Branch 257, Lantzville, for their assistance in the compilation of this history. The following are people who gave us support and encouragement:

Arnold Adams, Branch 631 RCL. Kingson, ON.

Barry's Bay This Week

Belleville Intelligencer

Betty Vezina, Branch 23 RCL. North Bay, ON.

Bob Tracy, Air Force Association of Canada, Ottawa, ON.

Branch 211 RCL. Bowser, BC.

Branch 36 RCL. Fernie, BC.

Branch 92 RCL. Salt Spring Island, BC.

Bruce Mitchell, Camille Belanger and Jacques Aubin, Dover Bay School, Nanaimo, BC.

Carol Foster Branch 65 RCL, Tofino BC.

Cheryl Gullage, VOCM, St.John's NF.

Christine Hogan, Branch 560 RCL. Kingston,ON.

Connie White, Branch 181 RCL. Bancroft, ON.

Donna Kelly, Branch 9 RCL. Kingston, ON.

Doug Cole, Portugal Cove, NF.

Father Bob Coote, Branch 23 RCL. Lunenberg NS.

Frank Burns, 105 Wing Air Force Assn. of Canada, Amherst, NS.

John McIntyre, Branch 99 RCL. Belleville, ON.

Jon Walters, *The Meridian*, Parksville, BC.

Kathleen (Hanlon)Williams, St.John's, NF.

Ken Thorne, Branch 137 RCL. Napanee, ON.

Kingston Whig Standard

Linda Sawyer, Secretary, Pacific Command RCL

Malahat Branch 134 RCL. Shawnigan Lake, BC.

Merv Unger, *Island Living*, Nanaimo, BC.

Maureen McMurrer, Branch 10 RCL. Borden-Carleton, PEI.

Nanaimo News Bulletin

New Seniors Magazine

Patricia Bennett, Jean Lord and Cathy Howe, Branch 15 RCL. Brampton, ON.

Paul Keddy, Branch 49 RCL. Mahone Bay NS.

Paul Pelchat, Branch 10 RCL. and Ray Thorne, Past President Quebec Command, Sherbrooke, PQ.

Peter McCullough Branch 18 RCL. Temiskaming, PQ.

Rick Buchanan, Branch 10 RCL. Amherst, NS.

Ron Smith, RCHA Brigade Assn. Kingston, ON.
Ruth Mooney Branch 86 RCL. Cartwright, MB.
Sandy McNiff, Branch 513 RCL. Dorchester, ON.
St. John's Evening Telegram
Ted Brothers, Vancouver Island Military Museum, Nanaimo, BC.
Victoria Times Colonist
Wilma Stevens, RCL Zone Commander, Qualicum Beach, BC.
We are sure that many more people and companies helped us gather narratives. Included among them are some who had given their names, which have been lost. We can only ask that our apologies be accepted.

—Gord Bell